AF573995

THE PHOTOGRAPHER'S BUSINESS HANDBOOK

THE PHOTOGRAPHER'S BUSINESS HANDBOOK

How to Start, Finance, and Manage a Profitable Photography Business

edited by

John Stockwell and Bert Holtje

A James Peter Associates, Inc., Book

McGraw-Hill Book Company
New York St. Louis San Francisco Sydney Paris
Hamburg Auckland Bogotá São Paulo
London New Delhi Mexico Tokyo
Johannesburg Panama Singapore
Montreal Madrid Toronto

Library of Congress Cataloging in Publication Data

Stockwell, John.
The photographer's business handbook.
Includes index.
1. Photography—Business methods. I. Holtje, Herbert, joint author. II. Title.
TR581.S6 770'.68 80-15296
ISBN 0-07-061585-3

1 2 3 4 5 6 7 8 9 0 DODO 8 9 8 7 6 5 4 3 2 1 0

The editors for this book were Robert A. Rosenbaum and Carolyn Nagy. Design and production were done by James Peter Associates Inc. The production supervisor was Paul A. Malchow. It was set in Souvenir Light Roman by Newtype, Inc.

Printed and bound by R.R. Donnelley & Sons Company.

Contents

Contributors

William J. Anton is the Executive Director of Professional Photographers of America, Inc. He has been in association management for over 20 years, holding various management positions with the New York Society of Certified Public Accountants, the Atomic Industrial Forum and the American Gas Association. He was appointed Executive Director of PP of A in 1975. A member of Chi Epsilon (Civil Engineering Honor Society), the American Society of Association Executives and the American Society for Training and Development, he was designated a Certified Association Executive (CAE) by the American Society of Association Executives in 1979.

Kermit L. Buntrock, photographic craftsman, Storm Lake, Iowa, has served as vice president and treasurer of the Professional Photographers of America. He is a past president of the American Society of Photographers and was winner of the National Award given by PP of A for service to his state association, the Professional Photographers of Iowa, of which he was also president. He has also been chairman of the Portrait Division and headed the Publications, Marketing and Affiliations committees for the national association. He is past president of the Storm Lake Chamber of Commerce and was the community's Centennial Chairman.

Steve Delloff is a freelance photographer and practicing attorney who currently serves as executive assistant for Motivation and Training Programs, Fair Lawn, New Jersey. A Henry Rutgers Scholar in History at Rutgers University, where he earned his AB, Mr. Delloff received his JD from New York University School of Law. He is listed in *Who's Who in American Law.* Prior to becoming an attorney, Mr. Delloff was associated with the Internal Revenue Service.

Rocky Gunn, M. Photog. Cr., S.I.I.P., is a working photographer, author, inventor, and lecturer, and is credited with pioneering the concept of the "love story" portraits of engaged couples. He is internationally renowned for developing the outdoor bridal portrait into a distinctive photographic specialty, and has authored articles and books on portraiture. At present, his studio photographs five hundred weddings a year.

Dr. John H. Hickman is Chairman, Management Studies, at Rochester Institute of Technology. He also teaches courses in strategy and planning, entrepreneurialism and finance there as well as at Louisiana State University and UCLA. He was also a member of the faculty of the University of Connecticut and developed courses on the social responsibilities of business at the Graduate School of Business. He has been Executive-in-Residence at the School of Business at Appalachian State University of the University of North Carolina. Since 1970, Dr. Hickman has been a partner and president of a private investment banking firm, active in management, planning and financial services, Foster, Hickman & Zaenglein. He is director of several public and private companies, and has been chairman of industrial and financial institutions listed on the New York and American Stock Exchanges.

Bert Holtje is president of Tek-Mark, Inc., an advertising and public relations agency. He is the author of twenty-two books and has written articles for many magazines. In addition to varied experience in photography, he serves as a consultant to a number of private and not-for-profit organizations. He has served as a guest lecturer on advertising and consumer behavior at several university graduate schools. He is a member of the Professional Photographers of America.

Ed Nano attended *Life Magazine's* school for the Armed Forces while in the Army Air Corps in 1940. After his discharge from the service, he traveled extensively in the U.S. and Canada as an editorial photographer, working on location, doing feature stories, covering news and sports. He was a photographic correspondent for numerous magazines, including *Life, Time, Fortune, Sports Illustrated, Architectural Forum* and *Business Week*. During this period he also worked for major advertising agencies and industry, doing photography for annual reports, facilities brochures and advertising. In 1959, he turned his attention to studio illustration for advertising, catalogs and package illustration. He serves as a consultant to several film and equipment manufacturers and has lectured to several art director and photographic groups. He has lectured at Winona School and Kent State University.

Ross Sanddal has been employed by the Hughes Tool Company for the past twenty-six years, where he is now manager of the Photographic Services Group in the Research Laboratory. He has been active in local and national professional photographic organizations for the past twenty-five years, having twice been president of the Society of Photographers in Industry. He has also held a variety of assignments in the Professional Photographers of America, currently serving on the Board of Directors and as Convention Committee Chairman. He has been a speaker at national, regional and state photographic meetings and is a contributor to various photographic publications.

Fred Schmidt has been in professional photography for thirty years, as a color technician, commercial photographer, writer and editor. He was Managing Editor of *The Professional Photographer* magazine for many years and is currently Editor of *Photomethods, the Magazine for Visual Communications Management.* He is co-author of *Opportunities in Photography,* a career guidance manual and serves as a consultant in photographic business and education. He writes and lectures on the status and future of imaging, and has appeared at seminars and conventions, including Professional Photographers of America and the Europhot Congress in Belgrade. He is a past director and officer of the American Society of Business Press Editors. He is a member of the American Committee of the Royal Photographic Society, and a member of several other professional societies.

Ted Schwarz is a member of the Professional Photographers of America and is a regular contributor to its journal. He is the author of more than thirty books, including such photography books as *The Business Side of Photography, How to Start a Professional Photography Business, The Amphoto Guide to Photographing Models, Freelance Photography, The Amphoto Guide to Real Estate and Architecture Photography* and others. He is a contributor to the Eastman Kodak *Practical Encyclopedia of Photography* and a columnist for *Camera Life Magazine.*

Arthur Shay, Veteran *Life* reporter and photographer, received *Life's* coveted "Picture of the Year" award for his picture of Russian Premier Kruschev visiting an Iowa farm. As a young *Life* reporter, and at one time their youngest Bureau Chief, Shay knew or worked with most of the great photographers of the Fifties. He still holds a *Life* record, 154 stories or parts of stories in the magazine in a three-year period. More than a thousand of his pictures have appeared on magazine, book and annual report covers. He has written and photographed 42 children's books and 25 sports instructional books. After an exhibition of his serious black and white photographs, Eye Corporation, a Chicago gallery, now offers Shay photographs to large companies as traveling exhibitions.

John Stockwell has translated a lifelong interest in photography into a number of books, articles and courses, in addition to working professionally as a photographer. Currently, he is the Associate Director of the McGraw-Hill Photography Workshop Sessions. He has been active in photographic organizations, and is a member of the Professional Photographers of America.

Preface

You're a photographer, or you're planning to be one. You feel you know a lot about composition, lighting, cameras, and equipment. But, do you know how to get the business that will allow you to use your talents? Do you know how to construct a profit and loss statement so you feel confident to take a well-earned vacation in Europe? Would you feel secure and at ease in an IRS audit? How much should you be spending on promotion?

Most creative people are alike. You figure that with talent and a growing list of assignments, you won't have to worry much about the details of running a business. It will run itself and pay you a handsome profit. For some photographers, this may be true. But, for most, it takes a great deal more than photographic talent to prosper in this competitive business.

This book is dedicated to all photographers who want to make money, but are reluctant to sacrifice their creativity in order to "nickel and dime" their way to business success. Each chapter in this book was written by a professional who has something important to say to you. Each has faced some problem you have faced or are sure to face sometime in the future. Each has gone on to solve these problems, and also to gain the respect of fellow professionals by contributions in the field. Many are authors, award winners, and sought-after lecturers.

In short, this book was created to make sure that you can devote most of your time and attention to the work you like—photography. Each chapter is short, practical, and to the point. We suggest that you read the book from cover to cover, quickly. Then, use it as a reference book when you're faced with any of the scores of day-to-day problems. If you have reviewed the entire book at the start, finding answers and inspiration will be easy.

Apart from helping you handle the routine business details easily, our intention is to provide you with information that will help you make your business grow and prosper. It takes talent, but it also takes solid business know-how to make a success of your enterprise. It's all in this book.

John Stockwell
Bert Holtje

1 | Entering the Photography Business

Kermit L. Buntrock

This chapter and chapter 8 are dedicated to a generation of photographers that promises to be greater than all that have preceded—better prepared scholastically, more sensitive, more creative. It is even possible that some members of this generation will have the wisdom to learn from the mistakes of others—because they know they won't have the time to make all of them on their own. This chapter is intended as a personal and close-up look at entering the photography business. If some of it reads like pontificating from Mt. Olympus, please excuse. It is done out of love for a generation that can bring new greatness to photography.

The Road Is Open

Midyear in 1976 he was a newspaper employee moonlighting in photography. Two years later he was owner of his own beautiful, artfully decorated studio, doing an annual gross of $50,000 and free of debt.

Tired of the rat race in an Eastern city where he was grunt man on a film crew, another young man pulled up stakes at the age of 28 and headed for his home area. In less than two years, without a cent of down payment, he was one-third owner of a thriving studio.

When his employer died, a hard-working young man obligated himself for $50,000 on a 7-year contract to purchase the studio where he had been an employee. The studio had returned the owner $19,000 on a gross of $65,000 the last year of his life. The widow reported later that the young man was enjoying success—and hadn't missed a payment.

A fourth young photographer apprenticed herself to a busy studio in a Midwestern college town and worked part-time through four years of college. Armed with her degree and a strong letter of recommendation, she went to the West Coast and caught on with a large photographic firm. Within two years she was head school photographer.

Another student put himself through four years of college by working as a photographic apprentice. By graduation day he had so impressed his employers with his dependability and management potential they purchased a studio and put him in charge. Within three years, using methods he had learned from his benefactors, he had turned a run-down business into a profitable one. Then he offered the owners a 10 percent per year return on their investment and became the owner of his own business while still in his twenties. Today he is a solid citizen and, respected by his peers, is going through the chairs in his state association.

Fantastic stories? Yes—but true in each case.

All had something a little bit special going for them, of course. The first photographer had a fine image in his community and a wife with a good-paying job in a bank. The second had the courage to ask. As he put it, "A fellow can have just about anything he wants—if he has guts enough to ask for it." The third was willing to work long hours and had the advantage of camera training by a master of photography. The fourth carried an all-important letter of recommendation from her college days' employer. The fifth got his opportunity because he had developed good habits early in life and was mature beyond his years.

Many Opportunities Available

So—there are many routes to a profitable photography business and the road is wide open for those wanting to own their own studios, especially those who are well-trained and are willing to pay the price in effort and self-discipline.

And the time is right!

Many of those who came back from World War II to start what are now successful photographic operations are nearing the end of the line. A lot of them—for one reason or another—have no one coming in behind them. Unless a promising young person with a love of photography and desire and ability to match comes along soon, those photographers will turn the key in the lock and a business that has taken a lifetime to build will be no more. This shouldn't happen.

One Master of Photography, immensely successful in his profession and an esteemed leader in his community, would like to turn his studio over to a young photographer who is as determined and qualified as he was when he started, but thus far he has been disappointed in those who have come to him. Somewhere there has to be the right person.

Another, also a Master and an internationally noted photographer of men, loves his profession so much he often works until midnight. He has an exceedingly profitable studio in a bustling city. Again, the person with the qualities needed to successfully follow him hasn't yet been found.

Good opportunities are available, but mostly for those who prove they are deserving. The answer is to become "the right person," and that could take some stretching.

Many of those now nearing the end of the line in professional photography will be tough acts to follow. They were hardened by the Depression and World War II. They made it big because running a studio was a downhill pull compared to what they had been through.

What will it take to convince these hard-nosed elders that there is a generation coming up that is sharper, better-educated, better-trained, and possessing more potential than the one of which they are so proud?

Set Some Goals

Having some well-defined goals will help. Successful people usually get where they want to go because they know where they are headed and why. The young photographer should know where he or she wants to be in 10 years, in 20 years, and at the end of the line—and the road map for the year just ahead should be a detailed one.

Here are some goals to consider:

1. Develop an inner peace—by recognizing that there is a power greater than your own and by working to best of your ability in every situation.
2. Earn the respect and trust of your customers—through the quality of your product and the thoughtfulness of your service.
3. Become a leader—through ability and dedication, rather than through taking political advantage.
4. Win the respect of your peers—through the integrity of your conduct and by giving generously of your knowledge and experience to help others in your profession.

5. Develop fiscal responsibility — through keeping wants less than your needs and by subordinating personal pleasures to the importance of paying bills on time.

Also consider that if a photographer doesn't have a deep-seated hunger for success, there should be some pretty strong compensating factor. Bear Bryant, the eminently successful football coach with a long career, started life on a vegetable wagon. The memories of that method of making a living were so vivid he decided early that in no way was he ever going back on that wagon! That gave him incentive.

Find a Formula

An outstanding photographer used to claim that he could make it if someone dropped him in the middle of a desert. He was making the point that he had a formula that would work for him under the toughest circumstances.

This sort of thing happens all about us. A person builds a successful business in one community, sells at a big profit, moves to another area, and repeats the process. That person has a winning formula!

Build a formula of your own as early in life as possible. The young man cited as an example at the start of this chapter has a simple and solid formula: "quality work, good service, and tasteful, imaginative promotion."

He advertises "Photography with a special touch" and he puts meaning into it by being sensitive to the needs of his customers. When he covers a wedding he carries along such thoughtful items as safety pins, needle and thread—and aspirin. He provides a glass of water in the dressing room of the bride and another one at the altar in cases where there is danger of fainting. No wonder his wedding business is booming!

What's a Photography Business Worth?

At the Buntrock-Salie Studio in Storm Lake, Iowa, when we decided to pass the baton to a couple of young people trained to come in behind us, we asked our accountant to establish a price that would be fair both ways.

By averaging the profit over a three-year period and then multiplying by four, he came up with a figure of $90,000, plus interest. At first glance this seemed to be a big price for a second-floor studio in a town of 8,500. How many times, however, can you buy a going concern at four times its earnings? So the selling price, large as it was, probably was a bit low. On the other hand, it was quite an improvement over the "inventory, plus a bit of blue sky" formula that has been used on so many studio sales in the past.

The purchaser should make sure that the figure used is the true profit and not the owner's take-home amount. The latter will give a false reading. Profit is what is left over after all expenses have been paid, including a salary to the owner—and salaries to members of the immediate family if they work in the business. In cases where the studio is located in a building belonging to the owner, a reasonable rent should be charged against the business.

The "four times average earnings" formula can be shaded one way or the other depending on local conditions, but the use of this formula in the Storm Lake and other sales has led to considerable mutual satisfaction, so the system must be pretty close to being fair both ways. It gives young people with talent and little money an opportunity to get into a going business on contract—and it provides the seller with a solid reward for the years he has put into building a profitable operation that deserves to go on living.

Under this formula the contract should be spread over seven to ten years. This will permit the purchaser to pay for the business out of earnings, with enough left over above the regular payments to take care of interest and income taxes.

There is some risk for the seller in this, of course. With little or no down payment, he will be left holding the sack if the purchaser doesn't make a success of the business. That's why it is so important to pick the right persons and then train them to a point where failure is out of the question.

If all else is forgotten, remember this: Never buy or sell a studio without involving your accountant and your attorney. They are fellow professionals and they will bring knowledge and objectivity to the bargaining table with them. What you pay them can be the wisest money you ever spend.

Go After What You Want

Here's something for the young person who isn't fortunate enough to have an inside route to studio ownership. Find a progressive town with an active chamber of commerce and no full-time photographic studio. Ask for a meeting with the chamber's board of directors, show your credentials, and tell your story. Emphasize that you are hungry for success, willing to work hard, possess business integrity, and have a desire to add an important new dimension to the community.

Admit that your start-up fund is small—or nonexistent—and that you will need someone in the community to build and equip a studio for you, or remodel and equip a vacant building in the business block. Progressive communities don't like empty buildings on main street. You can pledge to return one per cent per month on the investment.

This one isn't easy to pull off, but in nearly every small community is some well-motivated person with a strong chamber of commerce spirit and money to invest who might take a "flyer" on the right young person. An option to purchase should be included just in case you hit it big really fast, as sometimes happens.

Another option is to lease a going business from someone who wants to retain ownership for some reason. The person could be someone hoping that a grandchild will grow up to enter the business and so would like to keep the opportunity open with good management for the interval.

The benefit to you is that you would be working at the thing you love and possibly making enough so you could purchase your own studio when the grandchild takes over. Of course, there is always the possibility that the grandchild will grow up preferring a banjo to a camera, thus leaving you to continue under favorable circumstances.

Opportunities Unlimited

Large commercial studios, in-plant photographic departments, medical institutions, photographic schools, and color labs all provide opportunities for the eager young photographer who wants to go some other route than owning a studio. Our advice here is to choose the situation that will be most fulfilling and go after it. And don't pass up the color labs. Many of them could benefit by hiring bright young people who have been behind the camera. Don't be easily discouraged. Keep knocking on doors. Persistence does pay off.

Example: A bright young man registered as a freshman at Buena Vista College and then applied for a part-time job at the Buntrock-Salie Studio. We told him we liked his approach, but were well-staffed for the rush season. Next afternoon he was back wondering if anything had turned up—and the next afternoon, also. Guess what. Before the week was out one of our employees came to us with eyes shining and the news that she and her husband were adopting a baby and she wanted to stay home to be a full-time mother. We released her with our blessing and when the young man appeared that afternoon on schedule he had his job—until he graduated. Today he is a university business professor, with his doctorate, and is consultant for one of America's large corporations. The world moves over for people like that and it will for you if you have what it takes and you go after what you want.

Prepare!

Now you know some ways to get into photography. To stay in, you will need *preparation!*

Some say that photographic education is the wave of the future. It is more than that. It is the tide of the present. Never have so many been so busy teaching photography to so many. This exists at all levels: state universities, private colleges, area community colleges, adult classes, proprietory schools, high schools, junior high schools, and short courses and seminars ad infinitum.

The word is out: "Get knowledge—a lot of it—and get it fast."

There are photographers today who are making it big without a college degree—some without even a high school diploma—but it's going to be an uphill battle to do it that way in the days ahead.

Those who are serious about being a credit to photography, to themselves, and to their communities, will need a four-year degree just to stay even. For one thing, it will take that long to learn the things that will be needed for success—technical knowledge in photography, art appreciation, composition, color basics, psychology, salesmanship, business methods, marketing, a liberal arts foundation, and by all means, speech and newswriting. Too many in our generation have shortchanged themselves on the latter two.

The photographer who can speak with ease in an interesting manner can build an image rapidly by appearing before civic groups, luncheon clubs, and women's organizations. Most people find photography a fascinating subject. When you can sell yourself and your product in this subtle fashion, why not do it? Write a good speech—or get a prepared slide show from Kodak and move out on the circuit. It will benefit you greatly.

Learn to Write

A newswriting course can also be a solid investment for the photographer who runs his or her own business. Most editors are receptive to fact-filled stories written from the reader's point of interest about things photographic. They are busy people and don't always have time to cover the honors you have won, the conventions you have attended, or the public exhibits you have planned; so write the stories on your own and deliver them in person ready for print.

Here's an additional tip for those who live in communities covered by weeklies or small dailies. Set part of your gross aside for newspaper advertising. Editors like to pride themselves that there is no connection between the advertising columns and the news they print, but it is still wise to show your good will by voting for the editor's product with some of your advertising dollars.

There will be many pluses in life for the photographer who can write a good news story. Such a photographer's business letters will be more to the point, letters to friends will be more interesting, and memos to the staff more easily understood. Many photographers have been president before their time by volunteering to edit the association bulletin and then doing such a good job the top position came without a struggle.

Learn as Long as You Live

After you have finished your formal education, keep on learning as long as you live, even in retirement. Too many people with college degrees close their minds, feeling that they already know what they need for success. Not so.

The thirst for new knowledge—the desire to do it better tomorrow than it is being done today—should be a driving force all of your life.

A. D. "Tony" Wichers, who had more merits from the Professional Photographers of America for the excellence of his work and service to the profession than any person in the world when he retired, could be found up front at every convention he attended, listening intently and taking notes. This, even when many of those on the platform had been taught by him. If they had learned anything new along the line—or had a better way of doing it—he wanted to be in on it.

When those at the top of the profession know that there is still much to be learned in photography, who dares to close his mind after getting his degree?

Attitude Is All-Important

A director of a successful technical school that has more applicants than seats in its photographic courses and a 90 percent record on placements, listed attitude as the most important attribute for the graduate.

"We have placed graduates with good technical know-how who have been fired within three weeks simply because they didn't have the flexibility to adapt to the situation," he said.

It is difficult for young people who have more education than the person for whom they are working to have the patience to change things gradually. The wise ones do.

A studio owner who has put in a lifetime developing a formula for success that has worked well usually isn't too enthused about changes that haven't been tested, even though the idea sounds great to the proposer.

A nationally prominent photographer recently sold his successful business and retired. Asked how his successor was doing he replied, "He's in trouble. He wanted to change things too fast and he is losing business that I had for years."

This should be a two-way street, of course. The infusion of fresh ideas by imaginative, ambitious young people can be a fine thing for the profession, but the proposers should remember this: If you want to know who has the final say, just look for the signature on the bottom of your check.

Exhibit Integrity

A young officer in Vietnam, who knew that he would never make it back home to see the son who was born after he left for combat, wrote to his wife: "Darling, when our son gets old enough to know, please tell him that the word is *integrity*."

He said it the way it is.

The individual who keeps a promise on a handshake deal, no matter how expensive that might turn out, who refuses to cut corners, who keeps a trust when it would be expedient to do otherwise, who gives as much when alone as when he or she is being watched, has a character trait that will pay dividends throughout life.

This will be hard to believe, especially when you see the fast-buck artists and the corner-cutters getting rich while compromising on principle. Just hold on. The wheels usually come off for those fellows sooner or later. If they should get to the end of the line without being found out, you can be sure they have paid the price in mental torment.

And they have missed the satisfaction that is yours when you can look in the mirror and say, "Hey, you may not be pretty in that glass—but you are beautiful to the world."

That you are, for sure!

Boost That Community!

Be an energetic, enthusiastic booster for your community. It will pay dividends to your business and to you as a person. People respond favorably to a person who works unselfishly for the common good. Eventually this reflects at the cash register.

One person, with sufficient drive and ability, can transform a community. By working through your church or synagogue, your chamber of commerce, your service club, and your lodge, you can join your strength with others in making your community what you want it to be.

Your benefits will be solid ones. Your image as "a good guy" will be enhanced as you demonstrate that you are more interested in the benefit that will accrue to others than you are in the personal gain or fame that might grow out of your efforts. You will better yourself by rubbing shoulders with well-motivated people possessing ability and imagination; and you will have the deep satisfaction that comes from knowing that you have done something to make tomorrow better than today.

The Greeks had a phrase for it. Consider this oath of the citizens of Athens passed on to us by Pericles: "I declare that our community shall be an education to the world; I declare that I shall ever strive for the ideals and sacred things of the community—both alone and with the many."

Dedicated photographers should be important people in the community. So program your days, delegate less important details to others, become superefficient with your time—and give to your community the leadership of which you are capable.

Love That Customer

It is possible to be a success in a photographic enterprise on a 9 to 5 schedule, but you will be passing up business. For example, you may be excluding a lucrative market that involves photographing working people in the family. They usually drag their feet on the deal, anyway, and there will be few occasions on which you can get them before your cameras during business hours.

This means that if you want to serve this market well, you will need to work cheerfully after hours, Sundays, and holidays. If you do this, you can play with satisfaction at times when others are working.

When a family finally makes the decision to have a group portrait taken, the photographer who turns off the enthusiasm with an uncooperative attitude in finding a convenient time for the customer is doing a disservice to himself and to the profession.

Love the customer who comes through the door needing your services at times other than your regular hours and stretch yourself cheerfully to meet that need.

Many people go to the successful photographer because he or she stands tall in their eyes. Be that kind of person. You can, you know.

2 | Choosing the Right Type of Business

Dr. John H. Hickman

As a photographer going into business for yourself, your two most crucial decisions will be what services you plan to offer the public and where you choose to locate your business. Your initial selection of services and location will direct the development of your business plan and have far-reaching effects on the ultimate success of your venture. It is essential that you allow your own personal preferences in these choices to be guided by information developed through market research. This will be the first topic covered in the chapter.

Once you've decided on services and location, the next consideration is entry. The pluses, minuses, and situational factors of buying a going concern versus starting from scratch will comprise the bulk of the chapter.

The last topic considered will be the legal aspects of starting a business. You must choose the form of organization you feel will be best for you: proprietorship, partnership, or corporation. Finally, you will have to select and register a name for your enterprise.

Market Analysis

After settling upon the general geographic area in which you wish to live, you have to determine which locations are appropriate for the particular set of services you intend to offer. Prior to your decision to become an independent photographer, you should have developed a pretty good idea of the type of work you wanted to do. Perhaps you wished to pursue commercial accounts, such as fashion or catalog photography. On the other hand, you may be oriented toward personal services, including family portraits and wedding albums. You might even choose the mobile lifestyle of the freelance action photographer.

From this point on, further decisions will involve a meshing of location and service considerations. From a business standpoint, you must determine whether there is a sufficient need for your proposed services in the selected area at a high enough price and low enough cost to allow you to make a reasonable profit.

Location selection and its effect upon professional services offered can be studied on three levels: choice of a city (or town), choice of an area within that city, and choice of the particular site of the business.

The original choice of a city may be based upon personal preferences, such as favorable climate, presence of friends or relatives, or knowledge of local characteristics. However, it is not a wise policy to expect the patronage of friends and relatives to be very profitable. Your decision should also be influenced by present conditions within and future prospects of the city. A photographer interested in the high-fashion trade would find little stimulation in Littletown, USA, but would thrive (competition allowing) in New York City.

The suitable city would be one on the economic upswing, rather than on the decline or on an even keel. Factors such as climbing population and wealth, aggressive community organizations, and increasing business activity are positive indications of a growing community. Diversified industry is much preferable to a single town industry. A one-industry town can be plagued by seasonal fluctuations in prosperity and by strikes, which can bring your own business to a halt. The number of competing studios in the city also has a bearing on your decisions. Overcrowding obviously should be avoided. Sources quote from 6,000 to 10,000 as the number of people required to support a photography studio in a given area, but this depends on the type of services offered. Suppliers of essential goods and services should be within a reasonable distance to minimize cost and conserve time.

Once the city has been selected, concentrated attention must be brought to bear on the trade area you want to develop. Market research will be especially fruitful in this evaluation. A good location is essential in linking the market and the services required. It is the objective of the business person to discover the services in demand by the customers in the prospective trade area and to offer those he is able and willing to perform.

In general, a photographer interested in specializing in high-priced, individualized portraiture should investigate areas whose residents have greater-than-average incomes. In this general area he should seek a shopping environment evincing a certain level of sophistication. Case in point: Three-quarters of all studios are located in regional or community shopping centers and malls. On the other hand, studios deriving much of their volume from commercial accounts can be more flexible in location because their appearance is of secondary importance.

Location also places constraints on studio size. High downtown rent might limit the size of the studio to the point where the photographer could not perform the type or level of services he had originally intended. Furthermore, the rise in fixed overhead expense resulting from the high rent could make it impossible to make a profit no matter how much volume the studio handled. On the other hand, the central location might bring in rentals from other photographers who need a studio for occasional days of shooting. Regular short-term rentals could defray the overall cost of the downtown location and allow the leasing of a large studio.

In order to project your expected income, you have to first determine the limits of your market or trading area. Then estimate the number of customers in this market and how much of the market you expect to attract. As mentioned earlier, a study of demographic and behavioral characteristics of the market was undertaken to determine whether this was the particular market that you wanted to serve. Now you are interested in the total purchasing power and expected sales volume of your chosen market.

Segregate your prospective trading area on a detailed local map and plot your competitiors' locations. Estimate the population of the demarcated area with the help of census tracts, which give the exact number of people living in each ten-block area. Trading area maps can be acquired from trade association reports, chambers of commerce, or city newspaper offices, and census tracts from the county government. If figures on the present sales volume for your selected area cannot be obtained from trade association reports or the local chamber of commerce, then it would be necessary to develop an estimate of the annual expenditures for photographic services per person or family. If such information cannot be obtained from other local photographers, then assistance should be sought from university research bureaus or market research firms.

After arriving at the likely sales volume by multiplying the estimated expenditures by the population selected, you have to determine how much you can claim. A gross measure can be found by dividing the likely sales volume by the number of competing photographers in the area. Since you are new to the scene, you probably won't attain the average, but the ball-park figure will let you know whether it's worthwhile making the effort in this market.

A more rational, albeit subjective, approach would be to assess your competitors, take stock of your drawing points, and work out a set of expected market shares. Visit your competitors' studios and observe their level of business. Develop impressions of the way they do business and treat their customers. Talk with the customers about their satisfaction with present services and their needs for the types of services you plan to offer.

After learning how the present business is divided among the competing studios, consider your own advantages. Your location will place you closer to customers in certain areas. Established contacts and other photographers' dissatisfied customers are a good source of early business. Special skills and unique services will attract a number of customers. A well-presented "grand opening" promotion will give you the opportunity to make permanent customers out of first visitors. Gauging the influence of these factors and estimating the expected market shares of competing photographers, you can derive the proportion of total sales you can achieve.

Assuming that the sales volume is satisfactory in the market surveyed, you are ready to select a site for the studio. If you are planning to buy a going concern, then you obviously are restricted in your choice. Starting your own business will provide you with a greater diversity of locations. In both cases, you are faced with the same concerns. You have to insure ease of access, evaluating such factors as traffic flow, parking facilities, street or mall location, and availability of public transportation. In neighboring settings, it is a good policy to maintain some distance between rival studios, but this precaution has not proven necessary in large, community shopping malls. The building in which the studio will be should be in good physical condition, have an attractive exterior, and provide display windows for your work. The lease arrangement should be carefully scrutinized by your attorney. Inquiry into the history of the site might reveal a series of unsuccessful tenants, thus exposing the location as a "loser." The availability and capacity of utilities and services such as electricity, water, sewage and garbage disposal, and freight delivery had best be verified. The building should be large enough to provide room for expansion.

The Cost of Going into Business

Now that you have a market to serve, a set of services to provide, and a location for your studio, you should determine the investment necessary to accomplish your goals. The approach developed here presumes that most photographers would attempt to find a situation that satisfies them before figuring out the costs involved. Indeed, the location and set of services offered determine a number of costs that were previously unknown, such as rent and special equipment prices.

A detailed explanation of financial needs and arrangements will be deferred to the following chapter. Here we will confine ourselves to mentioning a few trouble spots and presenting a break-even model for photographic studios.

Cash flow shortages ultimately doom a business to failure. This deficiency nearly always results from shortsighted planning outlooks. To avoid this situation, the fledgling photographer-business person should maintain enough cash reserves, whether through outside income, savings, or personal loans, to provide himself with minimum subsistence for at least a year. Furthermore, there should be sufficient cash on hand to run the business. A good working figure would be the necessary start-up costs plus three months cash expenses. The major share of your investment will be in fixed assets, such as equipment, remodeling charges, and studio fixtures. Although these items are generally financed through long-term arrangements, monthly payments will have to be provided for in your estimate of cash expenses.

You can get the information you need to make preliminary cash projections from a multitude of sources. The firms you plan to do business with, namely suppliers, contractors, and lessors, will generally provide most of the information necessary. Professional advisors, such as bankers, lawyers, and accountants, and business agencies, especially the Small Business Administration and the trade associations, stand ready to supply whatever data they can. You might even be able to enlist the aid of a friendly competitor. Photography journals and government publications are additional sources that frequently yield helpful information.

A good measure of the financial success of an enterprise is its return on investment (ROI), which is calculated as follows: The cost of goods sold is subtracted from the total annual sales to find the gross operating profit. All other costs and expenses reduce this amount to the net profit before taxes, which is then divided by the total investment to form the percent return on investment.

William Park's[1] break-even analysis and supporting schedules are useful in revealing the magnitude of the expenses and revenues involved in a studio enterprise. The typical studio is 600 square feet (general range, from 200 to 1,700 square feet) and serves about 6,000 people. Approximately $29,000 has been invested to get the business operating and annual sales of $62,750 are needed to break even. A word of caution before we proceed: all figures

---

1. William R. Park and Sue Chapin-Park, *How to Succeed in Your Own Business,* (New York: John Wiley & Sons, 1978)

represented as "typical" are to be taken as useful guides, not absolute dictums that must be achieved.

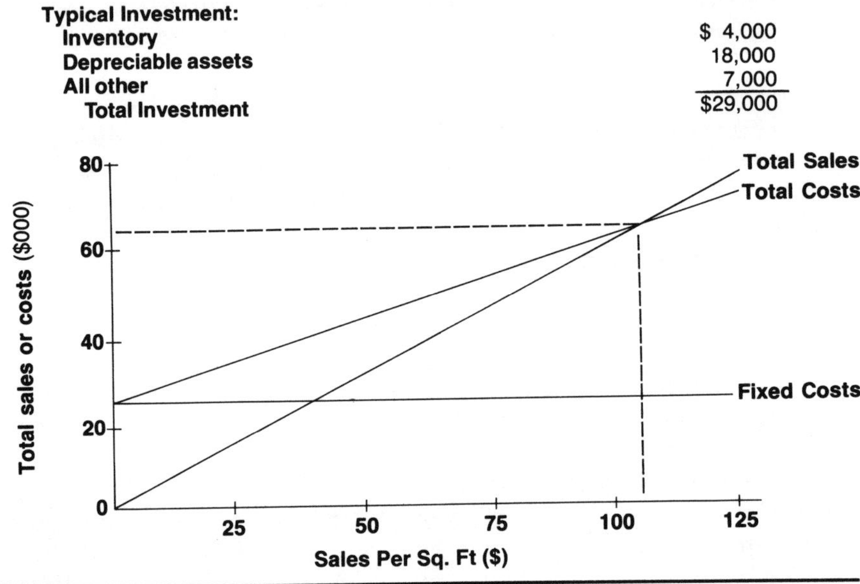

Typical Investment:	
Inventory	$ 4,000
Depreciable assets	18,000
All other	7,000
Total Investment	$29,000

Range of Income Statements:	Low	Typical Operation	High
Sales per Square Foot	$50	$110	$165
Net Annual Sales	$30,000	$66,000	$99,000
Less Cost of Goods Sold	14,000	30,800	46,200
Gross Margin	$16,000	$35,200	$52,800
Fixed Operating Expenses			
Rent and utilities	$ 7,800	$ 7,800	$ 7,800
Fixed payroll	15,000	15,000	15,000
Other fixed expenses	2,300	2,300	2,300
Total fixed expenses	$25,100	$25,100	$25,100
Variable Operating Expenses			
Variable payroll	$ 2,600	$ 5,700	$ 8,600
Other variable expenses	1,500	3,300	5,000
Total variable expenses	4,100	9,000	13,600
Total Operating Expenses	29,200	34,100	38,700
Net profit (loss) before taxes	($13,200)	$ 1,100	$14,100
Typical Operating Ratios			
Net profit/net sales	—	1.7%	14.2%
Net sales/total investment	1.0X	2.3X	3.4X
Net profit/total investment	—	3.8%	48.6%

While it is unlikely you will do as poorly as the "low" operation, you would be doing exceptionally well to achieve "typical" status during your first year. Lest you be confused by the "typical" net profit of $1,100, this figure represents earnings over and above the $15,000 fixed salary received by the proprietor. Thus, this could be considered a bonus for successful operations. The cost of goods sold would include such inventory items as film, print paper, and developing chemicals.

Net profit/net sales, also known as the profit margin, usually increases with an increase in sales, since fixed expenses, by definition, are constant. Net sales/investment indicates the rate of capital turnover. A high rate signifies efficient use of invested capital. Described earlier, net profit/total investment (ROI) is the most critical financial ratio in the business. If you see that the ROI is higher than the cost of capital, you would profit from increased investment in your business. If the reverse is true, then you would fare better investing your earnings from the studio in other ventures.

The break-even point is the intersection of the total sales and total costs lines. Graphically, total sales start at zero and narrow the gap with total costs, which begin at the value of the fixed costs and increase at a lesser rate than do total sales. After the break-even point, sales exceed costs by widening margins and profits are generated.

The formula for break-even point (BEP) is:

$$\text{BEP} = \frac{\text{FC}}{\text{1-VCR}}$$

FC stands for fixed costs and VCR the variable cost rate. The VCR is the ratio of the sum of the cost of goods sold and variable expenses divided by total sales. For the typical operation described here,

$$\text{VCR} = \frac{30{,}800 + 9{,}000}{66{,}000} = .60$$

Thus, the break-even point would be:

$$\frac{25{,}100}{1\text{-}.60} = \$62{,}750$$

Sales of $62,750 are required in order for this business to realize a profit. Sales per square foot become

$$\frac{\$62{,}750}{600} = \$105$$

Buying a Business

Now that you have decided to open a photography studio, you are faced with the choice of entry. The major considerations involved in buying an existing studio are treated in this section; an examination of the alternative of starting your own business follows. Either option has advantages and disadvantages, so a careful, practical evaluation of opportunities at hand should be performed.

Reasons to buy a going concern include:

1. The cost and effort required to plan and start up a new operation are eliminated. Revenue and profits are already being generated.
2. The uncertainty inherent in projecting sales expenses of a new enterprise is alleviated by the availability of the operating records of an existing studio.
3. It provides an established clientele.
4. The facilities, such as equipment and fixtures, are in good working order.
5. The location has proven favorable for successful operation.
6. Financial relationships have been developed with banks and trade creditors.

Each of these reasons must be evaluated for the studio under consideration to determine whether they do in fact hold true. Even if they are legitimate advantages, they must be weighed against the following disadvantages:

1. The purchase price may be overstated, which would put a drain on future profits.
2. A disagreeable landlord will make your tenancy arrangement unpleasant and worrisome.
3. The established customers may be detrimental to the continuing success of the business.
4. The physical facilities may be old and obsolete. Major expenditures may be required to modernize the studio layout and building exterior, and to purchase new equipment.
5. The location may no longer be favorable, if the neighborhood has deteriorated or major access routes change.

6. The purchaser inherits any ill will of the existing studio, including troublesome relationships with banks and suppliers.

Satisfactory answers to questions about the present and future condition of the business must be obtained before purchase can be reasonably entertained.

1. Has the studio been consistently profitable? As a potential buyer, you should study the firm's books, bank deposits, and income tax returns for the last five years. If the seller refuses to release these records, then you have grounds for suspicion of the purported profitability.
2. Is the sales volume of the business increasing, decreasing, or remaining stable? Examination of sales records (cash and credit) would shed light on this concern.
3. Are profits and expenses consistent with sales volume? Refer to the comparative statistics for photography studios published by the trade journals. Significant variations from standard profits and expenses should initiate an investigation of the discrepancy.
4. Is the firm solvent? Study of the balance sheet and use of various financial ratios will give a quick approximation of the soundness of the business. However, an audit by a public accounting firm might uncover problems that you missed. The liquidity of the firm is its ability to pay debts as they become due. The current ratio and quick ratio are good measures of liquidity. Current ratio equals the current assets (cash and easily convertible non-cash assets) over the current liabilities (due within a year), and should be at least 2:1. Quick ratio is the relationship between the most liquid assets (cash and accounts receivable) and the current liabilities. The ratio had better be in excess of 1:1. Another useful rule of thumb is a 50 percent proprietorship ratio, found by dividing the owner's investment by the total assets. As long as this ratio is over 50 percent, the owner has a greater right to the assets than do any creditors.
5. Is the equipment modern and in good condition? Is it properly valued in terms of the original charge and subsequent depreciation? Besides a visual check, scrutiny of purchase invoices and depreciation calculations is in order.
6. What are the terms of the lease and when does it expire? Review the lease and option to renew agreements.

7. Why does the present owner wish to sell? He or she may have a legitimate reason, such as poor health, advancing age, an urge to move elsewhere, or a desire to try another line of work. On the other hand, he or she may be looking to escape from a troublesome business situation.

8. What are the present owner's intentions after the sale? To assure that he or she does not enter into competition with you after the sale, insist on a clause in the sales agreement specifying that he or she doesn't open a studio within X number of miles for five years.

9. Are all liabilities correctly stated on the balance sheet? Contracts and other obligations should be closely studied. Another clause in the sales agreement fixing responsibility for any other claims on the seller is advisable.

10. How do the customers and the general public feel about the business? Some ill will may be discovered through interviews with customers or neighborhood surveys. If it is substantial, the future success of the operation may be jeopardized.

11. What is the reputation of the business among other photographers, suppliers, and local businessmen? Charges of poor credit risk, unprofessional conduct, or mediocre craftsmanship may be difficult to overcome.

12. Are there any nationality, religious, or political factors in the area that would hinder the buyer's successful operation of the business? It is still a reality today that if the neighborhood populace predominantly embraces a single religion, nationality, or political persuasion, then a photographer who is not a member of that group would have difficulty in developing a successful studio.

13. Would the investment make as high a return as could be made by starting a new firm? This answer depends on the purchase price, which is the subject of the following paragraphs.

Your purchase price decision should be based on the future earnings potential of the studio under consideration. From the point of view of the seller, he or she is entitled to a price over and above the market value of the assets sold if the business has been consistently profitable. This bonus, or good will, represents the benefit of public recognition and patronage to the business and becomes an asset on the balance sheet when the transfer of ownership takes place. As the prospective buyer, it is in your best interests to check with customers, suppliers, and local businessmen to assure that this good will will reside in the studio rather than disappear when the former owner leaves.

The value to be assigned to good will frequently can be derived from the income statement using the capitalized earnings approach. The amount to be capitalized is the business income remaining after the owner's salary has been deducted. The rate of capitalization depends on the riskiness of the enterprise. A rate of 20 percent is generally used for normal risk situations. The net value of assets used is ignored in this calculation since it is realized that adequate assets exist to produce surplus earnings.

If the net income was $10,000 and the rate of capitalized 20 percent, then the capitalized earnings would be determined by dividing $10,000 by .20. The maximum amount you should pay for this studio would be $50,000.

Starting a New Business

There are several valid reasons a photographer might want to start a business from scratch. Perhaps you didn't find an existing studio that really appealed to you. Then again, you may have discovered in your market survey that the expanding population of the community has taxed the capacity of existing studios and another is needed. Also through your survey, if you learned that the customers were not satisfied with present quality or variety of the services offered, you might be tempted to correct this deficiency by setting up your own studio.

Starting from scratch lets you:

1. Select the set of services you wish to offer.
2. Choose a location and design the type of layout you prefer.
3. Purchase technologically advanced equipment and supplies.
4. Establish working relationships with suppliers and bankers of your choice.
5. Avoid the legal commitments and binding precedents of an existing studio.

Disadvantages you will have to contend with include:

1. Raising capital may be extremely difficult and discouraging. Without a record of proven performance, loans are scarce.
2. Numerous problems in assembling necessary resources, such as a location, equipment, and supplies.

3. Start-up expenses may be higher and the time necessary to get under way longer than anticipated.
4. Because of the lack of an established market, sales generally are low initially and build up only gradually.
5. A basic accounting system has to be devised and implemented.
6. Difficulty in working out the "bugs" that crop up in the initial operation.

Type of Business Entity

Because of legal and tax implications, it is advisable to consult a lawyer when determining the best type of legal entity to fit your particular situation. Besides the traditional forms of sole proprietorship, partnership, and corporation, the recent subchapter S corporation form merits serious consideration.

Sole Proprietorship

This form is becoming increasingly popular because it combines the advantages of a corporation and a partnership. There is limited liability of the stockholders, but no taxation of the business entity. Instead, the stockholders include their proportionate share of profits and losses in their individual gross incomes. The requirements are not that stringent: a domestic organization, one class of stock, and fifteen or fewer stockholders.

Partnership

A partnership is the voluntary association of two or more people to carry on a trade, with each partner contributing some combination of capital, property, labor and skill. Discretion demands that contracts be prepared by a lawyer, spelling out each partner's rights, duties, and share of the profits or losses. Besides offering a wider range of skills, this form is more effective than a proprietorship in raising financial resources.

Unfortunately, each partner is personally liable for all debts and the actions of all partners in creating obligations for the business. The partnership is automatically dissolved by death or withdrawal of a partner, unless specific provision be made to the contrary.

Corporation

Because of its existence as a separate legal entity, the personal liability of the owners is limited to the original investment. Acquisition of capital is relatively easy. However, the obstacles to and disadvantages of incorporation do not make this route particularly attractive to photographers. An attorney is necessary to guide you through the procedure for formation, if indeed you are eligible. Fees range from $300 to $1,000. Taxes tend to be higher, because of a double taxation arrangement. Recordkeeping and reporting are far more extensive and time-consuming.

Subchapter S Corporation

This type remains the favorite of both portrait and commercial photographers. There is relative freedom of action and control, entry and exit. The profits are yours and so is the full responsibility. This requires that you possess or have access to all the abilities necessary to run a successful photography business. The business has no legal existence apart from the owner, so you are accountable for all liabilities, to the full extent of your personal assets.

Choosing a Name

If you purchase an existing studio, you may want to retain the name if the enterprise is successful and well-regarded. Otherwise, observance of a few empirical rules will facilitate a good choice of a name for your studio. Keep it short, simple, and easy to remember. The name should indicate the service offered or noteworthy features of the concern. Family names say nothing about the nature of the business, so don't use your surname unless it's well-known. Avoid shopworn words and phrases, such as "quality." Check with the county clerk to make sure you're not using a name someone else has been using.

Registration is required in the case of an assumed or coined name, or when only the first or last name of the proprietor or partner is used. The company name and full name of each owner should be filed with the county clerk. This action protects other individuals who deal with the firm and puts on record the actual owners of the business.

3 | Financing the Photographic Business

Ted Schwarz

The difference between success and failure as a professional photographer usually has little to do with your skills behind the camera. Every large city is likely to have one or more moderately competent photographers earning excellent incomes while a brilliantly creative individual is going out of business. The reason? Most probably the competent photographers were properly capitalized while the unusually talented photographer in financial trouble put too little effort into fiscal preparedness. This is such a common problem that 95 percent of all new businesses, including photography studios, are likely to fail in the first two years. Fortunately, your studio need not be one of them.

Setting Up the Studio

The first step toward determining your studio's financial needs is to analyze your market area. What clients can you realistically hope to serve? What types of jobs will bring the greatest amount of repeat business? Which types of jobs are you least likely to handle?

For example, Linda Lenscap is a photographer in a major industrial city. There are manufacturing plants, a large number of advertising and public relations firms, corporate headquarters, and other businesses, all of which can use the services of a skilled photographer. Since Linda wants to specialize in heavy industry, advertising, and related commercial fields, she recognizes that she should plan a studio that is located in such an area that will be most practical for her clients. She will need equipment to handle these accounts but will have little use for cameras, lights, etc., which might be needed if she were to seek primarily portraits and weddings. Naturally, she will want to handle all the business she can get while she establishes her reputation in the industrial field but, eventually, such assignments as portraits will be eliminated from her offerings.

Tom Tripid lives in Dead-At-Night, a rural community with minimal business activity. A small manufacturing plant is the community's biggest nonagricultural employer, but it employs about 75 people and has relatively little need for year-round photography. No matter what Tom's special interest, the only repeat business on which he can count will be portraits, weddings, and school photographs along with some scenic pictures for postcards to be sold to tourists. Tom will regularly be making use of relatively small cameras and lighting primarily designed for studio use. View cameras and extensive floodlighting might be a help in the manufacturing plant, but it will be of little practical use for any other activity he might undertake.

Both Linda and Tom will occasionally be handling similar assignments in the years ahead, but the number of such overlapping assignments will be limited. If they equip themselves for everything they might encounter, Linda will have a large quantity of small camera equipment she will seldom use and Tom will have large format cameras he will rarely call upon.

The same situation that faces Tom and Linda faces you. Although every new studio is likely to have to take all the business that comes its way, the area in which it is located will dictate the bulk of the work it will handle. It is essential that you recognize this fact and plan your basic equipment around the needs of the majority of your potential assignments. This may mean making do with less than ideal circumstances for a small portion of your work but that is not a serious problem.

Being objective, Linda can save herself money by finding a studio location in a relatively low-rent industrial area. This may mean an older section of the community such as a warehouse location. She will not be relying on drop-in customers who need to be impressed with her facilities. She will be getting her business by going to the offices of various corporate executives and selling them on her services. All she needs in terms of a studio is space large enough to handle the photography of the type of products she will most frequently be called upon to record. Much of her work will be on location, so her close proximity to an industrial area can be a distinct advantage.

Tom's circumstances are quite different. He will be able to count on the major manufacturing plant as a client but the work for the plant will be limited.

Most of the pictures will be taken on location. The product photos will also be taken on location if the item is large, such as earth-moving equipment. If the product is small, it can be photographed in space no larger than that which is necessary for recording a full-length portrait. Thus Tom will not need the extensive square footage Linda must have.

Tom's studio location is going to have to be more expensive than Linda's, however. Since portraits and weddings will be the major source of his income, Tom's studio needs to be located in an attractive part of the community. It must be readily accessible to the people who live in Dead-At-Night and be furnished so it is a pleasant place in which to have one's picture taken. A nicely furnished waiting room is essential, it should have adequate wall space for displaying photographs, an area for a receptionist (even if Tom will not have one for a while), and a place where a portrait subject can check his or her appearance. This entire studio must please the aesthetic sense of the customer instead of being merely functional.

The portrait studio will need just three lights to handle normal sittings, plus whatever portable lighting equipment will be used at weddings. Usually this means one or two electronic flash units with rapid recycling and at least one spare unit to cover accidents, breakdowns, etc. Two 35mm cameras or medium format cameras with at least a wide angle, normal, and short telephoto lens will be essential. Two bodies using the same lenses are a must and three provide an extra margin of safety. If more than one format is used, something the new studio owner should avoid when possible, then two bodies per format are essential.

The studio handling commercial accounts can also use the basic three-unit lighting system. However, these should be portable for location use and far more powerful than might be necessary for portrait purposes. A quartz lighting system of perhaps 3,000 watts minimum could be used here rather than the relatively low light output provided by studio electronic flash units typically used by portrait photographers. Barn doors, umbrella reflectors, and similar accessories can be used to modify the lighting for portraits and model poses. The only electronic flash equipment needed will be similar to that used for weddings. However, the industrial studio will be likely to use them only when handling annual reports, executive portraits taken in-plant, and similar assignments.

The industrially oriented studio will want to begin with no equipment smaller than medium format. Usually the swings and tilts of a view camera are essential, though some photographers find the medium format systems totally adequate. Again a minimum of three lenses will be necessary, along with one or more extra backs. At least two bodies are also needed. Some photographers who use equipment with shutters built into their lenses find that it pays for them to have either two lenses of the same focal length or two lenses that offer similar fields of view when that particular lens will be used frequently. A mechanical breakdown will thus not limit your handling of assignments during the repair period.

Operating costs must next be considered. You are going to have to pay rent, utilities, insurance, an answering service, and other bills during the year. You will need to be able to transport your equipment to and from location. You will also need money to meet lab bills in advance of payment from the client.

Advertising costs are another expense. The studio specializing in portraits and weddings will need to advertise in area publications, perhaps on radio and/or television, in high school and college newspapers, and in other areas. The studio selling to industry will need hand-out material such as illustrated brochures, high quality portfolios for showing clients, business cards, and related items. In addition, there will be many hours spent out of the studio trying to obtain new clients. This selling time is essential and must be covered by profits from financially productive periods. After all, you must have a salary to survive.

As you can see, the money you will need to start a studio is fairly high. You cannot expect to make a profit the first year and you will have slow going the first two or three years at least. Therefore let us explore how to reduce financial needs to a minimum and how to obtain the financing you will need in advance.

Figuring Costs

I am assuming that you are not considering going into business for yourself without some professional experience in your background. Perhaps you already work for a photography studio or the photography department of a company. Or you might be a part-time freelancer, selling photography services during the hours you can be away from your regular job.

A second assumption that must be made is that you have experience in the field in which you hope eventually to specialize. If you have five year's experience photographing babies in people's homes and have done nothing else, you should not be considering opening a studio specializing in industrial photography. Not only will you probably lack the needed skills to handle such assignments at first, you will also reduce your chances for financing, a situation discussed more fully later in this chapter.

Because you have been moonlighting or otherwise engaged in photography, you already own some camera equipment, probably some lighting accessories, a gadget bag for transporting it, and, perhaps a tripod. You may also have customers whose business you can rely on in the future. After all, if your work has not been so good as to enable you to obtain repeat requests for your skills in the past, you are not being realistic about going professional on a full-time basis.

The cameras and accessories you own are assets of your business and will be important when you seek financing. Make a list of everything you own and have a camera dealer write in the current market value. The list should be typed and should include serial numbers. A space by each item should be used for writing in the price. Finally, the name of the appraiser and the store for which he or she works should be placed at the bottom of the list.

If your camera equipment is a few years old, you may be surprised to learn that its used market value is higher than the price you paid for it new. A Leica M-4 body could be purchased new for approximately $350 during the first couple of years it was on the market. Seven years after its introduction, that $350 body could be sold *used* for just under $500 due to a combination of collector interest and a drop in the value of the dollar as compared with the German mark. Thus your assets may be far greater than the cash outlay needed to buy that equipment and this is to your advantage.

Next decide the *minimum* equipment you will need to work full time. You want to purchase the least number of items necessary to insure your ability to handle the majority of assignments you can realistically expect to receive on a regular basis. The portrait-studio owner may have an occasional request for architecture photographs requiring a view camera with swings and tilts, but that is the only use the photographer will have for that equipment. The majority of the assignments will need nothing larger than medium format. Thus owning a view camera is a luxury that should be avoided until architecture can be a regular, profitable aspect of the studio's business. It is always better to turn down an assignment for which you are not equipped than to buy the equipment needed to photograph the assignment. However, you can often rent specialized equipment to handle specialized assignments.

Shop various dealers to see what the new equipment will cost. If you can buy the items used, so much the better. Be certain they have been checked by a competent repair person and that you have a few days to run enough film through the camera to insure everything works. If your community is too small to have much in the way of used cameras, contact the major camera stores in a large city such as New York. You can spot their advertisements in the various amateur photography magazines and the majority are both honest and lower-priced than most small dealers.

Make a list of the items you need to buy right away and their prices. If for some reason you will not seek a loan for several months, this price list should be updated at that time.

Next make a list of your other costs. What rent are you likely to pay for the size studio you will need? Realtors can be of help here, and utility companies can provide information on the cost of fuel for the property.

What will your telephone costs be, including an answering service or *two* answering machines (one for a back-up)? Remember that the phone company will also have a fairly high initial installation fee.

How much money will supplies cost? These include business cards, a stock of film, letterhead, billing forms, model releases, customer order forms, envelopes, and similar items.

How much will equipment maintenance run? A minor overhaul of an intricate camera body can cost around $100 in many shops and the overhaul may be needed as often as once a year or as seldom as every five or six years, depending upon the camera and its use.

Will you need to supply your own air-conditioning units? What about furniture? Stands? Seamless background paper? Props? Flood bulbs? Batteries?

An accountant may be needed to help you establish a record-keeping system. You may need a lawyer. You will have insurance payments to make. All these costs can be estimated in advance and should be included in your figuring.

Contact the various media representatives in your area as well as a yellow pages salesperson. Find out the cost of advertising and decide how much you will want to do each month.

How will you live while you are starting your business? Do you have a working spouse whose income is sufficient to meet all household expenses for several months? Do you have a cash reserve to cover living expenses that will never be touched for business purposes? Will you be working a part-time job in addition to running your photography business? You should allow for profit with every assignment but your assignments are likely to be so few, at first, that the total net must be plowed back into the business.

You will also need money to be able to pay your bills on time. Most businesses are willing to extend a discount if you pay immediately upon receipt of your bills. This may only be one or two percent, but that amount adds up quickly in the course of the year.

You can also save money by avoiding credit buying whenever possible. It is estimated that long-term credit buying can add as much as 40 percent to the price of equipment. There are some tax advantages to credit buying, but when your business is new, the cost of the credit may reduce your net to such a level that you can not stay in business long enough to have a tax advantage.

Once you finally know your definite and projected costs for at least the coming year, prepare a statement listing all these items. You will have an entry for camera(s), another for lenses, a third for lights, background equipment and tripods, a fourth for your darkroom (if any), a fifth for film and related supplies, a sixth for all office supplies including business cards, chairs, desks, and a waiting room area, and so forth, to as many categories as are necessary.

Next show such items as rent, taxes (projected), license fees, insurance, utilities, personnel salaries, costs for an answering service or answering machines, general operating expenses, and so on. The two lists should cover every possible expense you can imagine including those which might prove unwarranted as you actually start in business.

Now make a list of your tangible assets that can be utilized for your business. This means your equipment value, of course, but also the cash value of your life insurance; your house, if you own one; and nonessential items you could sell for cash such as a second car, a motorcycle, or even a stereo system, though this latter item might be useful in the studio to provide background music for models. Consider your savings account, land you might own, stocks and bonds, collectibles with a liquid value and anything else convertible to cash. These must all be items you are willing to use as collateral for whatever type of financial arrangement you have to make, not assets you wish to retain at all cost.

Finally, prepare a financial statement showing your income taxes for the past three years with special emphasis on the income from photography. Detail the types of assignments you have handled on a freelance basis and how these relate to the type of work you will be doing when you have your own studio. You want to be able to show that there is reason to believe your studio will have customers right from the start. This is why it is essential that you be handling the type of work in which your studio will specialize. If you are currently doing industrial work exclusively, potential creditors will be concerned about lending you money to open a portrait business. Your photographic reputation is in industry and you presumably have no contacts in portraiture. It may be months before you establish yourself, in the meantime piling up massive debts from which you may never be able to recover. However, if you are going into industrial specialization, there is reason to believe you will have clients because you are already working with companies in the field.

Financing Your Business

The most logical source of financing is a bank. However, what you may not realize is that you can get at least three different types of bank loans. The first is a straight business loan which will be based on your personal credit, collateral, and your future business prospects. The latter is determined by looking at your financial records covering the last three years as they relate to professional photography. You will have to show what type of professional work you have handled and what your expectations for the coming months may be. The stronger your current base in terms of clients and the more realistic your expectations based on past work, the more money for which you will be eligible.

The second type of bank business loan is one which is backed by the Small Business Administration. Your area banker can put you in touch with the nearest SBA office. If you are approved for an SBA-backed loan, you will need far less collateral. The SBA insures the loan against default, taking the loss rather than the bank. This is usually the best approach to a normal business loan and will result in the best terms, so far as dollar amount, you can get.

The third approach is for the photographer with money in the bank. Suppose you have savings totalling $12,000 and need $10,000 in order to establish your business. You know that $2,000 is all the cash you require for emergency purposes, yet you dislike the idea of reducing your savings by spending the $10,000 for your business venture. The alternative is to put the money into a certificate of deposit (CD) and use that as collateral. Both banks and savings and loans institutions offer CD loans at rates that are currently 2 percent and 1 percent, respectively, more than the interest paid by the CD. This works out to far less expense for you than a conventional loan.

Another source for money is a credit union. This may be a professional photographers' association credit union, the credit union where you currently work, or a spouse's credit union. At times the credit union will be happy to give you a business loan even if you will be leaving the place of employment that allowed you to join in the first place. At other times you can only get a loan for the period during which you are employed by the member organization.

A credit union's business-loan rate may seem as high as a bank's on the surface, but you will usually find that the charge is based on the declining balance. This means that your interest payments are effectively reduced as you pay the loan, making your total cost for the loan less than for a bank loan.

If you have life insurance with a cash value, borrowing against the cash value can provide you with a source of income. The interest charged is usually extremely low, often two-thirds to one-half the bank loan rate.

Investigating Alternatives

What happens if you cannot obtain the working capital you need? The first step is to study your financial statements and review your current clients in relation to future prospects for business. Perhaps you have been overestimating your immediate potential. Perhaps you are being unrealistic about the requests that will be made for your services. You may not be ready to take the step toward full-time professional work or you may need to narrow your plans until you have a firm base of customers for your business.

There is also the chance that, when you study your statements, you will recognize that there is no reason for you not to get the loans. You have genuine reason to feel your venture will succeed. Being turned down for loans does not diminish this genuine potential of your future business.

When this second situation occurs, see where you can cut corners, perhaps by going after the type of customer whose needs will not require you to have high overhead. For example, suppose you want to open a portrait studio but can't get quite enough money to cover rent in the location you feel would be best for your business. Instead of opening a studio somewhere else, why not start by working out of your home, without a studio. Advertising is done in the media and your business telephone number is actually your home listing. You can also utilize an answering service if this works best for you.

Instead of running a studio, you can become a location portrait-photographer specialist. All your work can be done in the client's home or office, or in an outdoor setting. Your advertisements stress "environmental" portraiture. They speak of photographs taken to show people as they really are rather than unnaturally posed in the studio. In a sense, you make a virtue out of your poverty, creating a market where the customer might actually be insulted if asked to come to a studio.

The same is true with weddings. The engagement portrait can be taken in the bride-to-be's home. A full-length portrait of the bride in her wedding gown can be taken inside the church or synagogue, in front of an interesting-looking building, or in a park. It is the "natural" way to handle bridal photography.

Naturally you will go to the customer's home to show samples of your work when operating on location. But this works to the bride-to-be's convenience and will never be seen as a cost-cutting measure.

Commercial photography will have to be limited to on-location work. This means that work for advertising firms cannot be accepted unless you have room to set up enough of a layout to effectively tell the story. If you can work on location with various settings, the ads will also be easy to handle.

Public relations work, annual reports, and similar assignments can be handled no matter what your base working conditions. These can be avidly sought with no fear that you will be unable to deliver. Architecture and real estate photography are strictly location projects, of course.

Industrial photography is another potential maket for you, if you live in an area that has numerous factories. If you are in a rural area, you may still be able to find one or more industrial operations to photograph.

Consider services you can offer in clients' homes that are meant to provide you with income while saving to open an actual studio if you must start from your home. Pet photography in the home, photography of valuables for insurance purposes, and party photography are all possibilities. School photography is an ideal business venture for the undercapitalized photographer who can only survive if no studio space is rented.

When you work from your home, your biggest cash outlay, other than for equipment, will be for advertising and promotion. You must get your studio name to the attention of potential clients. This might be through direct mail to brides-to-be whose engagement announcements appear in the newspaper, through display advertising in various area publications, through brochures shown to public relations firms and advertising agencies, and by other means. Plan a monthly budget that is seasonally adjusted according to the type of work you handle. More couples get married in June and December than in other months, which means that the wedding photographer should begin advertising most heavily from six weeks to three months in advance of those dates, with a reduction in spending during the period immediately following those times. Annual reports are generally fall or winter projects, so you should begin your push to handle them sometime around late summer. Keep track of when such reports are prepared by the businesses in your area, then vary your promotion efforts if the timing varies from the fall and winter schedule.

As you begin to handle assignments, you will be faced with the question of equipment purchases. You will encounter assignments that can either be handled better with some lens or camera you don't presently own or which can *only* be handled with something you lack. The immediate tendency is to go out and buy the item. It seems to make sense to add equipment as you can use it, building your resources accordingly. Unfortunately, this may not be a realistic method for handling the matter.

Before buying any lens, camera, or accessory beyond those which are part of your basic equipment, consider how often you will use the item. For example, suppose you specialize in advertising photography and a client decides to have you include a picture of the building with the work you have been assigned. Normally you only handle product photographs, often with models, so you lack perspective control equipment. This is an important client so you immediately buy either a view camera or a perspective control, wide-angle 35mm camera lens. You take the necessary picture, the client is thrilled, and you are equipped for the next such picture demanded of you.

From a business viewpoint, the purchase of the perspective control item is not necessarily a good idea. Suppose you spent $500 for the item and earned $100 for the photograph. The lens is 20 percent paid for in your mind.

However, since architecture photography is foreign to your normal work, that means the lens could go unused for several months or as long as a year or more. It is generating no income and is actually draining your studio of profits.

But a lens or camera can't rob you of money, can it? Surprisingly, the answer is that it can. You may have earned $100 in the theoretical example, but you spent $400 more than that. If that $400 were in a savings account, you could be drawing interest on the money. Every month the item is not bringing income to your business, it is robbing you of bank interest.

Because of these factors, no item of equipment should be purchased without projecting your realistic future needs. How many times in the coming year can you expect to put the item to use? How much money can you expect to earn with that item handling whatever assignments you can realistically expect to obtain? I do not mean anticipated income based on your entering a new field, such as architecture, when you are currently known for advertising work only. I mean income based on the type of work you know you will continue to receive, though utilizing the special perspective of the new equipment.

If you cannot see yourself using a lens, camera, or whatever enough times in the course of the first year of ownership to at least earn back its cost, you probably should not buy it. You might want to turn down the assignment, suggesting another photographer who is both properly equipped and skilled enough to handle the job. Or you might want to rent or borrow the item, thus being able to accept the assignment while keeping your cost to the minimum.

Never fear turning over an assignment to another photographer. It almost never costs you money in the long run. The client is usually so pleased that you have been honest about your limitations and concerned enough about his or her needs to recommend someone who can handle the work that he or she remains loyal to you. The client continues sending you all the work you can handle.

Most camera stores do not maintain a line of rental items. The owners rent only the used equipment taken in trade, which has probably not been inspected by a repair person. This may present no difficulty but it is best to run some film through the camera, operating the flash if such lighting will be used, a day or two before you need it. This should be processed and checked to be certain the exposure will be accurate.

An alternative is to use one of the major city dealers for rental. A number of large camera dealers in New York have a special rental stock covering every possible item. These potential resources should be checked in advance so you can use them when you have enough assignment lead time to allow for shipping.

If you must rent a lens, camera, or other item for an assignment, be certain to increase your charge to cover the needed item. This is not a hard and fast rule, however. There may be instances when you know the client is on a strict budget, the rental cost is relatively minor, and the need is never likely to arise again with this client. Under such circumstances, assuming the client is a regular one, you may wish to absorb the rental cost to insure further good will.

If you are friendly with other photography studio owners, you might consider forming an equipment pool. If there is specialized equipment you each could use on an occasional basis, and if your needs are not likely to occur at the same time, you might jointly purchase the special optics, bodies, etc. You divide the cost equally among you and store the item(s) where it can be obtained by anyone who needs it. This is preferably kept in a locked cabinet with a sheet for signing the item in and out.

For example, suppose you want a quality, prime fish-eye lens but know you may only use it a half dozen times a year. Such a lens is likely to run from $300 to over $1,000, depending upon the particular brand, focal length, and f-stop. By sharing the cost with others, it might prove practical for the amount of money you would each have to invest.

Or you might want to get an ultrawide or medium-format camera. Again your needs will be limited and a shared purchase could be the answer.

The same situation can be carried over into services as well. You might find that two or more studios can support a full-time darkroom technician who is a fast, skilled worker. The darkroom could be set up in one of the studios, the square footage carefully measured so the exact portion of the rent needed to cover the space can be determined. The rent and cost of the equipment will be shared but the darkroom technician's time and supplies will be paid according to who uses this person. The technician will be given a record book into which the name of the photographer is noted along with the services performed, the chemicals, paper and other supplies used, and the client's name. Then the total hours are added for each photographer each pay period and the photographers pay according to their percentages of the time. Supplies are billed to the appropriate client, though these will be less than might otherwise have been possible because supplies for two or more studios will be purchased in larger quantity than for one. This means a discount for bulk purchases if you shop carefully.

Cash Flow

Cash flow is always a problem with a photography studio. With portrait customers it is essential that you receive payment for each service—sitting, proofs (if an additional charge), prints, framing, etc.—upon completion. You can keep the public happy while insuring immediate payment by honoring the bank credit cards. When people are able to charge their purchases, they are likely to buy far more than when they must pay cash.

Commercial accounts with advertising agencies and others should also be encouraged to pay immediately. One approach is to offer a slight discount for payment within ten days of receiving the bill. A somewhat smaller discount can be offered for payment within 30 days.

Credit should be extended with great care, even to major businesses. Many firms are notorious for putting off paying bills until the last possible moment in order to utilize the cash for other purposes or to obtain maximum interest. Be certain you investigate the credit ratings of both companies and individuals, however, before allowing delayed payments.

There are several ways to handle credit accounts. A talk with your local commercial credit agency will be a start, and many office supply stores have credit application forms that are excellent. In addition, you can contact the National Association of Credit Management, 475 Park Avenue South, New York, New York 10016, for help. Along with other services and aides, the NACM offers a book entitled *Everyday Credit Checking* written by Sol Barzman and published by Thomas Y. Crowell. Barzman's background is not in the photography business, but the information he supplies is applicable to the studio owner.

A new business can prosper only by keeping all nonessential expenses to a minimum. If you can get by without opening a formal studio during the early months of your professional career, you will be dollars ahead when you finally rent space outside your home. If you limit the assignments you seek to only those you can handle with minimum equipment, you will again avoid having overhead erode your chance for a first-year profit. And if you have enough initial capital to carry you through the lean periods, you can be certain that undercapitalization will not harm you the way it has devastated so many other beginning studios.

4 | Your Place of Business

Bert Holtje

The chances are that your photographic specialty will pretty much determine the location and complexity of your place of business. For example, a freelancer who shoots mainly for travel magazines will have need for little more than a place to put a phone and his files. But an industrial photographer might need a building that could hold an 18-wheeler. A realistic estimate of the major markets you serve is perhaps the best way to begin your search for a business location.

Later in this chapter the special problems related to the major fields of photography are discussed, but for now let's look at some of the general considerations.

Only an Office

If your shooting is always done on location, and you use a commercial lab for processing, you will have no need for anything more elaborate than an office. However, it is very important to have an office that is really a work place. Don't use a corner of your breakfast table to write bills and your shirt drawer to store records. Even if your office is in your home, it is important to set aside a space that is used for nothing else. It doesn't have to be a big room. It doesn't even need to be a room. Pieces of interesting and practical furniture can be found that look like decorative chests when closed, but become self-contained mini-offices when opened. Such furniture can enhance any room, and as long as you use it strictly for business you'll be in good shape. But, as soon as you begin to use it to make up your laundry lists or to write personal letters, you'll be in trouble. Sooner or later everything will blend into one big heap, and you will find yourself taking twice as long to handle routine business chores.

We have seen people build a complete office into a closet. When the door is closed, there is no office to see. One ingenious photographer built a rollaway desk into a closet, with shelves and files occupying the space above the desk. Even the phone was in this closet. All he did was open the door, roll out his desk and he was in business.

Of course, if you operate this way, you are probably away a lot of the time. Therefore, you need either an answering service or an answering machine. Most photographers we talked to seemed to prefer the answering machine. Each felt that the sound of his or her own voice was more personal than the voice of an answering service.

There is little chance that local ordinances will give you problems when you have nothing more than an office in your home. It's only when you have people coming and going that you will run into trouble. However, it's best to check your local laws just to make sure.

The Home Studio

There are many photographers operating from home studios rather than in commercial buildings. If you plan your home business carefully, there are numerous significant advantages.

Whether your home-studio is in a house in the suburbs, in a brownstone in the city, or in an apartment, certain requirements remain the same. First of all, the question of proximity to your market is paramount. If you are doing portraits, for example, and specialize in executives for public relations work, you will want to be near the businesses in which these people work. A house in the suburbs may appeal to you, but there is little chance of getting a highly paid chief executive officer away from his company and out into the suburbs for a portrait, no matter how good you are. In this case, you should think of a location where you can combine an apartment with your studio. And be sure to give some thought to lab needs if you are planning to do your own processing.

Whether you locate in an urban apartment or in a suburban house, another requirement is to have separate entrances for your living quarters and for your office. Also be sure that your personal quarters are not apparent to your clients. Nothing tears down a professional image faster than the family pet or your kids nosing around the studio.

When you use your home, you will be able to write off on your tax form expenses on that portion of the home used for business. (There are many legitimate business deductions; see Chapter 7 for further information.)

When the studio is located in a suburban house, it is often possible to make use of the basement for the lab. If such a darkroom is in your plans, be sure to check the basement carefully for dampness. It's not uncommon for suburban basements to be damp, especially when the weather is hot and humid. And heavy rains can turn a normally dry basement into an indoor swimming pool. While few basements are this bad, you should be especially watchful for normal dampness since it is bad for equipment as well as supplies. An inexpensive humidity indicator will help keep tabs on the moisture content in the air, and a dehumidifier will usually eliminate the dampness. If you see the moisture level of the air going above 50 percent, it's a good idea to run the dehumidifier.

A Studio in a Store

A storefront gives you the opportunity to display your work. Such a display would be impossible in a home studio, unless the home is located in a commercially zoned area. Most photographers get very little immediate walk-in business. But when people walk by a studio with a display window and see your work, they will start thinking about having some pictures made. The photographer with a home studio will generally have lower operating expenses, but it will be necessary to spend more on promotion and advertising. The photographer with the storefront will have rent to pay, but the window display will probably be all the promotion he or she will need to sustain a steady flow of business. However, many photographers who use their homes as studios have overcome this problem by arranging to have ongoing exhibitions of their work at other locations, such as bridal shops and toy stores. This problem is covered in detail in the chapter on advertising, but you should give it some thought now if you are not sure what type of location will be best for you.

The store location you choose should be compatible with the type of photography in which you specialize and the types of stores run by your merchant neighbors. For example, if you are doing portraits, look for a location near clothing stores, beauty parlors, and jewelry shops. When people visit stores such as these, they are thinking about themselves and the idea of having a portrait made has immediate appeal.

It's important to note that the strongest benefit of a studio in a store is the regular exposure you will get. Therefore, be careful to choose a store in a high-traffic location. The shopping malls tend to have the kind of traffic that most photographers need. However, some of the older neighborhood shopping areas can be just as effective even though the total traffic may be less. If the kind of people you want as customers shop in the smaller centers and they see your window display, such a location can be just as good as a high-traffic place in a big mall.

There is no substitute for direct experience to determine which location will be best for you. If you have found a store you like and are thinking of renting it, station yourself in the area for several days and make an informal count of the people who go into the nearby stores. Ask yourself if these people are the people you want for customers. Do they have children in tow? If so, you should be able to build a baby and child photography business. Are they buying expensive clothes and jewelry? Those who do often like to have themselves photographed wearing their purchases. Are the neighboring merchants willing to cooperate? You can often arrange with other business people to steer business your way, either for mutual benefit or for a recommendation fee.

You will also need to know something of the parking facilities and the proximity to residential neighborhoods. If the center is a good distance from the residential areas, and the parking spaces are limited, your traffic may be limited. Don't stop at what you see, though. Check with the local planning board and find out if any housing developments are going to be built in the area in the near future. The location may be marginal now, but if you are the only photographer in a shopping center that will soon serve an entirely new neighborhood, it could be the right location.

Stores come and go. You will want to know if there was ever a photographer in the center before you. Ask the local merchants or the chamber of commerce. If there was a photographer in the area and he or she has left, be sure you know the real reasons before you make your decision about moving into the same studio.

What should you do if there already is a photographer in the neighborhood? There may be more than enough business for two or more photographers, but you can be sure that the photographer who is there now will not tell you that. You will have to determine this for yourself by getting a feel for the volume that is being done and for the potential of the entire area. Of course, you may get a toe hold by specializing in an area that is not important to the photographer who has already staked out a claim.

To Rent, Buy, or Build

While rent is a business expense and can be deducted from your taxes, you will always be at the mercy of the landlord and high rent could put a squeeze on your budget. However, there are times when renting is the best way to go.

If, for example, you are not too sure of the most suitable location for you, it's best not to buy or build a studio right away. By renting first, you will be able to get a feel for the area and the business that you can develop. If you find yourself in this situation, try to get the shortest lease possible. Most landlords want to tie up their property for three to five years, but you should try to get a one-year lease at first. Business may not work out, and you could find yourself stuck with rental payments and no business. Or, you could find that your business has grown beyond your expectations, and your present space is too small.

However, be sure to have a renewal clause in the lease so that you have the option to stay at a favorable rent if the studio proves to be adequate and the area turns out to be a gold mine. But most landlords will recognize what you are doing and will want to rent to you at a higher rate at the termination of the lease. Even though it may cost more, it's probably better to renew the lease than to sink a lot of money into buying a building when you are not ready for this step.

Once you are sure that your business is on a strong footing and that your specialty is in demand in the area you have chosen, you should negotiate a long-term lease. For signing a long lease, your landlord should be willing to hold rental increases to a minimum. After all, you are guaranteeing that you will be using his space for a long period of time and that is worth quite a bit.

When you rent space for your studio, there are a number of points that you should keep in mind. You will probably have to do quite a bit to the premises in order to make them usable. You may have heavy power requirements and have to bring in extra electrical service. You might want to do some internal building to include not only a studio area, but a place for your darkroom, storage, props, office, dressing room, reception room, and a spot for displays. Be sure that you have in writing just what you plan to do and what the landlord will allow you to do before you sign anything. If you neglect this, you may find that when you move, all of your lighting and other installed equipment will become the property of the landlord.

Perhaps the best buck you will spend when you sign your lease will be for an attorney's review. Most leases are standard forms, but even when they are used, there are special conditions that can cause trouble for you later on. It's a one-time cost, and can save you headaches in the future.

Buying or building involves essentially the same commitment. If you buy or build just for your business, you had better have the volume to support it. However, many photographers who have recognized the value of property ownership have also discovered that it's often wise to acquire a building in which there will be other tenants. Some photographers just look for a "taxpayer," or another business to share the freight and the space. Others recognize that there can be more to making money in the photography business than clicking the shutter. The ownership of income-producing property adds a dimension of stability to a service business that is hard to beat if you suddenly find yourself unable or unwilling to work at the photographer's trade any longer.

Of course, the acquisition of such a building is a big undertaking. However, you will be surprised at how much easier it often is to acquire a big building compared with a small building in which you may be the only occupant. Banks and other organizations that loan money for such enterprises will see that a fully rented office building, in which you will have your studio, is a moneymaking asset. In other words, they are less likely to have trouble with such a facility than they would if it were to house only your studio because the risk is spread over a number of tenants.

If you plan it properly, your income from other tenants should cover your expenses to carry the building. If you maintain the building with care, its value will rise, and when you decide to quit the business, you will have an asset that can be turned into profit. Building or buying your own building is a big step, but most photographers who have done it say it's an excellent investment.

Selecting the Best Location for Your Business

Most people who go into business for themselves try to locate their business in areas that meet their personal requirements. It's ideal if this works out, but your first consideration must be proximity to your market. You may like to live near the water where you can sail your boat and do a little fishing, but if your clients are advertising agencies, you had better think of a summer home for personal pleasure and a studio near the agencies for business. This may seem like a blinding glimpse of the obvious, but you'd be surprised at how many of us let our personal feelings overrule good business judgment.

In the pages that follow are some hints on where to locate different types of photographic specialties for maximum impact. The points are general but related to each specialty. However, as a specialist and a person seeking to build a business in a specific area, you should use these thoughts as aids in planning your location to meet your individual requirements.

Wedding Photography

The wedding photographer works in and outside the studio. This means that logistics are very important. Your studio should be near most of the churches and synagogues in order to offer the most convenience. In most suburban locations, this is seldom a problem. Towns are not that big, and the churches and synagogues are seldom more than a few minutes apart. However, if you are thinking of locating in a big city, or in a rural area where the distances may become a problem, you will have to solve the problem in other ways.

For formal photography, your studio should be able to accommodate more than just the bride and groom. Often, the albums you shoot will include pictures of the entire wedding party. This could be quite a crowd, and you should be prepared to handle them all in the studio.

There are, of course, wedding photographers who have no studio at all. These people take all their pictures in the homes of the bride and groom, at the church, and at the reception. But, whether you need a studio or not, you should still be near enough to the residential areas where your clients live in order to discuss their plans with them.

If there is a department store in your area that does a big wedding gown business, you might inquire about leasing a department. Many department stores are made up of individual entrepreneurs who lease space from the store owners. If you can arrange to lease such a location, insist on being either next to or very near the bridal shop. Just as importantly, you should conclude an agreement with the proprietor of the bridal shop well in advance of signing a lease. If the bridal shop owner already has a photographer that is routinely recommended, the location could be of little or no value to you.

School Photography

Typically, school photography consists of mass-produced images on location. For this reason, a studio is unnecessary. Commercial processing labs provide special school services that include several sizes of prints packed neatly in a standard package.

For some types of school photography, such as senior pictures, you might need a studio convenient to the school you are serving. The actual space need not be large for this type of business, but should be so arranged that many sittings can be handled in a short time with a minimum of confusion. Generally speaking, this will mean a fairly large waiting room or staging area, and an arrangement that permits easy, flow-through traffic.

Public Relations Photography

Don't confuse advertising photography with public relations work. Advertising photographers work mainly with products, but the public relations photographer is concerned with pictures of people who are seeking to enhance their public image. You might be interested in doing theatrical work, handling celebrity shots for industry, schools, radio and television stations, publications, hospitals, and political parties.

Most public relations work for businesses involves shooting pictures for annual reports, publicity releases of executive promotions, and general corporate-image work. If this is your forte, you should locate as close to the industrial or business areas that appear to hold the most promise for your business. If this is not apparent from preliminary scouting, you can often get good advice from local and state business organizations. Many states publish industrial and business directories that list businesses by geographical areas. Armed with this information and a local map, you should be able to pinpoint the best spot for your studio.

The studio is generally very important for the photographer who does corporate public relations work. Executive portraits are easier to shoot when you have the control afforded by a studio. Of course, there is some excellent work being done by photographers who work with their clients on location. However, most still feel the need for a formal studio.

Architectural Photography

Except for a few well-known professionals who specialize in architectural photography, most pictures of buildings are taken by those who have a general studio business. You will want to be near the major concentration of architects.

The top architects work all over the country and the world, however, and when they need photographs they rarely use local talent if the job is important. They hire a top pro and fly him or her to the site to do the job. This is the kind of specialty that takes quite a bit of time to build, but when you have established contact with the architects and owners who buy quality photography, you will have a solid business.

Pick your location to give you easy access to your potential clients. Architects seldom congregate in tight little areas, but you will find that major cities have their enclaves. A tour of the yellow pages with a local map should give you an idea of where you should be.

You should also think of a location that will give you a place to display your work. The chances are slim that you will work from a storefront location. You might consider an office near the architects with whom you want to work. If the building will allow it, try to arrange a regular display of your work in the lobby to catch the eyes of the architects and building owners.

Obviously, architects and owners will be your major sources of business, but don't rule out real estate people. The real estate people who will mean the most to your business will be those who are dealing in office and industrial buildings, or those who specialize in very expensive homes. The realtor selling typical homes is generally interested in low-cost file shots for his office or sales book.

When you think of architects, don't limit your thinking to those whose work is on the ground. Naval architects are another source of photographic business. Every one, from those who design pleasure craft to those whose vessels carry thousands of tons of cargo, have a need for photography. Photographing a ship is essentially the same as photographing buildings. You have tough perspective problems and most usually work with natural light in an outdoor situation. Those who design and those who build the ships often have extensive photographic requirements. If their work isn't being handled internally, you might plan to locate near their offices or the shipyard where the work is being done.

Fashion Photography

The fashion photographer usually has heavy studio and lab requirements. Quite often the clients need the pictures in a hurry, and the photographer should have the tight control over processing that is possible only with an on-premises lab, or a reliable nearby lab.

If you are going to do work for department stores, the chances are that you will be doing most of the work on location. Department stores usually have the space and all the props needed to give good fashion images. However, if you are working with fashion manufacturers you may have more of a need for a studio. Be sure to determine just how each manufacturer works and what his or her preferences are before you commit to a location. In either case, you will have to be quite near your clients. Fashion is a fast-breaking business, and when pictures are needed in a hurry you will have to be ready to jump. Your studio should have ample facilities for models to dress and apply make-up. Security should be an important consideration if expensive garments, such as furs, are photographed.

The General Studio

The general photo studio is best located in an area that has a high level of foot traffic. A downtown business area or a shopping mall is a good spot. Seldom do people decide on the spot to walk in for a picture when they see your display. But regular reminders created by your ever-changing window exhibit will eventually make them curious enough to stop in for information.

When such people do stop in, you should have a well-planned selling area. This area should feature your best work, and also show the flexibility of your service. When most people think of having portraits of family pictures taken, they think of trooping into a studio and saying "cheese." You should choose your place to include adequate space to handling the selling. Most people really have very little idea of what can be done, and tend to think of nothing but the stereotyped poses that ordinary photographers specialize in.

In addition to a good space for display and selling, your studio will have to be big enough to accommodate groups, pets, and the odd assignments that often show up.

Advertising Photography

Perhaps the advertising photographer has the most varied life, and the most demanding at the same time. He may be shooting a china place setting in a carefully controlled studio situation in the morning and the coal conveyor in an electric power plant in the afternoon. This is a bit extreme, but most photographers who choose this type of work will find themselves in such situations.

You will have need for a studio. But what kind of studio? If you are doing food layouts for magazines or food-processing companies, you will need a kitchen.

If your specialty is manufactured industrial parts, you may need a studio in which big pieces of equipment can be rolled in. On the other hand, most of the industry in your area may be limited to the fabrication of small parts and require a smaller studio. For example, the electronics firms on the West Coast seldom make anything that can't be photographed in an average-size studio. But, if you plan to specialize in automotive photography, you may have to arrange for a place in which one or more trucks can be photographed.

The best advice we can give you here is to try to get a feel for the size of equipment that makes up the bulk of the industrial output in your area and gauge your studio size and location accordingly.

Will You Need a Lab?

There are no ready-made answers to this question. However, there are a few guidelines that apply to everyone. Think about this first: Few photographers can make as much money doing lab work as they can doing photography. However, if you are doing photography that requires considerable darkroom manipulation and you have a reputation for being the best, you can do it and charge accordingly. Under these circumstances, a lab will be an asset.

Most photographers we queried prefer to have their lab work done outside to let them spend their most productive hours either taking pictures or selling their services. The number of labs has increased so greatly in the past few years that there is sufficient competition to insure that you will get the best prices.

If you do consider the use of your own lab, you must choose a place where the work can be handled cleanly and safely. The lab may be part of your studio, or it can be placed at another location. Whatever you decide to do, be sure that the site you select can be kept clean with a minimum of effort.

Insurance

It goes without saying that all of your equipment should be fully protected by insurance. But you must give some thought to the kind of insurance you need for your place of business.

If, for example, you are doing fashion work and you have models in your studio often, you should carry enough liability insurance to cover them in the event they are injured and are unable to work. Your liability insurance should include your work outside the studio as well as within.

Also, check to see if your automobile insurance includes coverage for models you may transport to and from the shooting location.

Security

The kind of security you need depends on the location of your studio and the natural protection it already offers. If yours is a storefront studio, the shopping area is probably patrolled by the local police and there may even be additional surveillance arranged by a merchants' association. Under these circumstances, you may need little or no additional security. However, if you find the personal services lacking, you should consider installing one of the many different types of intruder alarm systems. Some systems will sound an alarm right on the premises, trying to frighten off the intruder. However, as thieves get more sophisticated they have come to realize that such warnings rely almost entirely on the willingness of those who might hear the alarm to call the police. Most people don't want to get involved, and will ignore the alarm more often than not.

Most photographers have found that the alarm systems that do not tell the intruder that his or her presence has been detected, but alert a private detective bureau or the local police to, be most effective. If some valuable props are frequently left overnight, you might even consider hiring a private guard on a part-time basis.

Conclusion

The preceding comments have been made with the particular needs of a professional photographer in mind. A photographer is also a business person and good business sense should prevail in the choice of a business location. You should answer such questions as:

1. Will the location I have in mind support a photographer?
2. Are the facilities adequate and fairly priced?
3. Is the location stable or is the area deteriorating? Is there a potential for growth?
4. What municipal services are available to business? Is the area protected, are the streets swept, and are the roads maintained?
5. Is parking readily available? This is especially important if you are photographing weddings or other fairly large groups that arrive in a number of cars.

The most important question you should answer is this: Is the cost of the location such that I can reasonably expect to pay for the space and still make an acceptable profit? High rent or an uneconomical building can be a drag on any business.

5 | General Management

Dr. John H. Hickman

A large number of business failures can be attributed to poor management. If you realize that your managerial ability is on a much lower level than your skill in photography, do not make the mistake of starting your own studio without professional help. You could lose your life savings, damage your business creditibility, and cripple your self-esteem.

Managerial failures result from difficulties or mistakes in analyzing customer needs, securing adequate financing, finding the correct location, and /or in expansion. Here are some specific difficulties in each of these areas.

Customer Needs

1. Inaccurate or incomplete judgments about what customers need or want.
2. Inability to attract new customers.
3. Poor monitoring of factors affecting the market for future photography services.

Financing

1. Shortage of funds for necessary photographic equipment
2. More likely, inadequate working capital for day-to-day operations.

3. Unsatisfactory credit arrangements with studio customers.
4. Record-keeping systems incapable of a) signaling when corrective action is necessary or b) providing a basis for managerial decision making.

Location

1. Poor judgment in the original selection of a location.
2. Inability to notice changes in circumstances that make the location less desirable.

Premature Expansion

1. Growth ambitions that are inconsistent with the studio's financial capability.
2. Expansion that is not based on the existence of a legitimate business opportunity, supported by adequate market research.

Planning and Pricing for Profit

Planning for profit requires the preparation of financial reports to indicate what you have done in the past and/or intend to do in the future. At the very least, you should develop an income (profit and loss) statement and a balance sheet.

The income statement summarizes business operations for the period, resulting in a profit or loss. Preparation of monthly statements is recommended for close monitoring of activities. If you are just opening a studio, an income statement based on the experiences of local photographers will be helpful as a basis of comparison with your own results. A simplified monthly income statement might look like this:

Sales	$5,000
Variable Costs	2,200
Operation Margin	2,800
***Fixed Costs**	2,300
Net Income	500

***Include semivariable, semifixed expenses**

The balance sheet depicts the total assets owned by the studio, the amount of debt still owed for them, and the owner's equity in the business. It shows the financial condition of the studio on a given date. Important considerations are the current assets available to pay current debt and the proportion of debt to owner's equity. The following is an example of a balance sheet:

Current assets:		
Cash	$ 3,000	
Accounts Receivable	4,500	
Supplies	2,100	
Total Current Assets		$9,600
Fixed Assets:		
Equipment	20,000	
Furniture and Fixtures	5,000	
Less: Depreciation	10,000	
Total Fixed Assets		15,000
Total Assets		24,600
Current Liabilities:		
Accounts Payable	3,000	
Notes Payable (in one year)	2,500	
Total Current Liabilities		5,500
Long-Term Debt		7,500
Owner's Equity		11,600
Total Liability and Owner's Equity		24,600

A major reason why many studios find themselves in a financial bind is the failure of their owners to identify relevant costs and keep suitable records of them. Lack of accurate cost information leads to the illusion that operations are more profitable than is the real case. This is clearly an undesirable situation for a prudent business person.

The nature of cost has to be clearly understood if all costs are to be accounted for. Besides real costs such as rent and employees' wages, implicit costs have to be set against revenue to determine profit. Implicit costs are those that would be charged for your services if you rendered them to someone else. Interest on the capital you have invested in your studio, rent of a building you already own, and payment for your own services are the major items in this category. Another means of classification is between fixed and variable costs. Fixed costs are incurred whether business is being conducted or not, and do not vary much over the short term. Rent, heat, and license fees are representative examples of fixed costs. Variable costs, of course, change with the amount of production and include such items as film and chemicals.

Analysis and compilation of cost data will enable you to construct a budget, which is one of the fundamental tools of planning for profit. Preparation of a budget forces you to plan the future activities of your business carefully. It should be constantly updated and kept flexible enough to allow adjustments based on future needs.

Planning for profit and development of a budget requires a systematic approach. One method of attaining these goals consists of the following steps:

1. Establish your profit goal.
2. Estimate your expected level of sales.
3. Tabulate your expenses for that sales volume.
4. Determine your estimated profit based on expected sales and expenses.
5. Compare this estimated profit with your profit goal.
6. Devise alternative measures to improve profit.
7. Study how costs and profits vary with changes in sales volume.
8. Analyze your possible alternatives from a profit standpoint.
9. Adjust your plans if advisable. Express your overall plans in the form of a budget.

Let's take a closer look at each of these steps.

1. Establishing your profit goal.

The desired profit should be a specific target figure based on several factors. As manager and chief photographer, you are entitled to a reasonable salary. Furthermore, you should receive a return on your investment in the studio. The target figure should be comparable to the interest you would receive from investing your money in other ventures, plus a bonus for the risk you are taking. For example, assume your initial investment in the studio was $25,000 and subsequently you have added $10,000 to purchase new equipment. If you had invested a similar sum of $35,000 in bonds or stocks, you might have received a seven to eight percent rate of return at little risk. Because you are investing in your own business, you deserve a risk premium because of the greater uncertainty involved. At a rate of 12 percent, your investment should net you $4,200 after taxes, in addition to a reasonable salary. Allowing for a tax rate of 30 percent, the profit needed before income taxes is $6,000.

Investment in Studio	$35,000
Rate of Return	× .12
Return Desired	$ 4,200
Estimated Tax	+1,800 (30%)
Profit Needed Before Taxes	$ 6,000

2. Estimating sales

For a new enterprise, the initial sales forecast can be determined according to the methods proposed in chapter 2. After several years in the business, you can use the prior year's sales as a base for the forecast of the upcoming year. Factors affecting the new estimate include market conditions, expected activities of your competitors, level of sales promotion, and forecasts of business activity made by experts. Such experts include business magazine writers, government specialists, and professional forecasters. Through this information and awareness of your studio's sales trend, you can predict a percentage increase (or decrease) in sales for the upcoming year.

3. Calculating expenses for estimated sales volume

After collecting and classifying costs for the past several years, you can estimate the expenses for the coming year. The expected values depend on the planned sales volume, the promotional efforts to reach this sales level, improved methods of production, changes in scope of operation, and economic conditions.

The cost of goods sold includes the cost of film, paper, and chemicals, and varies directly with sales volume. Other expenses will be adjusted according to whether they vary directly, change somewhat, or remain the same with volume changes. Usually, the costs have to be boosted several percent to allow for inflation.

Item	Last Year	Expected This Year
Cost of Goods Sold	$24,000	$27,000
Salaries	23,800	25,500
Promotion	3,000	4,000
Rent	3,600	3,600
Insurance	2,500	2,500
Depreciation	2,200	2,500
Utilities	1,600	2,100
Maintenance	1,200	1,260
Interest	1,000	650
Taxes	1,600	1,600
Miscellaneous	1,500	1,700
Total	$66,000	$72,410

Determining profit

Profit, of course, is found by deducting costs from sales revenue and is expected to increase this year to $4,590 before taxes.

	Last Year	This Year	
Sales	$70,000	$77,000	(10% increase)
Costs	66,000	72,410	
Profit Before Taxes	$ 4,000	$ 4,590	

5. *Comparing estimated profit with profit goal*

Since the estimated profit falls short of the profit goal of $6,000, further steps must be taken to improve profit performance.

6. *Alternative measures to improve profit*

Measures can be taken to improve sales revenue, cut costs, or bring in other types of income. You can increase the number of jobs done by boosting sales promotion, improving quality, performing a wider variety of services, or by decreasing prices for your services. However, slashing prices can result in cutting your own throat. Instead, you should price for profit and sell such benefits as integrity, reliability, and high quality. This policy will work to your advantage in the long run.

Expenses can be reduced by keeping a close eye on your disbursements, by securing better deals with vendors, and by increasing your productivity through adoption of improved methods and techniques.

Additional income can be earned by renting your studio to other photographers on a part-time basis. Providing services to other photographers, such as developing film and enlarging prints, would be another source of revenue. Outside jobs, such as school and party pictures, have long been a large part of many photographers' businesses.

7. *Costs and Profits Vary with Changes in Sales Volume*

In step 3, you listed the costs expected for a 10 percent increase in sales volume. Now it is important to separate these costs according to their fixed, variable, or semivariable nature. This classification will allow you to construct a break-even chart and a profit table to study the relationships between sales levels, expenses, and profits. As the volume of sales changes, the costs of doing business and the subsequent profit also change.

Item	Estimated Cost	Fixed Cost	Variable Cost
Cost of Goods Sold	$27,000		$27,000
Salaries	25,500	$23,500	2,000
Promotion	4,000		4,000
Rent	3,600	3,600	
Insurance	2,500	2,500	
Depreciation	2,500	2,500	
Utilities	2,100	1,200	900
Maintenance	1,260	1,000	260
Interest	650		650
Taxes	1,600	800	800
Miscellaneous	1,700	1,700	
Total	$72,410	$36,800	$35,610

Break-even Chart for Studio

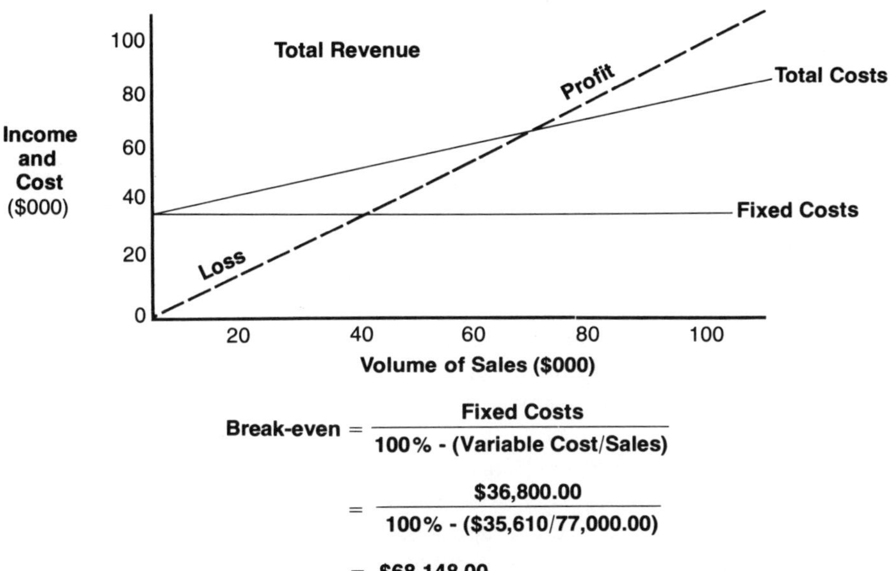

$$\text{Break-even} = \frac{\text{Fixed Costs}}{100\% - (\text{Variable Cost/Sales})}$$

$$= \frac{\$36{,}800.00}{100\% - (\$35{,}610/77{,}000.00)}$$

$$= \$68{,}148.00$$

Break-even analysis does more than specify the volume at which total cost equals total income. It will show the impact on profit if fixed costs increase 10 percent and sales jump 15 percent, or if variable costs rise 10 percent and volume drops 12 percent, or various other combinations. The marginal income (or profit) is derived from the break-even equation. For every $1.00 of sales increase, the marginal (variable) cost is $.46 (35,610/77,000) and, therefore, the marginal income $.54. From this information, we can construct the following table:

Sales Volume	Fixed Costs	Variable Costs	Profit
$60,000	$36,800	$27,600 (60,000 × .46)	−$ 4,400
70,000	36,800	32,200 (70,000 × .46)	1,000
80,000	36,800	36,800 (80,000 × .46)	6,400
90,000	36,800	41,400 (90,000 × .46)	11,800
100,000	36,800	46,000 (100,000 × .46)	17,200

8. Analysing possible alternatives

You can use marginal analysis as an aid in your decision-making process. For instance, is it feasible to increase promotional costs $1,000 to gain $7,000 more in revenue? The marginal cost of additional sales is $.46 and the marginal income $.54. This income includes the fixed costs as well as profit. Therefore, any extra income is useful in reducing fixed costs even if it does not add directly to profits. Marginal profit of $3,780 for the $1,000 investment in promotional activity makes this a very favorable option.

You should exercise care not to drop your price more than 54 percent to make a sale because then you would be paying out more in variable costs than you would be bringing in. Other questions answered by marginal analysis include the effects of price hikes, cuts in fixed costs, and reduction in variable cost in profit.

9. Planning adjustments and budget

The economic benefits postulated by marginal analysis must be evaluated along with your other goals. If you want to experience yearly growth in sales, you won't accomplish this by increasing price to improve profit, because you lose a certain percentage of customers. Cost reduction also might boost profits, but result in laying off your part-time photographer or reducing services to customers. The alternatives that you do select should be incorporated into your income statement and detailed budget for the approaching year.

Your pricing strategy depends on a multitude of factors. Desired profit, fixed and variable costs, services offered, type of clientele, and projected studio image are among the major determinants. Pricing was an implicit feature of the planning for profit routine presented above. Since it is an essential component of the total marketing plan, the pricing strategy should be formulated during the start-up phase of the studio and periodically reevaluated by the owner of the business.

Three components of the price are the variable costs, the fixed costs, and the profit margin. To simplify matters when calculating the price for a job, variable costs would include out-of-pocket costs such as those for film and paper. The rest of the costs plus the expected profit could then be accumulated in an "overhead" account. Thus, your salary and costs that are variable in nature but difficult to assign directly to a project (promotional expenses) would be included in this fund. The overhead rate is the total overhead divided by the number of hours the studio operates per month. Each job you perform should be priced according to this hourly time charge plus the variable costs involved.

Once you have developed the target price for a service, you have to weigh other considerations. A commercial studio will generally make less profit on each sale, in order to keep its prices lower and thus gain a larger volume of sales. A specialty studio, on the other hand, usually attracts customers for reasons other than price. There is, of course, the opportunity of acquiring additional business by lowering prices, but the photographer has to seriously consider whether this practice would be helpful in the long run. Going the other way, more complex jobs may be priced at a level that will give you a higher than normal rate of return. Services offered for the sake of completeness that you don't really like to do may be priced extremely high to discourage that kind of work.

Again, operating costs should be closely followed to insure their proper inclusion in the budget from which prices are calculated. Furthermore, you should compare your prices with those of other photographers to satisfy yourself that they are not grossly out of line.

Business Habits

Development of proper business habits will make you a success both in customer relations and studio management. In the former area, your customers will want prompt, efficient service and a "personalized" relationship with you. They will come to you because they expect you will give them high-quality, considerate service. This in turn will assure you of a permanent clientele, assuming you fulfill their expectations.

Consideration ranks extremely high as both a business and a personal attribute. Finding ways to please other people, tactfulness in customer relationships, and understanding other people's points of view will pay dividends in the long run. Besides, winning an argument is an empty victory if it results in losing a customer. Honesty also is a fundamental quality for long-term business success.

Good judgment involves the ability to think logically and to evaluate a situation rationally. This faculty enables you to plan intelligently, solve problems in a logical, step-by-step fashion, and make appropriate adjustments in your business. An extension of good judgment is the knack of seeing problems from a business point of view (as opposed to a technical perspective). Without this attitude, you will not see and respond to problems as a business person should.

Reliability is an important element in determining your reputation in the community. Keeping appointments on time and having the job finished when promised regardless of personal inconvenience will establish you as dependable. Accuracy, thoroughness, and attention to detail will enhance your reputation.

Success in business is not possible without a strong measure of aggressiveness. Determination and diligence in the performance of your business affairs are necessary to get your enterprise started and to keep it going and growing.

As mentioned earlier, proper business habits will aid you in developing skills in management. Skills are necessary in each of the four functions of management: 1) planning, 2) organizing, 3) controlling, and 4) improving performance.

Planning involves formulation of both the immediate and long-range steps to achieve your business objectives. Goals are set, strategies and tactics planned, policies established, priorities mandated, and resources budgeted. The budgeting of financial resources was covered in the section on planning for profit. The budgeting of personal resources, i.e. time management, also merits discussion.

Time management has two major elements: 1) ranking the importance of duties and 2) making effective use of timesavers. In the photography business, serving the customer takes precedence over all other duties. But the time not required for customer service should be effectively used to accomplish other tasks in the order of their importance. Developing film and preparing prints are daily occurrences, but other, managerial duties also have to be done. Keeping adequate records for tax purposes, making tax payments on a timely basis, completing other government-issued paperwork, arranging for adequate insurance coverage, and paying creditors when due are a few of your business responsibilities. It's a good practice to record the deadlines for these obligations on your desk calendar or some other reminder device so that they are not overlooked. As they become due, they should be included on your daily memorandum along with your routine tasks. When you have some free time during the day, you can consult your list and work on the most important or urgent job remaining. This system will help you complete essential work on time and avoid wasting time on routine work that is less urgent than something else on the list.

Organizing your business, the second management function, means gathering the resources to accomplish specific activities under the guidance of a responsible individual. Since your studio may be a one-person operation, it may not be necessary to delegate duties. Nevertheless, segregation of the resources to carry out different activities is a vital feature of the purchasing managing, and record-keeping processes.

Controlling insures that the work done conforms to the studio's objectives and standards, and falls within the allotted time and budget constraints. Measuring, evaluating, and correcting performance are the skills required in this phase.

Improving the studio's performance requires careful assessment of the likely impact of a change on the studio's overall situation. Decisions should be based on an evaluation of past performance, consideration of the present circumstances, and anticipation of future events. Most of the changes have to be beneficial if the output of the studio is to be significantly improved.

Personnel

When you originally opened your studio, you probably did all the work yourself. But as business expands, you need to free yourself from the more routine tasks to concentrate on challenging photographic and managerial functions. However, it is not advisable to hire an additional employee unless the revenue from having this employee is significantly greater than the cost of hiring him or her. A photographer, for instance, should receive but 20 to 30 percent of the billings he or she is responsible for. A receptionist-secretary cannot be evaluated in this fashion; her value depends on her ability to handle routine tasks that would tie up the photographer-owner and limit the amount of revenue he could bring in. In the interim before a full-time employee is necessary, you might find it feasible to hire retouching, lab, or other photographic services on a temporary basis or employ an assistant on a part-time basis.

Good employees are a business' most valuable asset and careful selection of personnel is critical to protect the reputation of your studio. Specify in advance the range of jobs you want the new employee to perform. A comprehensive job description will help you find the person to fill your particular needs and save you time by screening out applicants who don't qualify.

Once you have determined your needs, actively pick someone to fulfill them. Don't trust the right person to find you. Solicit suggestions from friends, other established photographers, university professors, and placement advisors. Call government employment agencies, private employment services, and your professional society. Check want ads in local papers and trade magazines. Unemployed and underemployed photographers are not a scarce commodity.

As the owner of a small business, you should establish hiring, training, and personnel retention programs that stress employment opportunities offered by a small studio and not found in the larger studios. Varied work experience, increased responsibility, and recognition of the individual's special abilities should be emphasized. Formal on-the-job training and continuing educational programs at local universities provide the firm and its employees with good, inexpensive training opportunities. Fringe benefits may be relatively limited compared to those a larger firm can offer, but a profit-sharing plan will certainly help attract and hold good employees.

Training employees is a continuous process. Do not expect too much from a trainee in a short time. Allot sufficient time and your undivided attention to training. Have the new employee learn by performing under actual working conditions. Follow up on your training, reemphasizing important points and keeping him or her up-to-date on new developments and procedures.

6 | Accounting and Cost Control

Steve Delloff

Keeping Business Records

Good business records are essential to the success of almost any enterprise. Virtually any question involving the finances of your business can be answered if you have a good set of records. You need not be a trained bookkeeper or accountant to maintain good records. However, you must be thorough, neat, and accurate. Get in the habit of doing your paperwork when you have the time to concentrate on it with no distractions. Keeping records is as important to your success as taking good pictures. You can't keep track of costs and profits if you don't have the figures to refer to. Don't rely on shortcuts like "double your material and lab costs to determine price." This *might* result in realistic pricing or it might not. You won't really know *unless* you have records to refer to.

There is no one way to keep a set of business records. A method of record keeping that is satisfactory for a small operation may not be satisfactory for a larger business. You should investigate various types of record keeping systems and adopt or modify one that fits your particular business needs. Like other facets of running a business, a record-keeping system must be evaluated periodically to determine if it is satisfactory to the business. As the business grows or changes, very often the record-keeping system needs to be changed too.

Generally, the tax authorities do not require any particular type of records. However, they do require that the method of record keeping be suited to your business: that it clearly reflect your income and that it be consistently applied so that accurate comparisons may be made from year to year.

Accounting Methods

The two most commonly used accounting methods are 1) the cash receipts and disbursements method, and 2) the accrual method.

A person using the cash receipts and disbursements method records income when it is actually or constructively received. An example of constructive receipt of income would be interest on a savings account. Although the actual entry of the interest on your passbook may not be until January 3, the interest for the last quarter ended December 31 was constructively received by you on December 31 and would be included as income for the period ended December 31. Deductions or credits are taken in the year in which actually paid, unless they should be taken in a different year to reflect income clearly. If you prepay three years of insurance to get a favorable premium you should only deduct the amount of the prepayment attributable to the insurance for one year to clearly reflect your income. The remaining portion of the premium will be deducted in the years to which it is attributable. To deduct the entire premium in one year would give a larger expense figure than is justified. You cannot defer *income* under the cash receipts and disbursements method.

An accrual method user accounts for income when a right to receive this income comes into being. A right to receive the income exists when all events that determine your entitlement to the income have occurred. Assume you have done a portrait job and have delivered the prints to the customer on December 31. The customer does not pay until January 3. Under the accrual method, you record the sale as income for the period ended December 31 because your right to receive the income occurred at the time you delivered the finished prints to the customer. The fact that you weren't paid until January 3 is not relevant under the accrual method. Expenses under the accrual method are deducted in the year in which all events have occurred that create a liability on your part. On the same portrait job, you sent negatives to the lab for printing. You received the finished prints and the lab invoice on December 29, but you didn't pay the lab until January 3. Since the lab did the work you ordered and sent the finished prints to you, the events occurred that created a liability on your part to pay them as of December 29. The fact that you didn't actually pay until January 3 is not material here, either.

While either the cash receipts and disbursements or accrual method can be used by any business, it is often difficult for a business person to determine when an item is "accrued" either as expense or income. It is usually simpler for the small business owner to operate on the cash receipts and disbursements method.

Bookkeeping Methods

The two basic methods for maintaining financial records are 1) double-entry bookkeeping, and 2) single-entry bookkeeping.

In the double-entry system, items are first entered in a journal and then summary totals (usually monthly) are entered into a ledger. There are as many journals used as are necessary to give a complete financial picture of the business. The double-entry system is self-balancing—debts must equal credits, thus it is relatively easy to catch errors. For this reason, the double-entry system is used by most large businesses.

The single-entry system records only the flow of cash, accounts receivable, and accounts payable. Under the single-entry system, the main emphasis is placed on the profit (or loss) of the business. Other items are not covered by the single-entry system. However, it is possible to use a modified single-entry system that will give a complete picture of business operations.

Record-Keeping Procedures

Your records should indicate all your receipts. These receipts should all be deposited in your business account. All your expenses should be recorded and paid by check wherever possible. You should have a cross-reference system between bills and checks so that it is possible to easily associate the bill with the check that was used in payment of it. Likewise, your receipts should indicate the date the money was received, who paid you, for what purpose, and the amount of the payment. If you extend credit to your customers (check, credit card, or store charge) you will also need to note the method of payment. See figure 1 for a method of recording expenses. This type of format can be prepared for a standard 8½ X 11-inch, three-ring binder, or you can buy an account book in the stationery store. If you have many transactions with one particular business, it might be helpful to set up an account sheet for that business (see figure 2). If there is any need to check, for example, on XYZ Photo Lab accounts, it can be done quickly from the XYZ expense sheet. Your unpaid bills should also be recorded or filed in such a way that you can always tell who has not been paid and how much in total is due. One way to do this is to place all bills in an "unpaid" box or file. Any system you adopt is good, so long as it works for you. The essence of good record keeping is to be able to keep track of your transactions and locate all needed documents as quickly as possible.

An example of a record of income is shown in figure 3. Sales slips may be purchased at the stationery store, or you may have your own printed. They should be consecutively numbered, have a space for the customer's name, address, telephone number, work ordered, amount, sales tax (if applicable), total, and deposit taken. You can use a three-part system in which the original stays in an accounts receivable file until paid; the second copy is the customer's receipt, and the third copy goes with the customer's

Date	Bill #	Nature of Expense To Whom Paid	Check #	Amount
05-2-78	001	XYZ Photo Lab - Jones order - process & proof	001	$ 60.00
05-26-78	002	ABC Photo Supply - 3 bulbs	002	$ 45.00
05-26-78	003	Anytown Power & Light electric for May 1978	003	$150.00
05-28-78	004	ABC Photo Supply 20 rolls CG135-36	004	$ 80.00
05-28-78	005	DEF Supermarket - 4 rolls towel paper	CASH	$ 2.50
06-01-78	006	Able Realty Corp. - rent for June 1978	005	$500.00
06-03-78	007	XYZ Photo Lab - Mc Duff order - 8 × 10 custom	006	$ 24.00
06-06-78	008	XYZ Photo Lab - Holtje order - 11 × 14 Kodalith	007	$ 15.00
06-10-78	009	XYZ Photo Lab - Spencer order - 16 × 20 custom	008	$ 40.00

The BILL # to the right of the date is put on the bill or invoice so that one can associate the bill with the check used in payment. It is also helpful to put the check number of the check used in payment on the bill. This system can also be used for cash payments as shown. In this case, the register receipt or sales slip should be marked "cash" in addition to the BILL #.

Figure 1. Record of Expenses.

work. When the customer picks up the work, the customer copy is stamped "paid" and returned to the customer as a receipt; the accounts receivable copy is stamped "paid," removed from accounts receivable, and entered into the record of income; the third copy is stamped "paid" and kept with the customer's negatives in the studio. By looking at the accounts receivable file, you can determine who has work outstanding and how much is due. If a deposit is taken and/or work is paid for in advance, this should be clearly indicated on the sales slip.

Another record that you should keep is a 3 X 5 or 5 X 8 file card of your customers. This is kept in alphabetical order and has the name, telephone number, address of the customer, how they came to you (advertising, word of mouth, walk-in, etc.); your comments (children, pets, etc.); and the sales slip numbers of all work you did for them together with a description of the work and the dates (see figure 4). The more information you can obtain about your customers, the easier it will be to sell them because you will know their preferences: what they ordered before and what they might be interested in. A job record card such as shown in figure 5 is very useful to keep track of time and materials used for each job type so that you can accurately keep track of costs and determine pricing. You will, if you keep these cards faithfully, have ready reference to see what services you have that give you the most profit and which are the least profitable.

Accounting for Expenses

In the discussion of record keeping of expenses, no distinctions were made between different types of expenses. However, your expenses fall into several categories:

1. Expense in purchase of assets used in your business. These are called business assets. They may be tangible assets such as a camera, or intangible assets such as a franchise. Usually, these assets have a usable life of more than one year and the usable life can be reasonably estimated or determined. If they meet these general criteria, the business assets may be depreciated—that is, a portion of the cost of each asset may be recovered through an annual deduction over the usable life of the asset.

2. Expense in purchase of materials to be held for sale to others whether these materials are in their original form or become part of something else. Film purchased for resale to your customers would be an example of a material in its original form held for resale. Wood and glass used in making frames would be an example of material becoming

part of something else, the wood and glass become part of the frames. The general name for this type of item is "inventory."

3. Expenses for general business operations—wages, rent, repairs, travel, entertainment, insurance, taxes, expendable supplies, utilities, advertising, charitable contributions, educational expenses, etc.

EXPENSES PAID TO XYZ PHOTO LAB

Date	Bill #	Customer Name Type of Service	XYZ Inv #	Check #	Amount
5-2-78	001	Jones - process & proof 6 rolls	13579	001	$60.00
6-3-78	007	McDuff - 4 - 8x10 custom color	13850	006	$24.00
6-7-78	008	Holtje - 4 - 11x14 Kodalith	14250	007	$15.00
6-12-78	009	Spencer - 2 - 16x20 custom portrait	14283	008	$40.00

Figure 2. Expense Sheet.

RECORD OF INCOME

Date	Sales Slip #	From Whom Rec'd. Service/Product	How Paid	Amount	Sales Tax	Total
5/27	001	Jones - process & proof 6 rolls - portraits	cash	$120.00	$6.00	$126.00
6/8	002	McDuff - 4 - 8X 10 custom color portrait	check	$ 48.00	$2.40	$ 50.40
6/15	003	Holtje - 4 - 11X 14 Kodalith	cash	$ 30.00	$1.50	$ 31.50
6/20	004	Spencer - 2 - 16 X20 custom color portrait	Master Chge	$ 80.00	$4.00	$ 84.00

Figure 3. Record of Income.

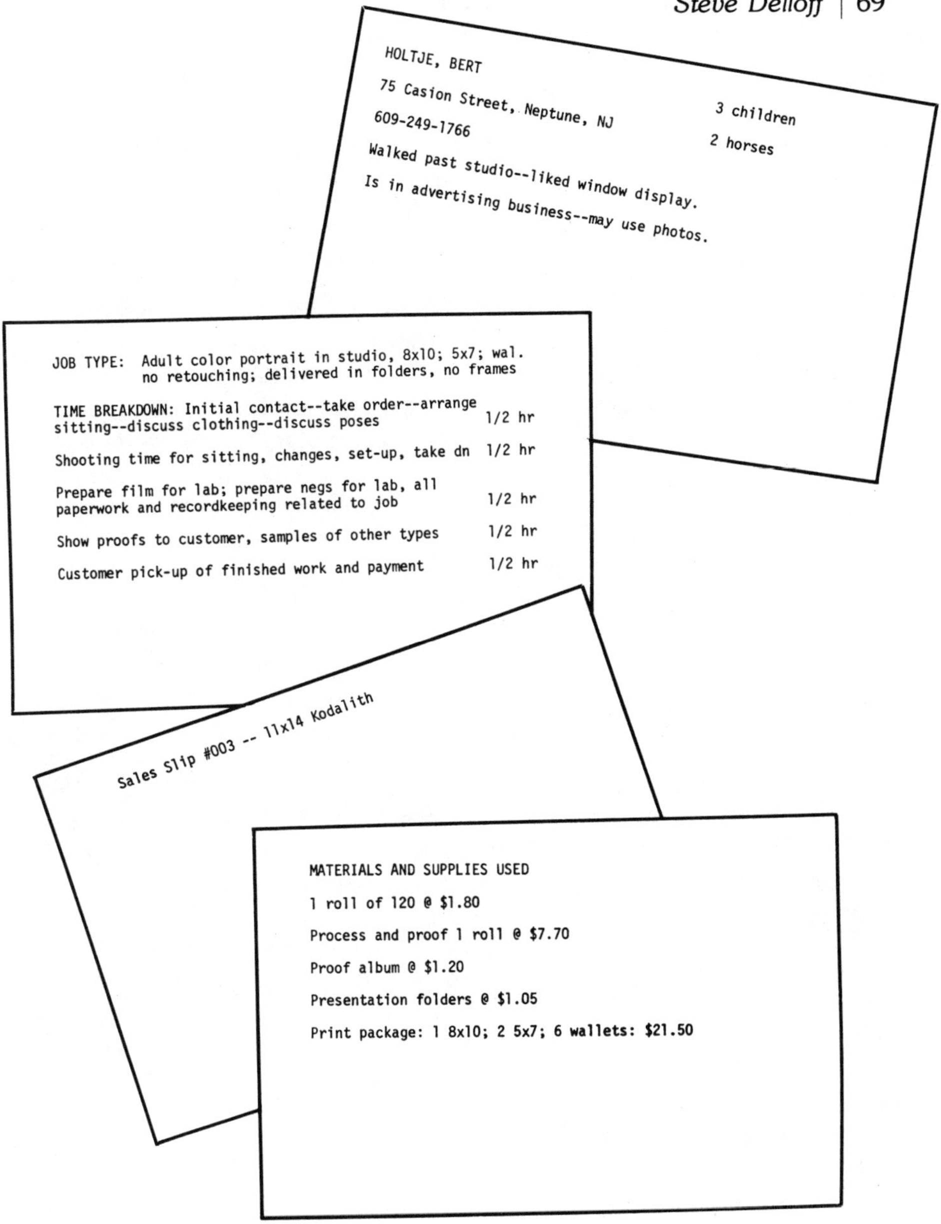

HOLTJE, BERT

75 Casion Street, Neptune, NJ 3 children

609-249-1766 2 horses

Walked past studio--liked window display.

Is in advertising business--may use photos.

JOB TYPE: Adult color portrait in studio, 8x10; 5x7; wal.
no retouching; delivered in folders, no frames

TIME BREAKDOWN: Initial contact--take order--arrange sitting--discuss clothing--discuss poses 1/2 hr

Shooting time for sitting, changes, set-up, take dn 1/2 hr

Prepare film for lab; prepare negs for lab, all paperwork and recordkeeping related to job 1/2 hr

Show proofs to customer, samples of other types 1/2 hr

Customer pick-up of finished work and payment 1/2 hr

Sales Slip #003 -- 11x14 Kodalith

MATERIALS AND SUPPLIES USED

1 roll of 120 @ $1.80

Process and proof 1 roll @ $7.70

Proof album @ $1.20

Presentation folders @ $1.05

Print package: 1 8x10; 2 5x7; 6 wallets: $21.50

If you plan to sell anything except your photographic services, that is, if you are going to sell film, flash bulbs, frames, and other goods to your customers, you have to segregate the expense for these items since they are your inventory and are accounted for differently. You can do this by making a sheet called "Inventory Expenses."

INVENTORY EXPENSES

Date	Bill #	Item, Supplier	Check #	Amount
6-25-78	010	ABC Photo Supply - 20 packs, Polaroid type 668	009	$50.00

If you buy items that are both for your *business* use and to be sold retail, you must segregate them. In the example above, you bought Polaroid 668 film; you use this for test shots in your business *and* you sell it retail to your customers. You must segregate that which you use as a photographer from that which you sell to your customers. All purchases should first be recorded in the record of expenses (the master list). If you purchase a large number of business assets, you should prepare a sheet entitled "Business Asset Expense" and make entries similar to those on the inventory expense sheet. If you have only one or two purchases of such items a year, you can make the entry only in the record of expense sheet and denote by some code letter that the expense was for the purchase of a business asset.

Taxes

As a business person, the studio owner is subject to a variety of taxes. The individual owner must report profit or loss from self-employment to the federal government on Schedule C of Form 1040. A partnership would report its profit or loss to the federal government on Form 1065 (US Partnership Return of Income). The corporation reports its profit or loss on the appropriate form in the 1120 series.

State laws regarding taxes required of a business person vary. You can usually obtain information, forms, and advice from the agency that administers the tax. Normally these agencies can be found in the telephone directory. However, if you are not clear as to what your state requires of you, seek professional legal and/or accounting advice. Some local authorities (cities and counties) also impose taxes on business people. Once again, contact the tax authorities to find out what is required. If you're not sure, get professional advice.

If you have employees (other than yourself) you will be required to file a federal quarterly employment tax return. This return lists your employees' names, social security numbers, amount of taxable wages, amount of tax and social security withheld from their wages, etc. You are required, generally, to establish a special bank account to deposit monies that you deduct from your employees' wages. Your local Internal Revenue Service office (listed in the telephone directory) will be able to advise you of the procedure for obtaining an employer identification number, as well as the procedure for filing employment tax returns. They will be able to supply you with the necessary forms and instructions.

There is no particular form prescribed for keeping payroll records, but your records should include, at a minimum: *the amounts and dates of all wage payments subject to employment and social security taxes; the names, addresses and occupations of employees receiving such payments; the periods of their employment; the periods for which they are paid while absent due to sickness or personal injuries and the amount and weekly rate of such payments; their social security account numbers; their income tax withholding exemption certificates; your employer identification number; duplicate copies of quarterly and annual returns filed; the dates and amounts of deposits of withheld monies made.* If you have employees, you may also be required to file an annual federal unemployment tax return. Forms and information can be obtained from your local Internal Revenue Service office.

States and local governments vary in their employment return requirements. Usually, if a state has an income tax, it will require that you withhold tax from your employees' wages as does the federal government. You will probably have to file a periodic employment tax return and remit the money you withheld. You will most likely be required to file some type of unemployment insurance return. Questions about employment returns and labor requirements can usually be answered by your state department of labor office. If you aren't sure of the requirements, get professional help.

As a self-employed person, you are not covered by withholding tax on your income. The federal government, as well as many states with an income tax, require you, on a quarterly basis, to pay estimated tax. This is nothing more than a payment of a portion of what you estimate your income tax bill for the year to be. Instructions for estimated tax are included in the federal tax instruction booklet and in most state instruction booklets. If you're not sure of the requirements, contact the tax authorities.

Depreciation

As mentioned before, "business assets" are depreciated—that is, a portion of their expense is charged off each year. The starting point of the expense is what you paid for the item when you bought it as a business asset. Suppose you didn't buy the item for a business purpose, but you converted it from a nonbusiness to business purpose? In that case, the value assigned to the item would be its worth as of the time it was converted to business use. Suppose you purchased a new camera for your business that cost $500. Your depreciation would be computed on that $500 cost. However, if you bought the same $500 camera several years ago and used it for personal use and now are converting it to business use, is it still worth the same $500 as it cost new? In other words, what is the worth of the camera now as you convert it to business use? This determination of worth is something that you must do before you can depreciate the item. You can do this by having it appraised by a camera dealer who is familiar with prices of used equipment, or you can value it yourself by means of advertisements of used equipment, similar to the one you wish to value. The figure you arrive at must be the one which a willing buyer would pay to a willing seller for the equipment. Whatever figure you choose, you must have some "back-up" material that you can use to prove the value if necessary (written appraisals are helpful, so are advertisements of similar items) to the tax authorities.

Having determined the value of your equipment for depreciation, you must now figure its usable life. The Internal Revenue Service has published a series of guidelines for usable life of certain items grouped by class or type of item. While you are not bound by the Internal Revenue Service usable life, if you choose a different life, you must be able to support your choice. It may be that a certain piece of equipment that would normally have a usable life of six years has only a usable life of three years because you consistently have to use it under conditions that greatly lower its usable life. Or, the piece of equipment with a normal usable life of ten years is made obsolete in four years because of advances in technology and is now only usable as a "curio." In any of these cases, you may adopt the usable life that actually fits the equipment being depreciated, but you must be able to show how you arrived at the figure you did.

There are several methods of depreciating equipment. Under the straight-line method, you merely divide the value of the equipment by the usable life and the result is the annual depreciation expense. In the case of the $500 camera purchased new for business, assume it has a usable life of 10 years. The annual depreciation would be computed by dividing the value ($500) by its usable life (10 years) for a figure of $50 per year. The concept of usable life does not mean that the items will not be usable after this period. It is merely a guideline for how long a particular type of equipment generally lasts; a piece of equipment may last longer or wear out earlier than the usable life usually given for it. However, as a general rule, after the end of the usable life, there will be little value to the equipment. Should the equipment have substantial salvage value (what you can sell it for after its usable life) you must subtract this figure from the original value placed on it. Thus, if the $500 camera could, after 10 years, be sold for $100, your actual value for depreciation purposes would be $400. This is the $500 original cost of the business asset *less* the salvage value of $100. In this case, the annual would be $400 divided by 10 years or $40 per year. Generally speaking, under current Internal Revenue Service Regulations, you may ignore the salvage value if it is less than 10 percent of the original value of the equipment.

Two other commonly used methods of computing depreciation are the declining balance method and the sum-of-the-digit-years method. Both of these methods have limitations as to when they can be used for tax purposes.

A very useful booklet published annually by the Internal Revenue Service called "Tax Guide For Small Business" covers most of the tax points (and many accounting points) that a small business owner would need to know. There are examples to illustrate the text including filled-in tax returns, forms, and schedules. This booklet is usually available from the Taxpayer Assistance Section of your local Internal Revenue Service office. Other useful publications on accounting, taxes, and small business operations are produced by the Small Business Administration. Listings of available publications and prices may be obtained from the Superintendent of Documents, Government Printing Office, Washington, D.C. 20402.

Maintenance and Repairs

Maintenance and repairs are directly related to the usable life of an asset. In general, maintenance and repairs are both items of expanes. They are considered necessary to preserve the asset so that the asset can reach its usable life. Thus, periodic maintenance of an automobile is necessary to allow it to reach its usable life; repairs are also important. It is unlikely that an automobile would reach the end of its usable life (generally three years) if no maintenance or repairs were performed on it. However, where maintenance adds appreciably to the life of an asset, it is not an expense, but a capital expenditure or a capital improvement and is depreciated. Thus, repair of several shingles to the roof of a building would be a normal item of repair. Applying tar to seams and joints in the roof on an annual basis would be a normal item of maintenance. However, taking off the old roof and putting on a new one would be a capital improvement and it would be depreciated. The addition of a new roof materially prolongs the life of the asset (the building).

There is no one answer to questions involving depreciation, what is a business asset, what constitutes repairs or maintenance as opposed to a capital expenditure, and so on. Each problem must be answered by itself. As with everything else related to the tax system, you must be able to explain to the government, if called upon to do so, why and how you arrived at the result you did, together with the records necessary to support your point of view. As has been suggested in the past, if you are not sure about what you can or cannot do, seek professional assistance. It's hard to explain to a government auditor how you arrived at certain figures if you really aren't too sure yourself. It's also generally less expensive to pay a professional to advise you before you have problems than after you have them and have to get out of them.

Insurance

As a business person you face a variety of risks. Consider these possible situations:

1. A customer walks into your studio, trips over a wire, and breaks a leg. Liability insurance, which covers you for your liability for injury to a person or damage to the property or someone else, is necessary to protect you in this case.
2. A pipe breaks, shorting out your electricity and destroying a good part of your lighting system. Hazard insurance takes care of your loss here.
3. While on location, someone breaks into your car and steals your equipment. Theft insurance helps to reimburse you.
4. You plug your electronic flash contact into the wrong flash contact and get no wedding pictures; the customer wants to sue you. Professional liability (malpractice) insurance can be a help.

To adequately insure your property against hazards and theft, you must have a *complete* list of all the equipment to be insured, the serial numbers, descriptions, and proof of the worth of the equipment (including sales slips, receipts, bills, appraisals—anything that will establish worth). You will have to prove to the insurance company, should the need arise, that you lost a certain item that was worth so much money. A duplicate listing of insured items, together with the supporting material mentioned above should be kept in a safe location *away* from the studio (a bank safe deposit box is ideal). Thus, if your studio records are lost or destroyed, you will still have a listing of equipment.

The liability insurance coverage you purchase should adequately insure you against potential loss because of injury to person or damage to property. Usually, the cost differential, in amount of premium paid, between moderate and high liability coverage is not very great. It is generally to your advantage to have the most coverage you can afford. We hope it doesn't happen, but one lawsuit, if you are uninsured or underinsured, can easily put you out of business. Remember that generally speaking, the insurance company is only obligated to you to the limits of your policy. Thus, if you have a $25,000 limit, but you lose a lawsuit and have a $75,000 judgment against you, the insurance company is obligated for $25,000 and *you* have to come up with the other $50,000.

A *knowledgeable* insurance broker, particularly one who handles other photographic studios, is a good asset. Such a broker can usually suggest a package of insurance that contains liability and hazard policies tailored to your business operations. Probably the best way to locate such an insurance broker is to have one recommended to you by a person who is in the photographic field and has used the broker for a period of time. The same holds true of lawyers and accountants. Your competitors, trade associations, and suppliers, are good sources of recommendations of insurance brokers, lawyers, and accountants who have worked with photoaphic studios in the past and whose work has been satisfactory to those using them. Your insurance coverage should be evaluated periodically as to the amount of coverage and the type of coverage. Make sure you take inflation into account.

Types of Insurance

Other types of insurance that you may wish to consider are:

1. Accident/illness medical coverage, to cover your medical and hospital expenses if you are injured or ill.
2. Income continuation insurance, which provides income in the event you are ill or injured and unable to work.
3. Overhead expense insurance, which pays your overhead costs while you are ill or injured and unable to work.

If you have employees, your state will probably require that you obtain workers' compensation and disability coverage for them. Make sure you understand your state's laws and comply with them. One accident involving an employee can put you out of business if you aren't properly covered.

As a self-employed person, you are eligible to establish a pension plan for yourself and make regular contributions to it. However, if you have employees and you have a pension plan for yourself, you will probably have to establish a pension plan for your employees, too. Your banker is a good source to begin getting information on pension plans for you and your employees.

Comprehensive Example

Suppose you have been in business for one year, from January 1, 1978, to December 31, 1978. Your accounting period coincides with the calendar year. You have no employees; your state has a 5 percent sales tax, but you are not liable for any other state or local taxes; you keep your accounts on the cash basis and you sell nothing but your photographic services. You would report your self-employment income on Schedule C of Form 1040 (see figure 7). Your account totals are:

Advertising: $400
Cleaning service: $1,200
Cleaning supplies: $50
Expendable photo supplies: $250
Film: $550
Gas and electric: $1,500
Insurance: $800
Lab Expense: $3,000
Legal fees: $300
Postage: $75
Rent: $6,000
Repairs to camera: $75
Samples for window display: $350
Sign painting, promotional handouts: $500
State tax on sales: $1,500
Stationery supplies: $100
Telephone: $1,200
Total sales: $30,000

Your equipment is as follows: one 35mm SLR body worth $90, a 50mm lens for this camera worth $50, a 35mm lens for this camera worth $75, and a 135mm lens for this camera worth $35; one 2¼ SLR body worth $125 and one 80mm lens for this camera worth $175; one 4 X 5 view camera body worth $150; one 150mm lens for this camera worth $150, and one 210mm lens for this camera worth $325; two tripods worth $100 each; lighting equipment worth $300; furniture worth $1,000; a typewriter worth $250; and a cash register worth $250. When you began in business on January 1, 1978, you had all these items. Each has a usable life of 10 years and no salvage value after the usable life.

Form **4562**

Department of the Treasury
Internal Revenue Service

Depreciation

▶ See instructions.
▶ Attach this form to your return.

19

Name(s) as shown on return: Pete Photographer

Identifying number: 000-00-0000

Use this form as an attachment to an individual, partnership, fiduciary, or corporation return.

a. Description of property	b. Date acquired	c. Cost or other basis	d. Depreciation allowed or allowable in prior years	e. Method of computing depreciation	f. Life or rate	g. Depreciation for this year
1 Total additional first-year depreciation (do not include in items below) →						
2 Depreciation from Form 4832						
3 Other depreciation:						
Buildings						
Furniture and fixtures . . .	1-1-78	$ 1000	-0-	S/L	10	$ 100.00
Transportation equipment . .						
Machinery and other equipment .						
Other (Specify)						
35mm SLR body	1-1-78	$ 90	-0-	S/L	10	$ 9.00
50mm lens	1-1-78	$ 50	-0-	S/L	10	$ 5.00
35mm lens	1-1-78	$ 75	-0-	S/L	10	$ 7.50
135mm lens	1-1-78	$ 35	-0-	S/L	10	$ 3.50
2¼ SLR body	1-1-78	$125	-0-	S/L	10	$ 12.50
80mm lens	1-1-78	$175	-0-	S/L	10	$ 17.50
4X5 view camera body	1-1-78	$150	-0-	S/L	10	$ 15.00
150mm lens	1-1-78	$150	-0-	S/L	10	$ 15.00
210mm lens	1-1-78	$325	-0-	S/L	10	$ 32.50
Two (-2-) tripods	1-1-78	$200	-0-	S/L	10	$ 20.00
Lighting equipment	1-1-78	$300	-0-	S/L	10	$ 30.00
typewriter	1-1-78	$250	-0-	S/L	10	$ 25.00
cash register	1-1-78	$250	-0-	S/L	10	$ 25.00
4 Totals		$ 3175.00				$ 317.50

Individual, partnership, and fiduciary filers should include totals from line 4 on the corresponding lines of their regular depreciation schedule. Form 1120 or any of the Form 1120 series (Form 1120S, 1120F, etc.) filers should attach Form 4562 to their return and enter total of line 4, column g, on appropriate depreciation expense line in "Deductions" section of return.

Instructions

(Section references are to the Internal Revenue Code unless otherwise specified.)

Note: *Instructions for Class Life Asset Depreciation Range (CLADR) System are contained in separate instructions for Form 4832 (Class Life Asset Depreciation Range (CLADR) System). Also see Publication 534, Tax Information on Depreciation.*

Reasonable Allowance.—You may deduct a reasonable allowance for the exhaustion, wear and tear, and obsolescence of property used in a trade or business, or held for the production of income. The allowance is not allowed for stock in trade, inventories, land, and personal assets.

Charge off the cost (or other basis) to be recovered over the expected useful life of the property. Depreciation begins when the asset is placed in service and ends when it is retired from service.

In computing the depreciation basis for personal property other than livestock, you need not take into account salvage value that does not exceed 10 percent of the property cost or other basis. If the salvage value exceeds 10 percent, take only the excess into account. These provisions apply to property with a useful life of three or more years.

Depreciation Methods.—The various methods of depreciation you may use under section 167(b) are:

Straight Line Method.—Determine the depreciation for each year by dividing the

(Continued on back)

Form **4562** (1977)

Since all these items are business assets they can be depreciated. Using the straight-line method of depreciation the amount of depreciation attributable to each item would be its worth or cost divided by the usable life. The fact that you had some of the equipment prior to going into business is not important. If the equipment has been used entirely for business purposes since you went into business, you have converted it from a personal to a business asset and you compute depreciation from the day it was converted, based on the worth of the item at the time it was converted (see figure 6). Using the straight-line method of depreciation, the total depreciation for the year was $317.50. If you purchased an item during the year (and used it for business purposes for less than a full year) or if you converted an item from personal use to business use during the year (and used it for business purposes for less than a full year), your depreciation would be computed on the fraction of the year in which you used the item for a business purpose. Thus, if you purchase the view camera body on March 31, the depreciation allowable for the year would be 9/12 of the total of $15 or $11.25.

Another cost would be for travel and transportation. You have a car that you use partially for business and partially for personal use. You can deduct either the actual amount of expense (including depreciation) attributable to business use or a fixed amount based on business mileage (currently $.17/mile for the first 15,000 miles of business travel). Tolls and parking are additional. To facilitate computing your automobile expenses, keep a record of your travel as well as receipts of travel related expenses. It is also helpful to keep a daily diary in which you briefly indicate the physical location of the places you went as well as the reason you went there. The format below can help you keep track of your travel:

TRAVEL EXPENSES

Date	From	To	Mileage Start	Mileage Stop
5/23/78	Studio	XYZ Photo Lab	15321	15363
5/23/78	XYZ Photo Lab	ABC Hardware	15363	15378
5/23/78	ABC Hardware	Studio	15378	15403

In the sample, the trip to the XYZ Photo Lab would probably be self-explanatory. But, why did you go to ABC Hardware? A glance at your diary would show that you went there to do product shots. Business lunches, other entertainment expenses, tolls, and parking fees should also be recorded in the diary with a notation of where the bills and receipts for these expenses are located. This is not only very helpful at tax time, but it enables you to keep track of your time and eliminate or reduce wasted hours.

To complete the financial breakdown for the year, you traveled 5,000 business miles and had tolls of $15 and parking expenses of $10. During the year, you had no entertainment expenses. Your profit and loss statement as reported to the federal government on Schedule C of Form 1040 is reproduced as figure 7.

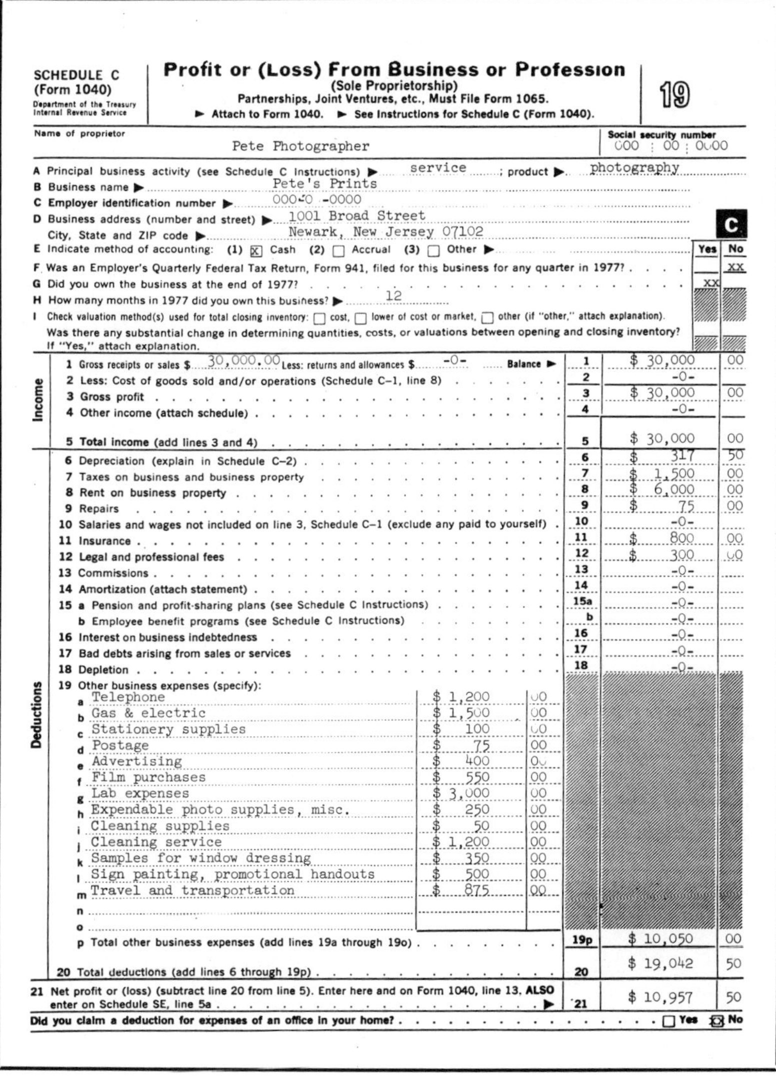

SCHEDULE C (Form 1040)
Department of the Treasury Internal Revenue Service

Profit or (Loss) From Business or Profession
(Sole Proprietorship)
Partnerships, Joint Ventures, etc., Must File Form 1065.
▶ Attach to Form 1040. ▶ See Instructions for Schedule C (Form 1040).

19

Name of proprietor: Pete Photographer — Social security number: 000 : 00 : 0000

A Principal business activity (see Schedule C Instructions) ▶ service ; product ▶ photography
B Business name ▶ Pete's Prints
C Employer identification number ▶ 000-0 -0000
D Business address (number and street) ▶ 1001 Broad Street
City, State and ZIP code ▶ Newark, New Jersey 07102

C

E Indicate method of accounting: (1) ☒ Cash (2) ☐ Accrual (3) ☐ Other ▶

	Yes	No
F Was an Employer's Quarterly Federal Tax Return, Form 941, filed for this business for any quarter in 1977?		XX
G Did you own the business at the end of 1977?	XX	
H How many months in 1977 did you own this business? ▶ 12		
I Check valuation method(s) used for total closing inventory: ☐ cost, ☐ lower of cost or market, ☐ other (if "other," attach explanation). Was there any substantial change in determining quantities, costs, or valuations between opening and closing inventory? If "Yes," attach explanation.		

Income

1 Gross receipts or sales $ 30,000.00 Less: returns and allowances $ -0- Balance ▶	1	$ 30,000	00
2 Less: Cost of goods sold and/or operations (Schedule C-1, line 8)	2	-0-	
3 Gross profit	3	$ 30,000	00
4 Other income (attach schedule)	4	-0-	
5 **Total income** (add lines 3 and 4)	5	$ 30,000	00

Deductions

6 Depreciation (explain in Schedule C-2)	6	$ 317	50
7 Taxes on business and business property	7	$ 1,500	00
8 Rent on business property	8	$ 6,000	00
9 Repairs	9	$ 75	00
10 Salaries and wages not included on line 3, Schedule C-1 (exclude any paid to yourself)	10	-0-	
11 Insurance	11	$ 800	00
12 Legal and professional fees	12	$ 300	00
13 Commissions	13	-0-	
14 Amortization (attach statement)	14	-0-	
15 a Pension and profit-sharing plans (see Schedule C Instructions)	15a	-0-	
b Employee benefit programs (see Schedule C Instructions)	b	-0-	
16 Interest on business indebtedness	16	-0-	
17 Bad debts arising from sales or services	17	-0-	
18 Depletion	18	-0-	

19 Other business expenses (specify):

a	Telephone	$ 1,200	00
b	Gas & electric	$ 1,500	00
c	Stationery supplies	$ 100	00
d	Postage	$ 75	00
e	Advertising	$ 400	00
f	Film purchases	$ 550	00
g	Lab expenses	$ 3,000	00
h	Expendable photo supplies, misc.	$ 250	00
i	Cleaning supplies	$ 50	00
j	Cleaning service	$ 1,200	00
k	Samples for window dressing	$ 350	00
l	Sign painting, promotional handouts	$ 500	00
m	Travel and transportation	$ 875	00
n			
o			

p Total other business expenses (add lines 19a through 19o)	19p	$ 10,050	00
20 Total deductions (add lines 6 through 19p)	20	$ 19,042	50
21 Net profit or (loss) (subtract line 20 from line 5). Enter here and on Form 1040, line 13. ALSO enter on Schedule SE, line 5a ▶	21	$ 10,957	50

Did you claim a deduction for expenses of an office in your home? ☐ Yes ☒ No

Costs

From the profit and loss statement, we can construct the operating statement for the business:

FIXED EXPENSES

Depreciation	$ 317.50
Rent	6,000.00
Insurance	800.00
Gas & electric	1,500.00
Telephone	1,200.00
Cleaning service	1,200.00
Cleaning supplies	50.00
TOTAL:	$11,067.50

SALES EXPENSES

Advertising	$ 400
Samples	350
Sign painting & promotion	500
Travel & transportation	875
Taxes	1,500
TOTAL:	$3,625

OPERATING EXPENSES

Film purchases	$ 500
Lab expenses	3,000
Repairs	75
Expendable photo supplies	250
TOTAL:	$3,825

MISCELLANEOUS

Stationery supplies	$ 100
Postage	75
Legal fees	300
TOTAL:	$ 475

Of total sales of $30,000 we can compute these percentages: Fixed expenses, 37 percent of total; sales expenses, 12 percent of total; operating expenses, 13 percent of total; miscellaneous, 2 percent of total. The remaining 36 percent was a net before-tax profit of $10,977.50. Assuming you work 260 days per year, you can compute a daily expense rate by dividing your expenses by 260 days. Thus, in our example, the fixed expenses of $11,067.50 plus sales expenses of $3,635 plus miscellaneous expenses of $475 gives a total of $15,167.50. Divided by 260 days, this comes out to $58.33 per day. This daily figure *does* not include the cost of film and other materials and processing. For a small studio operation it is easier to *add* these costs directly to the job. As the operation becomes larger, it can be made a part of the total figure. Finally, you must include a percentage for profit. We computed our before-tax profit as $10,977.50. Dividing this by 260 days, we have $42.22 per day. To this we must add the $58.33 per day, which is the daily cost for fixed expenses, sales expenses, and miscellaneous expenses. The total expense and profit figure is $100.55 per day or, assuming a 10-hour day, $10.05 per hour to make the same profit as for the year on which these computations are based.

Figuring Cost on a Job

Assume you have a customer who wants a portrait package consisting of one 8 X 10, two 5 X 7's; and six wallets, all in color. You will do these portraits in the studio. How much should you charge? First of all, how long will it take you to do the job? From your job record card you know:

1. First meeting with customer to discuss samples, poses, obtain information, and set up sitting:	**½ hour**
2. Shooting time for sitting (including set-up and take-down time):	**1 hour**
3. Preparing film to go to lab and preparing finished negatives for prints:	**½ hour**
4. Showing proofs to customer:	**½ hour**
5. Final trip for customer to pick up finished work:	**½ hour**

Your hourly rate (as figured above) is $10.05 per hour, or for this job $10.05/hour X 3 hours = $30.15. To this must be added the cost of materials:

One roll of 120 color film @	$1.80	**Processing & proof:**	$7.70
Proof album:	1.20	**Presentation folders:**	1.05
Print package (One 8 x 10, Two 5 x 7, Six wallets):			21.50

Total cost of materials = $33.25

To the hourly charge of $30.15, you must add your materials charge of $33.25. To make the same percentage of profit on this job as you did the year before, you must charge your customer a minimum of $63.40. Remember that the job record cards (figure 5) are a great help in determining times and materials used in different types of jobs. When you have enough data in the job record cards and daily diary entries, you may be able to figure out a different method to save time and thus reduce costs.

Know Your Costs

How can you determine if a certain job is unprofitable? Calculate how much time it takes you to do. Does this figure give you a profit? For example, you have a location job to do several black-and-white publicity photos. The customer is willing to pay $35 for the job. Should you take it? The trip to and from the location takes 1 hour; you estimate that it will take ½ hour to set up; actual shooting time will take another ½ hour; packing up your equipment will take another ½ hour; the time spent preparing the film to go to the lab is another ½ hour, and the return trip to the customer with the finished prints will take 1½ hours. Materials and lab services will cost $10. The total time is 4½ hours. Multiplied times our hourly rate of $10.05 we have $45.23 plus the $10 material costs, which adds up to $55.23. If you do the job for the $35 that the customer is willing to spend, you will lose money. Why? Subtract the $10 material cost from the $35 that the customer is willing to pay; this leaves $25. At $10.05 per hour, this $25 will be used up in about 2½ hours. However, you estimated that it would take 4½ hours for this job, so at $35 you will be selling below cost. In other words, this job will cost *you* money.

If you can persuade the customer to have the job done in your studio, you can make a profit on the $35 that the customer is willing to pay. How? You estimated round-trip travel to the location as 1 hour and you will have to make two trips; this accounts for 2 hours. You *must* charge for this time because it is unproductive for you—while you are driving to and from the location you cannot take pictures and make money. However, if you stay in the studio, you don't have these unproductive 2 hours because you can use them for profitable work. If you reduce the time for the job by 2 hours, the time becomes 2½ hours for the job. Remembering our earlier calculation, subtract the materials cost ($10) from what the customer is willing to pay ($35). Divide the remainder ($25) by the amount of time the job will take in the studio (2½ hours). This comes to an hourly rate of $10. Since your normal hourly rate is $10.05, you will lose about $.15 profit on this job ($.05/hour for 2½ hours). While it may seem like an insignificant amount of money, remember that when multiplied by a considerable number of hours and jobs, it adds up. Remember that when you're tempted to reduce your percentage of profit just to get a job.

How do you determine pricing *before* you have a complete set of records? Find out what your competition charges: make a telephone survey or go to other studios and ask. When you have a good sample, you will have a high and low for each type of job. You should be somewhere in the middle.

If you're well known or have a much demanded specialty, you can charge more. As you become established and take part in professional society meetings, you will find adequate opportunities to discuss price with your competitors. Price competition doesn't hurt anyone as long as prices don't go too low; they must always give a reasonable amount of profit if the business is to prosper. You'll also find various pricing guides in professional magazines and in book form. These guides are neither good nor bad; they are simply guides. They may help you when you are getting started, but the best source of pricing information is your own records. *Your records* are the only ones that relate to *your* business, *your* costs, and *your* profit. If you keep track of costs, you'll automatically adjust your prices to keep pace with inflation.

What Is Your Business Worth?

We've concentrated on profit and loss, but what is your business worth? What is your studio's financial picture as a whole? To learn this, you must make up a balance sheet. At its most basic, the balance sheet shows the amount of assets, liabilities, and capital (the investment in the business). Assets are usually grouped according to the ease with which they can be converted into cash. Current assets, like cash in the bank, are easily convertible. Fixed assets, such as land, buildings, etc. are not as readily convertible. You would expect to receive a current account receivable in 30 to 60 days. However, a long-term receivable like a mortgage may take several years before it comes due. Liabilities are also grouped by time of maturity. A current account payable would be paid in from 30 to 60 days. A long-term account payable, like a mortgage, may take some years to be paid off. Using the figures from the profit and loss statement, plus some others that you kept, you would have:

BALANCE SHEET AS OF DECEMBER 31, 1978

ASSETS	
Cash on hand (from checkbook)	$500.00
Accounts receivable (add up all unpaid sales slips)	250.00
Studio furniture & equipment	3175.00
less depreciation	317.50
	2857.50
TOTAL ASSETS:	**$3,607.50**

LIABILITIES	
Accounts payable (from file of unpaid bills)	$150
TOTAL LIABILITIES	**$150**
CAPITAL	**$3,457.50**

(Capital is the difference between assets and liabilities; it is also net worth)

Remember that the expense deduction for depreciation reduces the value of the business asset.

The basic profit and loss statement format as well as the balance sheet format are the same for a one-person business as for a multinational corporation. The large corporation will have more entries and adjustments on its balance sheet profit and loss statement because it does more business and has more complicated transactions than does the one-person operation. However, the basics are the same: for the profit and loss statement, total income less expenses equals profit (or loss) before taxes. On the balance sheet, assets less liabilities equals capital. This is referred to as the "net worth" of the business, i.e., what the business is actually worth.

The term "good will" is frequently mentioned in conjunction with accounting for business. Good will is an intangible asset (as opposed to a building, which is a "tangible" asset). It puts a value on the good reputation that the business has built up. It is a difficult asset to value because it is based on such factors as customer identification, customer satisfaction, repuration in the area, etc. For this reason, some accountants value good will at a nominal $1. If you bought an existing studio, chances are that some of the purchase price was for goodwill. In the sale of a photographic studio this would consist of such items as the name, negative files, lists of customers, etc. If you're opening a new studio, it is up to you to create good will.

Summary

Here is a list of the important accounting points to keep in mind.

1. You must keep accurate records of all items of income and expense.
2. Deposit all items of income into the business checking account; pay all items of business expense by check.

3. Make sure all entries are complete and legible.
4. File your records so that you can find them quickly.
5. Keep a record of what you did for each customer.
6. Keep a record of your job types including time spent and materials used.
7. Be aware of your costs! If you learn that your competitor is paying $500 for insurance coverage for which you are paying $800, find out why. It may be that the coverage is not the same. Or it is possible that your insurance broker is not giving you the best possible price. *Investigate* alternative sources of supply, from film to insurance. Don't stick with the same supplier out of habit unless you are getting the highest possible quality and the lowest possible cost from this supplier.
8. Keep duplicate records of equipment, insurance policies, legal documents—anything that you would have a hard time replacing or running your business without. There should be one copy in the studio with your other business papers and the other copy in a safe place like a bank safe deposit box.
9. Make sure your insurance coverage is adequate and update it regularly.
10. Keep abreast of business developments in your field. Learn about them and how they can be adapted to your business operation.
11. Be cost conscious! Know where your money goes. Remember that you are selling a personalized product that requires skill; always deliver a high-quality product to your customer.
12. If you have questions about legal, accounting, and/or tax matters, seek professional advice. Don't guess! If you guess wrong the results can be quite costly.
13. Good Luck!

7 | Merchandising Your Photographs

Kermit L. Buntrock

Professional photographers are fortunate people. They are dealing in a service packed with the potential to bring happiness and satisfaction far beyond what is being paid for it. When people will rush into a burning house—not for their precious jewels, but for a treasured photo album—you know that you are dealing in magic.

If our portrait studios could photograph all of the people who would like to have a picture made, who have talked about it many times, and who have the money to pay for it, our profession would be filled with people wading around in $20 bills up to their eyebrows.

What's needed is the nudge that will help people overcome their inertia and send them hurrying to have those professional pictures made before it is too late.

The enterprising hometown photographer needs to make it fashionable for people to have their portraits taken. Once this battle has been won, the snowball rolls downhill, getting bigger as it goes.

The key is to develop tasteful, image-building promotions that provide a valuable service for the community and customer while giving the photographer the profit he deserves through the traffic that is generated. This traffic can be restricted and selected, or it can be a broad stream, depending on the wishes of the photographer.

There is more gold in the hills than has yet been dug and the enterprising photographer is less than he or she should be if he doesn't go after it. The photographer should be a respected, influential, *affluent* citizen. What follows is written with the intent of making him or her that.

Media Help Is Important

Here again there is a formula. You help others and they help you.

Photographers who are in communities blessed with friendly, progressive newspapers and radio and television stations are fortunate. The media can be ideal partners in mutually beneficial promotions that help the community, the studio and the media itself. Here are some mutually beneficial programs that have the ring of success.

Anniversary Parade

Photographic studios that have built a favorable image with the aid of radio advertising should get enthusiastic cooperation on a promotion devised for couples who have been married 25 years and longer.

The station asks listeners to send in names of couples married 25, 30, 35, 40, 45, 50, 55, and 60 years who have an anniversary approaching. These are read over the air. When the name comes in, the station sends out a card something like this: "Congratulations! We are happy to wish you many more years of wedded life. In remembrance of this occasion we present you an anniversary gift of a 5 x 7 natural color portrait professionally made at Blank Studio. Phone this number for an appointment."

The five-year interval stipulation is to safeguard against "the sharpie" who might otherwise come in every year until enough gift enlargements had been received to take care of the entire family. The gift is in the 5 x 7 size so that the studio owner can upgrade to larger sizes with subtle suggestive selling. It is wise to keep this very low key, however, to avoid the appearance of a "come on."

This is truly a great promotion and there is a lot of personal satisfaction in it for the photographer. For the most part, the couples are respected people in the community who have been through thick and thin together. Usually they have children who have been putting pressure on them to be photographed. Here is the nudge that is needed to get them before the camera.

It should be made clear to the customer that the print is a gift from the radio station and not from the studio. You should not degrade your valuable product by appearing to give it away. Have a message typed on radio station letterhead that identifies the donor and deliver this with the gift print. When additional photographs are ordered be sure to start with your first print price, thus establishing the full value of the gift.

No money changes hands on this. The radio station doesn't charge for the advertising it does for the studio and the latter doesn't bill the prints given in the station's name. It is a mutually beneficial promotion.

There is a lot of spin-off from this program in addition to the sale of extra prints. The photographer who does the job right will book many future wedding, family group, and individual sittings as a natural follow-up. And the promotion pays big dollars and cents because of the pent-up demand for a photograph of Mom and Dad together. This is a high level service program that will build your image in your community.

Happy First Birthday

This program, similar to the anniversary parade, provides a steady flow of child sittings through the year. Again, the radio station does the fronting for the photographer through a portrait given in the station's name. Here's some suggested copy for the station letter mailed to the parents.

"Happy First Birthday!

"At the time of your new arrival, listeners were informed of the good news by this station. Now that the baby is growing up, we wish to send you our special gift: a 5 x 7 natural color portrait of the baby, compliments of this station.

"The portrait may be made anytime within 30 days before or after the baby's first birthday. Just call Blank Studio at this number and make an appointment. Then take this letter with you when the portrait day arrives. We hope you will treasure this gift for many years."

In a community of 8,500 this promotion has drawn as many as 225 sittings in one year, pretty evenly spread across the months, with an average extra print sale in excess of $29 each.

Here again is a solid, dignified, mutually beneficial program that benefits the public, the radio station, and the studio.

If the radio station traditionally has a booth at fairs and special shows in the area, tie in by providing a photographic exhibit of "Anniversary Parade" and "Happy First Birthday" portraits taken during the year, with the name and address on each photograph. This has a strong human interest appeal and will draw many visitors to the radio booth who will be impressed with your skill as a photographer. Your only cost for this image building is an additional print made at the time of the sitting and kept in your file until needed.

Child Personality Contest

Radio stations with good clout can do a real ''biggie'' in cooperation with a prestige studio that is still pushing for additional volume. The station lines up some nationally known singing star as the judge of a child personality contest at no cost through offering to plug the singer's recordings.

The lure of the nationally known star serving as judge and some prizes offered by the photographer will pull in sittings in surprising number. One midwestern studio in a county of less than 20,000 people pulled in more than 400 sittings in a three-week period.

The average per-sitting sale of extra prints isn't large on this one, but the intensive cooperative advertising campaign makes a big impact and additional business accrues to the photographer as a result. Again there is some image building by being linked to a big name.

Love That Newspaper Editor

A photographer's best friend isn't his dog. It's his newspaper editor. Fortunate, indeed, is the studio owner who has a good relationship with the press, even to the extent of blinking at some business that might be his except for some moonlighting news photographer.

It's a natural marriage. Both benefit when there is cooperation instead of hostility. The established studio can be a ready source for quick glossies of people in the news and the paper can be of immense help in building the image of the photographer by using news stories of his successes and by joining in mutually beneficial promotions.

Citizen of the Week

Most editors will agree that the biographical human interest story has a high readership, especially when it is about a well-known citizen and accompanied by a good portrait.

Here's a promotion that is easy both ways. The newspaper makes the selection and gives the name to the studio, which follows up by calling the person so honored and booking a sitting. A questionnaire devised to elicit the information the newspaper needs for the feature goes along in the proof envelope. The completed blank comes back to the studio with the returned proofs and then accompanies a glossy of the view selected to the newspaper office, again in the same envelope. This guards against one or the other getting lost in the clutter that exists in most newspaper offices.

The photographer gets his or her reward in the form of a credit line under the photograph and favorable mention in the story for cooperating in the program. Also, he or she has a valuable negative of a community leader for the possible sale of extra prints. At the very least, he or she can make a display print for the studio window, or a public exhibit later on. With the news article attached it makes a good attention-getter. Later the photographer can offer the exhibit print to the subject or the subject's family at a reduced price.

In rural communities a "Farmer of the Week" series is a solid promotion that builds a lot of good will because farmers generally feel that they are a neglected group and will appreciate the recognition all the more as a result. There are many other variations: Young Person of the Week, Churchman of the Week, and so on. The idea is to provide the incentive that is necessary to get people who need pictures in front of your camera.

Pioneer of the Week

If you are in a community that is proud of its heritage, as most are, you can get a lot of mileage out of photographing people who are old—and proud of it! How about a series geared to those born before the turn of the century? This one will provide human interest stories with widespread appeal.

One enterprising studio did a cooperative program with a newspaper observing its 80th year. All persons 80 years or older were invited to come to the studio for a complimentary portrait to be used in a feature article about them. A surprising number accepted. The newspaper editor followed up by giving a party for all those who were photographed. This was really frosting on the cake. When you can tie a public event to any of your promotions, there is extra mileage for you.

The Big Haymaker

All of the promotions discussed thus far are speculative from the standpoint that the photographer gets no front-end cash. The photographer obligates himself or herself for the cost of the sitting and a print in return for image-building publicity from cooperating media. Now, here's one that will provide full price for that first print, if the studio owner wants to run it that way. It is known as "portrait dollars," a steamroller coupon program that will bring terrific plus business.

The plan works this way. You go to some supermarket owner or manager, timing your visit to hit when he or she is looking for something new that will capture the imagination of customers who have become jaded with the promotions that have been used.

You lay it on the line in these words: "With portrait dollars, your customers will receive a prized portrait made by a professional photographer living in your community. This photograph will become more valuable with the passing years and will be a source of recurring good will for you as visitors admire it in the home. Here you have terrific traffic pulling power because of the sentimental value of a portrait."

If you can sell the promotion at 2 percent—less than most stamp programs cost—you can have $40 or more for that first print. Let's take $40 as the figure you want. You ask the customers to accumulate $1,000 worth of portrait dollars, given dollar for dollar on sales, over a six-month period.

From tests already run, you know that people will scramble for their portrait dollars—even grabbing them ahead of their change; and yet, because of human inertia, they will redeem only fifty percent of them, or less. You have already collected from the supermarket at 2 percent for all of the portrait dollars given out, so you reap the benefit of the inertia. In other words, your take will become 4 percent because you will be providing prints on only half of the portrait dollars for which you have already been paid. Multiply $1,000 by 4 percent and you come up with $40 for the first print. If you want more than that, just require the customers to accumulate more portrait dollars to qualify.

There are variations on the plan. You can tie in sustained, concentrated publicity for your studio by having a newspaper or radio station front for you in return for 25 percent. The advantage here is that you do nothing but make the portraits. The cooperating media does all of the other work, such as printing and distributing the portrait dollars and collecting for them. If your supermarket does $1,000,000 in business over six months, there will be $5,000 for the cooperating media and $15,000 for you—plus the sale of extra prints and the advertising bonanza.

This promotion can be broadened to include other businesses. It can be especially effective in a shopping center where the merchants pool their efforts in a traffic-building program. It can also be given as a favor by the radio station or newspaper to good customers, one from each line.

One midwestern studio, which has run portrait-dollars promotions four times, has had as many as 15 merchants cooperating at one time.

This promotion is so good that the photographer can shade the percentage a bit, if it's necessary to get the supermarket to go along with the plan.

Here is really a big one. It is clean, ethical, and dignified; and it builds business for the future. When you get all of the portrait-dollars customers giving photographs to relatives, you achieve a snowball effect. Many of those recipients will be giving photographs back the next year.

Capitalize on Grandparent's Day—and Other Holidays

Grandparent's Day provides a rare new marketing opportunity for the enterprising professional photographer. There's a lush crop out there ready for the harvest. Surveys disclose that a small percentage of people in this age group are photographed in any one year.

Here, again, the photographer will need a strong "motivator" to get these people before the camera. Very few will come in on their own.

An attractive, carefully worded gift card can be an effective device for achieving this objective. How about something like this: "Congratulations on being members of a very special group—the Grandparents of America. In appreciation for the rich heritage being left by your generation, we are joining in honoring you with a public exhibit of portraits—and we hope that you will be part of it. Just bring this card with you to our studio and we will make a complimentary sitting of you. Then select the pose you like best and we will make an enlargement from it for the exhibit. There is no obligation on your part for a purchase of any kind. Should you like the photograph in the exhibit, it will be available later at a special price. Call today for an appointment."

Your advertising should be beamed at the children and grandchildren, urging them to write in for the cards, which they can then pass along to the honored couple. This gets the grandparents over the modesty hurdle and they will be more likely to come for a sitting, "because someone they love wants them to be photographed."

Your exhibit can be personal, with invitations restricted to the couples photographed, and their relatives and friends, or it can be a big public event promoted as a program honoring a generation that has contributed much to the community.

Whatever it costs, it will be worth it to you as an image builder and as a winner at the cash register. With the possible exception of the high school senior, this type of sitting usually yields a higher dollar average than any other.

Grandparent's Day is a fine addition to the gift occasions that the professional photographer should promote with vigor. Valentine's Day, Mother's Day, Father's Day, Family Reunion Day, birthdays, anniversaries, and, of course, Christmas, should all be used with sensitivity to get people before the camera. And don't hold back on the sentiment. Love really makes the world go around for the photographer. "If you really love someone, give your portrait" is a line that should be universally used in our profession. One West Coast photographer who does a huge decorator business started it with "Put a little love on your wall." That kind of perception pays off at the cash register.

Boost Your Houses of Worship

Most photographers can benefit by identifying with "the church crowd." After all, here are the people who put a high value on love of home and family, with a resulting sentimental attachment for photographs of cherished ones.

The hometown photographer who forfeits the church directories to outsiders is doing less for his community than he or she should be doing. He or she should do the directory—in a quality manner—with a choice of proofs from negatives of good size rather than 35mm transparencies. The average sale will be about $30 per sitting in a normal situation. The photographer should figure $2 to $3 off the top for the cost of putting out the directory, because it should be a credit to the church and to the photographer. Even if the directory turns out to be only a break-even proposition, the photographer has gained by building for the future through exposure to people who can be of benefit with good word-of-mouth advertising.

Work Your Files

Experts will tell you that it costs less to get more business from those already trading with you than it does to create new business. This means that your files are a source of gold for you.

A nationally known West Coast photographer reports that a surge of business automatically follows his mailings to addresses taken from his files.

For the more aggressive, here's a road-tested idea that will bring in some extra dollars at a low period in the year. Send a mailing to a list selected from the sittings made during the year asking for permission to make a print for public exhibit. Explain in all honesty that the exhibit print will be offered for sale later at a reduced price. Provide an opportunity for enclosure of a check for the print in a return envelope. Then make up the prints, have your annual exhibit of professional photography, and let nature take its course.

One well-known studio sent out 500 letters and received 150 back, including 84 with enclosed checks of $19.95 each for an 11 x 14. By timing this for the first quarter of the year the studio owner can take advantage of the specials offered by many labs for that period, with extra profit to himself.

Use Sittings to Pull More Sittings

The imaginative photographer can increase camera-room traffic by using a pleased customer to pull in other customers, or to get more business later from the original client.

School photographers have increased their wedding business through the simple device of a discount card delivered with the senior order. The card can read like this: "We also take beautiful wedding pictures. When that big, wonderful day comes along for you, remember to invite us with our cameras to your wedding. Then use this discount card as a deferred graduation gift from us."

If weddings are nothing but hard work and no joy for you, use an alternative that will bring in family sittings. Enclose a card that reads: "Thanks for coming to us for your senior portraits. It has been a pleasure to serve you. Here is a bonus for you. This card is worth $10 toward the purchase of a 5 x 7 portrait of your family in natural color. Here is your opportunity to provide a family portrait that will become a treasure in the years ahead. Please make your appointment by July 1. Don't throw this card away. It is worth $10 to you."

Learn from Your Competitors

One of the big photographic chains realized a 40 percent response through a simple suggestion that the parent sit in with the child on a pose or two. What a payoff for being perceptive!

Here's a large company sensitive enough to realize that adults usually shy away from being photographed—not because they don't like pictures, only because they must be given a compelling reason for going before the lens. What more compelling motive is there than to be shown in company with someone you love?

Anyone who doesn't learn from this competitor and do the same for himself—or who doesn't take every family group he or she can assemble at a wedding, or who doesn't photograph Dad and Mother together after a family group—is missing out on a big market.

There is a demand for professional photography beyond our fondest dreams. We just need to be alert enough to recognize it when it's there, and take advantage of it with gain to ourselves while being of service to our customers in a personal, sensitive way.

Another thing the chains do with great profit is to run specials on copies and restorations at slow periods of the year, usually January, February, and March. Why should the hometown photographer be reluctant to do the same thing?

Why not do something a bit special by staging an imaginative promotion along with the price reduction, like putting on a local contest for the best use of photography in a building with some respected interior decorator as the judge? Additional weight can be given to the competition with your announcement that winners will be entered in a national Photographic Art for Wall Design competition sponsored jointly by Eastman Kodak and the Professional Photographers of America.

In the copy and restoration area, don't pass up the groups in your community that maintain lodge buildings—the Masons, Elks, Knights of

Columbus, etc. Sell them on the importance of preserving their heritage with photographs of their leaders down through the years.

If you have four lodges that have been in existence for 50 years, that adds up to 200 photographs or copy jobs. In many cases you can increase your sales volume through the skill you exhibit in matting and framing those historical pictures.

Invitational Sittings

Low periods can also be filled in profitably by using invitational sittings to bring in high income segments of your public. You can do the whole bit, one at a time: environmental portraiture of groups, sweet sixteen, charm portraiture of the mature woman, leaders in industry, and on and on.

This works especially well for the prestigious studio with a reputation for award-winning photography, since most people will then look upon the invitation as an honor.

If you haven't built your image to that point yet, you can help yourself in a hurry through the Certification Program sponsored by the Professional Photographers of America. By successful completion of a written test, submission of acceptable prints and proof of business integrity the full-time photographer can get in on a nationally marketed program that should be a terrific image builder. This program isn't in the future. It is here now.

Many Ways of Developing Additional Business

The aggressive photographer is limited only by his or her imagination in the things that can be done to increase business. With the terrific demand that exists for his product, can be as busy as he or she wants to be, managing and promoting business, clicking the shutter—and ringing the cash register.

For instance, the wedding photographer who is in a highly competitive situation can get out in front by teaming up with a jeweler who gives out a card reading like this: "Thank you for choosing Superb Jewelers for your engagment ring. In appreciation, we have commissioned the Blank Studio to make the announcement portrait of you for the newspapers. This will be done without obligation on your part. Please come to us again when we can be of service to you."

This gives the photographer the opportunity to meet the bride "personal and up close" at a time *before* she has been besieged by people who want to get in on her wedding business. Human nature being what it is, the jeweler may forget to send out the card. Guard against this by having your receptionist pick up the names and addresses once a week and mail out the gift card yourself in the jeweler's envelope.

Some perceptive institutions are making a good thing out of advertising themselves as the "full-service bank." Many photographers would be wise to follow the same line. If there is a portrait to be made in your community, you should want to do it, ranging from the dowager who drives up in her Cadillac down to the junior high school girl who wants a billfold for her first boyfriend. Treat that girl right and the chances are good that she will be with you for a long time.

Don't even shy away from taking "ping-pong" pictures. Your public knows the difference between those prints at a few cents each and the artistically matted and framed heritage portrait you sell for several hundred dollars.

One photographer with a national reputation even does a "one-shot" child promotion several times a year right in his studio, offering an 8 x 10, two 3½ x 5s, and eight billfolds for $4.85. He takes as many as 150 child sittings in one day, giving proof that, all things being equal, a lot of people prefer going to the hometown photographer over a stranger set up in the cluttered aisles of a store.

There is much to be said for building a plan for the entire year. Many successful chains have a calendar for their managers that tells them what to do on every working day. You may not want to go that far, but at the very least you should have a promotional calendar that will fill in your low periods with profitable traffic builders. Simply by keeping figures that you can separate into categories you will know which type of sitting provides the best return for your time and effort. Give priority to these in your advertising.

Yes, It Works!

Now, you ask, does this system of promoting your photography business with imagination and aggressiveness really pay off?

Back in 1947 a couple of World War II veterans teamed up to purchase a studio that had done a volume of $37,000 the previous year. Before they passed the baton 27 years later to a couple of young men trained to come in behind them, they had built their gross to $165,000 in a town of 8,500. Two years later, using the formula handed to them by their predecessors, the young men set a new volume record of $173,156.22, and increased profit in keeping.

Photographers are fortunate for another reason. The profession has many people who have spent a lifetime refining a formula for success—and then will share it all in an hour from a platform—or in a couple of chapters in a book.

8 | Photographic Advertising and Promotion

John Stockwell

Few businesses are in a position to benefit more from a carefully planned advertising campaign than a studio or individual photographer. Advertising is really the art of persuasion and few things can persuade as effectively as a fine photograph.

Advertising comprises various ways of bringing your skills and talents to the attention of potential buyers. It can be thought of as comprising two parts: the creative or idea part, and the job of planning, producing, and distributing your advertising message. Chapter 8 suggested various creative ways of getting business. This chapter will emphasize ways of using these ideas in your own work as effectively and as economically as possible.

Planning

Many advertising campaigns fail from poor planning. Too often, a decision to advertise is made at the last minute, which invariably results in poor execution. Money is spent in a hit-or-miss fashion on various media with the hope that something will happen. As a result, few people really appreciate how effective a good advertising campaign can be in producing high income, month after month, year after year.

The first thing to do is to set an advertising budget based on what you hope to accomplish in the coming year. Frequently, a budget is based on the previous year's sales; this guarantees a no-growth situation for the coming year. Instead, sit down with whatever records you have kept and try to create a chart that shows where your business comes from, and where you would like to be at the end of the year. A typical chart might look like this:

Chart 1 Source of business

Category	Last year's sales	%	This year's goal	%
Weddings	65,000	54	68,000	51
Portraits	32,000	26	35,000	27
Seniors	11,000	9	12,000	9
Commercial	12,000	10	15,000	11
Restorations	1,000	1	3,000	2
TOTALS	**$121,000**	**100%**	**$133,000**	**100%**

Set a sales goal for each of the categories based on your estimate of the market. In setting next year's goals, here are some questions to ask yourself:

- Did I miss some seasonal opportunity because I didn't plan far enough ahead?
- Am I spending too much time on parts of the business that bring in a relatively small return?
- Conversely, am I spending too little time on those aspects of the business that have the most potential for growth?
- Are any trends visible? In other words, are some parts of the business growing faster than others?

You can probably think of other questions to ask and the answers. The important part about this exercise in profit planning is the discipline of forcing yourself to review what you've been doing, and what you think is possible in the following year.

Typically, you may spend from three to eight percent of your gross on advertising. Keep in mind that the *commitment* to spend the money over the entire year is much more important than the *amount* of money you allocate toward advertising. Nothing will waste money faster than to spend a large amount of money in the beginning of the campaign, and when results are not immediately forthcoming, to pull back and stop advertising.

Spend your money according to your plan. Make some adjustments during the year to fine tune your efforts, but keep at it for the rest of the year. You will be surprised how this commitment to results will pay off despite some temporary misgivings.

Timing

Timing your efforts is just as important as budgeting for them. Again, too often not enough time is left for proper planning. As a rough rule of thumb estimate how long you think it will take to create a campaign for some seasonal promotion, then double that time. Anyone who has worked in a studio for even a short time knows that a lot of business is seasonal. It makes sense to time your efforts to take advantage of this seasonality and to plan for it far in advance.

It is extremely helpful to make a yearly calendar of promotional events that shows the year at a glance. Across the top, run the months of the year, while down one side indicate the various seasonal events you might want to exploit. A promotion-planning calendar might look as simple as this:

EVENT	MONTHS											
	J	F	M	A	M	J	J	A	S	O	N	D
WEDDINGS		PLAN		LAUNCH								
CHRISTMAS								PLAN		LAUNCH		
VALENTINE	LAUNCH										PLAN	
MOTHER'S DAY	PLAN		LAUNCH									
etc.												
↓												

Only a few aspects of a photographic business are shown on this chart, but the principle is clear. Plan far enough ahead to give time to launch the promotion at the opportune time of the year. Launch your program early enough to gain the maximum selling time for your promotional expense.

Once you've planned your yearly budget and decided on your monthly promotions, you can allocate your budget by month. The effect will be to spotlight your commitment to advertising for the whole year, broken down on a monthly basis.

Planning Specific Promotions

If you've planned your year's activities as we suggested, then this job will be automatically done for you.

If you want to increase your wedding business in June and August, you know how early to plan for it. If you see growth in your portrait business, then you can expect a good part of this business to come around the holidays in December. Summer months are big months for a photographer who specializes in outdoor portraits in customer's homes.

Certain seasons, such as Christmas and graduation, are universal throughout the country. On the other hand, there might be purely local celebrations that could mean a promotional opportunity for the alert photographer. If you're new to the business, then check with your local chamber of commerce for advice and guidance.

Your success in the coming year will depend a lot on how well you plan. Therefore, don't rush the process or try to do it strictly by guess. Take sufficient time to research your market and your past business history. Your first try will be a rough plan; succeeding thoughts will refine that plan. The end result should be a realistic plan for your year's activity spelled out in expected expense and income to be earned from each aspect of your business. Most important, your planning calendar gives you a timeable for profits.

Make or Buy?

This is a question every business executive who produces a product has to answer. In the area of advertising, it simply means asking yourself whether you should create your advertising yourself, or whether you should engage expert help. How you answer this depends a great deal on your own abilities and interests.

Photographers are engaged in creative work, and creative people can often carry this talent into other fields, such as advertising. Later in this chapter, we offer tips for making the most of your creativity in this field. However, here are some questions to ask yourself first:

- Instead of creating advertisements and brochures, can I earn more for my time by being a photographer instead of an advertising person?
- Are there services or people available at a reasonable fee who will understand my business and be able to help me grow?
- Do I really want to get involved with such things as buying space or time, working with printers or mailing houses?

While you can't divorce yourself from the advertising process (after all, you're paying for it and supervising its creation), you can minimize your involvement by working with an advertising agency, or go to the other extreme and produce all your promotional materials and ad copy in your own studio.

Many photographers choose a position somewhere between these two extremes. You can plan your advertising campaigns around advertisements, brochures, or complete promotion packages that are made available by the Eastman Kodak Company and various other suppliers and laboratories. In this case, you have the advantage of professionally prepared materials at an affordable cost. It would be impossible for a typical studio or photographer to go to the expense of creating and printing a full-color brochure in quantities of a few thousand or less.

On the other hand, you must realize that these standard campaigns are available to your competitors, and if you are both promoting the same package, it will be difficult for you to maintain a sense of identity in this look-alike situation.

Working with an Advertising Agency

A good advertising agency can save you a lot of grief in promoting your business. They can make market surveys and discover new sources of business; help build an image that is uniquely yours; create ads, brochures, and radio and TV commercials; and help you analyze the results. Needless to say, a full range of services like this can be very expensive. Normally, advertising agencies make their money on the commissions earned from the various print and broadcast media in which they place your advertising. Since studios are not big users of advertising space, as are supermarkets and department stores, the commissions are relatively low. The expenses must be recovered by means of additional fees and charges of various kinds.

If you decide to use an agency, the following checklist will help you get the most out of your investment:

- Who are their other accounts? Can the agency demonstrate with samples that they can sell an intangible like photographic services?
- Where will your account rank in the agency? Near the top or near the bottom? Both extremes are bad; try to be a middle account in terms of dollars spent.
- Precisely what services will you get for the money spent? Put things like this in writing to prevent misunderstandings.
- Do you feel comfortable with the principles of the agency? This is a hard quality to define, but you will recognize it after talking with the people for a little while. Do you trust them to understand your business and to do a good job?
- Finally, check into the financial stability of the agency. The agency places the orders and pays media bills. If they should go under, it is possible you may wind up paying twice for the same space. Your bank can help you here.

Working with Other Professionals

If you do not choose to use an agency, it is still possible to tap the creative talents of outsiders without spending too much money. Very often, freelance talent is available in your locality. Designers and copywriters, even if employed on a full-time basis, will often take on assignments to augment their incomes or to get a chance to do something different.

Finding them might take some work but the effort could prove very worthwhile. Ask other business people you know if they use freelancers. You can get some good leads this way, especially if their advertising attracted you in the first place. Call up a few printers in the area and ask their advice. Often, they work with clients who use freelancers, and they can suggest some names for you to contact. Finally, you can place a small help-wanted ad in your local newspaper. Stay away from the classified columns. Rather, place a two- or three-inch ad on the business page of your local paper.

Creating a Unique Image for Your Business

Nothing is more important to your long-term success than the image you project. As a creative person in a creative business, your every contact with the public should project this image. Your first investment in promotion should be the design of your logo. This is the symbol, name, or some unique combination of elements that instantly identifies your studio or business.

Take time in preparing your logo. Don't entrust it to a printer with some statement like "Pick a fancy type for my letterhead and studio name." Your logo should be simple and distinctive. It should be clear and recognizable when put on a small business card, and be impressive when reproduced on a large building sign.

Once you are satisfied with your logo, make it a signature on everything: letterheads, business cards, brochures, price lists, newspaper ads, albums, labels, and on your finished product. Consistency is important and will eventually pay off in identification and remembrance in the minds of potential customers.

An important point to remember when designing a logo is the fact that it will be used in a variety of media. Your logo should reproduce well in black and white or color. Some of your ads will appear in newspapers where simple black-and-white illustrations print best.

Getting the Most from Your Displays

A display of your work in the window of your studio is probably the most effective and least expensive way of turning lookers into buyers. It should be the starting point of every promotion you plan.

Display ideas abound, and your own planning will suggest others as the year progresses. You can build displays around portraits for holiday giving, special pricing, framing specials, restoration, or other promotional ideas you have in mind. It is much more interesting if you keep windows simple and change the displays frequently. Avoid an expensive display that is so elaborate that you have to leave it untouched for months.

A good way to tie your newspaper advertising into your window display is to mount a blow-up of your ad someplace in the display. This serves as a recognition point for people who have seen the ad and they identify it with your studio.

A display is a visual message; therefore, keep words to a minimum. At most, they should be price captions or other brief descriptions. A good way to test the attraction of your display is to take a picture of it. The window should be composed in an interesting fashion, just like photograph. If your window looks good in a black-and-white photo, then you probably have an eye-catching display.

Newspaper Advertising

Your local newspaper should be given early consideration as an advertising medium. However, in order to get the most from your investment, you should become familiar with buying space and preparing effective ads. Your planning budget described previously will help you set a budget for newspaper advertising. Often, when starting some new promotion or campaign, you might want to take a somewhat larger ad than normal in order to attract attention; later ads can be smaller and serve the function of reinforcement of the original message.

Newspapers sell space by the column inch or the column line. There are 14 lines to an inch, so if you know the line rate, you can easily figure out the cost of the ad you have in mind. For example; at $.50 a line, a space one column wide by one inch deep would cost $.50 times 14 or $7. If you wanted an ad to run 10 inches deep, it would cost you ten times that amount, or $70. An ad two columns wide by five inches deep would contain the same area and would cost the same.

Space is sold by the *open* rate or the *contract* rate. Don't be frightened away by the word contract rate. You merely agree to take a certain amount of space in a given period of time, and the newspaper will bill you at a lower rate, depending on how much space you've contracted to buy. If you do not buy the contracted amount, the paper will simply bill you the difference between what you agreed to take and what you actually took. For a small noncontract advertiser, the open rate applies. It is the highest rate for space and is charged for the casual, one-time user of space. By planning carefully a year in advance, you can take advantage of contract rates and probably even get a better position in the paper as a valued advertiser.

If you've hired an agency or a competent freelancer to do your advertising, then much of the work of preparing the ad will be done for you. You, of course, will have to give your agency the "meat" of your campaign—what you are selling, or what you're trying to accomplish in your advertising. They will have to come up with ideas for putting your message across.

If you plan on handling the ad yourself, these hints should prove helpful:

- Create the ad the way you would a photograph. Think of the layout as a photographic composition that has unity, movement, and a central visual idea. The only time a cluttered ad works is in the used or bargain equipment market; people will hunt through a jumble of small type looking for a sale.
- Keep the typography simple. Nothing says amateur more loudly than an ad that contains too many different typefaces. Three faces should be the limit. For this reason you should choose your type carefully for a logo. If you think Old English Script is an elegant typeface for your name, you may later find that it's impossible to harmonize with modern typefaces.
- If you use photographs they should be bold in design and tone. Newspaper reproduction is terrible at best; fine detail and subtle tones are muddied and lost. Large areas of solid black should also be avoided because such tones do not print deeply or evenly on newsprint.
- Often, it is easier to use professionally prepared ads available from Kodak and others. You can be sure their experts know the problems of newspaper reproduction.

Where your ad appears within the pages of the newspaper is important. Ordinarily, space is sold ROP, which is a newspaper term for "run of paper." This means that your ad will be placed any place at the discretion of the make-up editor. If you want a special position you have to request it at the time of ordering your space. Certain positions are considered very valuable and a premium is charged for the space. You will have to decide whether it is worth the extra price. If you're trying to build a wedding business, it certainly would make sense to pay a premium to get your ad placed among the engagement and wedding announcements because you know many more prospects will see your message in those pages.

One of the best sources of help in preparing newspaper advertising are the business representatives of the newspaper itself. They will have studies of readers' habits, income, interests, and the like, which can be helpful in planning a promotion. In addition, the staff can often help you in preparing an ad that will be both effective and attractive in newspaper format.

Brochures

It is hard to imagine any situation where an attractive brochure would not be useful as an additional selling aid. The brochure can sometimes be as simple as a price list, or it can be an elaborately printed booklet with color illustrations. A number of suppliers make available standard brochures that you can imprint with your name, and thereby have the advantage of professionally prepared advertising at relatively low cost.

If you have a specialty you want to promote, some special skills to make known to a specialized audience, or just special prices to announce, then you will have to prepare a brochure to serve your own needs. Fortunately, it need not be especially difficult or expensive if you know what you're doing.

The first thing you will have to decide is what you want to accomplish with the brochure. Do you want to show the full range of your services and capabilities to advertising agencies and other users of photographs? Do you want to present a selling message to a specific audience, such as brides-to-be? Are you introducing a new service such as restoration work? Do you want to use the brochure as a substitute for a personal presentation?

Once you've focused your objectives, then many of the pitfalls can be avoided. The most expensive flaw in the preparation of a brochure is to tell too much. If you're offering a wide range of service to a variety of different clients, it is impossible to appeal to them all in a single brochure. A bride-to-be, for example, simply is not interested in your capabilities as an industrial photographer.

Eventually, you may decide that a number of different brochures will have to be prepared to exploit various segments of the markets you are trying to reach. As a start, pick the most promising area and concentrate your efforts there.

Even if you plan on having a studio or agency plan your brochure, there are certain things you have to do in the beginning:

- Once you've targeted your market, identify two or three important selling points that you want to make to your prospects. If you're promoting weddings, you might want to concentrate on your ability to turn out formal portraits or lively candids, your wedding packages and what they contain, and perhaps some mention of your credentials, such as your years of experience, awards won, and so on.

- Merchandise your abilities and services. Everything you say should relate to the specific service you are trying to sell. Keep your story simple, repeat your main points several times in different ways, and err on the side of telling too little rather than turning prospects off with too much.
- Dramatize your story with interesting layouts and pictures. Let your prospect see your ability in the brochure. Again, compose your brochure with the same care that you compose a picture. The headlines, copy blocks, and illustrations should all be part of a unified whole that invites the reader's eye.
- Finally, and perhaps most important, is an action device or message. After your prospect has read the brochure and is interested in your story, *ask for action.* It is nothing short of amazing how many otherwise excellently prepared brochures fail on this point. Ask for an order, an appointment, or what have you. If possible, make it easy to respond by including a reply card. But don't leave the prospect feeling favorably disposed toward you without knowing precisely what to do next.

Writing the copy for the brochure can often be the most difficult part of the job. Unless you have experience or skills in this area, it is recommended that you find a copy pro who can take the raw information you supply and transform it into vibrant, selling copy. If you plan on tackling this job yourself, then some of the following information should be useful in preparing the most effective message.

Creativity can't be reduced to rules. Accept the following statements as guides that will work most of the time. Sometimes breaking a rule can be more effective than observing it too slavishly.

Good copy can usually be broken down into four parts:

1. The headline should attract attention with a strong statement of benefit that appeals to the reader.
2. Immediately afterward, the copy should relate that benefit to the reader, often by means of a subhead.
3. The bulk of the copy explains the service or product in benefit-oriented terms.

4. The ending should ask the reader for action—to send for more information, phone for an appointment, ask to see a representative, or whatever.

If you will refer to this four-part checklist every time you have to write an ad or construct a verbal presentation, you will never make a bad mistake and lose a prospect. Perhaps the most common failing among beginning advertising writers is forgetting about the prospects' interests and saying too much about ones' self.

Direct Mail

Direct mail is one of the most personal media you can use in promoting a business, a service, or a particular product. Years of experience show that it is one of the most effective types of advertising but also the one most misunderstood, and therefore poorly used.

What is direct mail? Essentially, it is a single communication addressed to a prospect through his or her mailbox. It can be a brochure, a post card, or a complete mailing package consisting of a letter, brochure, and some device to facilitate responding to the offer or announcement. Let's take these components one at a time.

The letter. Many direct mail experts say that every campaign should include a letter, even if it is not personalized. Instead of the prospect's name and address appearing on top of the letter, you can use a headline to attract attention to the message in the body of the letter. Of course, the most impressive way to begin is to personalize the letter by means of fill-ins or the use of an automatic typewriter. While expensive, these techniques can be enormously effective when you want to pinpoint your prospects.

The brochure. This has been covered previously. In most mailing pieces you can use the brochure that you created for some other purpose. This is especially true if your brochure is a statement of your capacities or a price list describing some services. If you are making some special promotion or an announcement, then you will have to create a brochure just for that purpose.

The response device. Classic mail order uses a reply card that makes ordering easy. As a photographer, you will be interested in having the prospects call you, request an appointment, or visit your place of business. All of these can be accomplished with a separate card in the letter. A good way to get people to come to your studio is to make the card a certificate or some other document of value that the prospect can exchange for a gift or discount.

Finally, don't forget the outer envelope that carries all these pieces of paper to your prospect. Most of the time you will use your regular letterhead and business envelopes. However, it is quite effective to add a "teaser" message on the outside of the envelope to get people inside faster. This message can be something like:

"Free gift certificate enclosed . . ."

"Save $10 on Christmas portraits . . ."

"Special, limited-time offer . . ."

You can think up many others depending on the job you're trying to do. Printing this message on the envelope usually entails extra expense, but most of the time it is worth the investment. The only time you should consider leaving it off is if you are using a personalized campaign with an individually typed name and address on the envelope. Then you want your letter to look as much as possible like a regular letter.

How to Use Direct Mail and What to Expect

Direct mail is a very personal medium and should be used much like personal selling. In other words, you choose a likely prospect very carefully, then use the mailing piece to sell that prospect on whatever item you're promoting. Choosing your prospect in direct mail means getting a mailing list of people likely to be interested in your product or services. While you have to accept the fact that you will reach many nonprospects in a newspaper ad or a radio commercial, you simply can't afford that extravagance in direct mail.

The other thing that surprises many first-time users of direct mail is the relatively low response that normally occurs. If three or four persons out of a hundred receiving your direct mail piece respond, you probably have a very successful campaign. All your direct mail budgeting must reflect this fact. Of all the things you can do to improve your response rates, refining your list to include only the best prospects is the best way to boost results dramatically.

Sources of Lists

Large scale direct-mail users, those who mail upwards of a million pieces a year, work very closely with list experts and brokers to discover the best lists to use in campaigns. Your efforts will be much more modest and it is unlikely that your mailing volume will run into the tens of thousands. For the most part, you will have to generate and compile the mailing lists yourself.

A list of names is useless unless they comprise people with some common interest or attribute that you can exploit. A list of names taken from a telephone directory, for example, is useless because the list includes every range of age, occupation, income, and interest. For direct mail to be successful, you have to pick a list that targets your prospect group. For example:

- A list of public relations directors of companies and plants in your area would be valuable if you're promoting your capability as an industrial photographer, especially for annual report work.
- A list of new mothers can be used for baby photography.
- A list of lawyers who specialize in accident work would be good prospects to cultivate if you want to build your business as a forensic or insurance photographer.

The list can be expanded endlessly. The important thing is to decide what type of business you want to cultivate with your direct mail, and then to build a prospect list in that area. Most of the time, your list will grow very slowly, depending on how and where you locate names.

Another important thing to do is to separate your list into various categories. As a rough guide, the following list can be used to sort your names into groups:

- The first and most important group is your customers. In any list, you should have some way of identifying past customers from just prospects. In addition, you might want to sort your customers by interest group, age, or size of purchase.
- The next most important group in your list is people who responded to some advertising you placed in the past. The fact that the prospect was interested in your services, even if it did not result in a purchase, suggests a higher level of interest than might be found in "cold turkey" prospecting.
- The next prospects are names obtained from newspapers, directories, or other commercial sources that identify the people by some attribute you can exploit. Examples are: names of new mothers, newly promoted executives, names of businesses that use photographs or photographic services, and so on.
- Under no circumstances should you use an unknown list or a list of names and addresses with no commonality of interest. In other words, sending a mass mailing to everyone in town by means of postal patron mailings is the quickest way to lose money.

Timing of Direct Mail

There are two ways of timing your direct mail and both methods have points to recommend them. In a typical studio situation, much of your business is concentrated in the summer around popular bridal months, and then around the end of the year when gift portraits are popular. Direct mail can be used during slow months to promote other services, such as copying and restorations, commercial work, or other services you want to expand.

The other method is to use direct mail according to a calendar found successful by many direct-mail practitioners. Curiously, the time of year that you mail affects the response, certain months bringing more business than others. On a scale of 1 to 10, the mailing months can be rated as follows, 10 being the best month:

Month	Rating	Month	Rating
January	10	July	7
February	9	August	8
March	7	September	8
April	7	October	9
May	7	November	8
June	6	December	8

As you can see from the table, busy months in the studio occur in places with less than maximum direct-mail effectiveness. Therefore, if you find yourself in this pattern, direct mail can work beautifully to smooth out income during the year. Mail heavily during normally slow months, and mail less during normally busy times.

Follow-ups

Many users of direct mail will do everything perfectly until they reach the final step of following up on responses. If you sent out a mailing and ask people to come in or phone for an appointment, make sure that every response is treated promptly and courteously. If you're offering a brochure, they should be printed and ready to mail. A valuable positive image created by effective advertising can be dashed in an instant if the follow-ups are handled poorly.

If you perceive that a response might be heavy, which is apt to happen if you're offering something free, then consider breaking down your mailing into groups that are mailed at intervals instead of all at once.

Broadcast Advertising

Radio and television are considered broadcast media, and because so many people listen to them, they are also called mass media. This should immediately tell you what you should promote in broadcast media and what you would be wasting your money to promote.

Products and services that appeal to a large segment of a population are suitable for broadcast advertising. Gift portraits, weddings, seniors, and the like can be reached economically by broadcasting. On the other hand, promoting a specialized service such as insurance photography would be too costly because the number of prospects for that service is limited in any general population group. Such prospects are best cultivated by direct mail that can be targeted to that specific group.

At first you might be confused as to whether to use AM or FM stations for your commercial messages. Actually, the choice is quite easy. Talk to the various station representatives serving your trading area and ask them what kind of audience they reach, and how much of that audience is tuned in at various times of the day. They can answer these questions quickly and accurately because stations do research in this area as a service to advertisers.

Many stations fall into fairly well-defined categories and the audiences line up according to these categories. Stations can be identified as rock, middle-of-the-road, classical, country-and-western, news-and-talk, and so on. The type of programming determines the type of listener, and hence the type of product or service most suitable for that audience.

Spoken commercials are the toughest to write and you should accept help from the station representative. As a listener, you might feel that a typical commercial goes on forever. When you try to write a one-minute message of your own, you may be surprised at how little can actually be said and suffer the frustration of trying to tell everything, including your name and phone number, in that small span of time.

The best commercials stress one simple theme or offer, and are repeated at frequent intervals. An easy-to-remember address or phone number is invaluable here because a quickly spoken group of numbers is very hard to remember.

The cost varies with the amount of time you are buying, the size of the station, and the time frame in which your commercial will be aired. Different types of listeners are attracted at different times of day, so you should discuss the change in audience carefully with the station representative.

Television adds two things: expense and visual appeal. Often this extra expense is worthwhile because photography is a visual medium and you can illustrate your product dramatically on TV. Television production expenses are much higher than radio and any investment in this area should be carefully weighed. Often, the station can help in the production and can use your print material as elements in the production. Much visual appeal can be gotten with a moving camera, zooms, and the like.

Television is sold much like radio, and each station has studies relating to audience size and composition. Generally speaking, TV stations are not as specialized in programming as radio stations. On the other hand, the audiences are more segmented depending on programming. Cartoon shows obviously attract mostly children, while adult males form the major audience for sports broadcasts.

Displays and Exhibits

This is one area that most photographers do not exploit to the fullest. While no one has to tell you to put a display of your work in your window, consider all the other opportunities for displays at other locations: in hotel lobbies and other places that attract groups of people, in florists' shops, in the infants' department of larger stores, in photofinishing outlets, and so on.

Many of these outlets can be cultivated on a cooperative or commission basis. Once you make a deal, show your appreciation by coming by frequently to replenish literature racks or to change the display. This keeps a fresh image facing the public and tells your benefactor that you appreciate the exposure.

If you're a freelancer without a walk-in studio, your portfolio will be your best exhibit. The best type has removable pages so you can change the pages depending on the client being approached. Even if you are competent in several areas, such as weddings and industrial photography, leave the bridal pictures out when calling on a company, and vice versa. This is an obvious caution, but it is amazing how often freelancers lug their total work output from one type of client to another.

Conclusion

Advertising is a vital part of your business and is essential if you want to grow both in reputation and in money. Several fundamental points are worth repeating:

1. Advertising should be budgeted for the year and a commitment made to spend that money according to a definite plan.
2. The commitment to advertise is more important than the amount of money allocated.
3. Choose a particular medium because it will reach the prospects you seek, and not because it is the cheapest or the most expensive, or what have you.

4. Finally, you should keep accurate records of the results of your advertising—number of appointments, sittings booked, requests for brochures, etc. This will tell you how to alter your budget for the next year to improve the effectiveness of your advertising investment.

This chapter could only touch on the highlights in the space available. Your library has books covering various aspects of advertising and they can be consulted for detailed information and strategies. In addition, companies serving the photographic field have a stake in your success and they spend a great deal of money creating professional advertising programs that you can tap at little cost. If you add all this expert help to your own store of personal experience, your advertising should be both professional and *profitable.*

9 | Public Relations and the Photographer

Bert Holtje

Few professionals are in a better position to make use of business-building public relations than photographers. Your work is graphic, artistic, inherently interesting, and it lends itself to mass exposure in print, TV, and all types of displays. In short, you have a lot going for you before you ever think about the specifics of a public relations program.

Many of the most successful public relations programs I have seen have been the result of an individual photographer's personal insight and foresight. The ability to see something unique that will help to build business, and the drive to make it work are often worth more than slavish attention to a list of public relations dos and don'ts. And, many of the successes were the result of trying to solve a problem, rather than starting from scratch with a what-do-I-do-next attitude.

Consider the situation of a general studio proprietor who had a personal interest in antique photographs. Although it amounted to only a small portion of his business, the owner relished the few antique restorations that came in. One day, the photographer discovered that many of the people who sought out restoration work were from a nearby senior citizens community.

The thought occurred that these people might be helped by setting aside one evening a month when all who were interested could bring their old pictures for a free evaluation. Not only would they be told something of how the pictures were made, but the antique value would be appraised as well as estimates given for restoration work. The photographer assumed that the restoration work obtained would at least pay for the evening.

While the restoration work was rather modest, there was another benefit never counted on. It sooned turned out that these people wanted pictures taken of themselves to send to relatives. The free clinics were really public relations projects, even though the first purpose of them was a way to enjoy old prints.

One professional interest led to the sale of professional portrait services. Eventually, the local newspaper carried a story about this work for these people, and the result of this public relations coup was an even greater demand for portrait services.

What Is Public Relations?

I've just done something that makes handbook editors cringe. I've used a term repeatedly, but haven't defined it. However, the example I cited has probably done more to position public relations than any traditional definition. But, in a book such as this, a working definition is obligatory, and here it is: Public relations is any message about a product or service created mainly to build prestige or good will for an individual or an organization. Most textbook definitions talk about public relations being free promotion, and advertising being the paid counterpart. In the main, this is true, but public relations services must be paid for, so the definition is only partially correct.

Now, we can get down to the very practical matter of using public relations to build your photographic practice. Let's not call it a business; practice is more meaningful. Professionals have practices, and you are a professional. You do continue to study, don't you? You are always expanding your knowledge of photography, apart from your personal experience. You do read the journals, and maybe even share your knowledge with other professionals. The emphasis will be on professionalism. With so many cameras in the hands of so many people who might be your customers, the best way to make a public relations program work is to have at its core a strong theme of professionalism.

Should You Do It Yourself?

Before I get into some of the techniques that have worked well for other photographers, you should think seriously about the amount and kind of work involved in a good public relations campaign. The word campaign implies that this should not be a spotty effort, that it should be an ongoing program that is working for you all the time. Unfortunately, many photographers undertake a PR (public relations) program when they first get started, only to drop it when business builds to a comfortable level. Then, when the business fades, they have to kick the wheel again. The most successful photographic professionals plan a campaign carefully and keep it up. I hope that you will do the same.

Most of the techniques described in this chapter can be handled by just about any photographer, but there are two requirements that you should consider before you decide whether to do it yourself or to engage a public relations consultant. One is time. If you plan your program correctly, it will take time, and you can't let the program slip when you are overwhelmed with business. The second is a skill with words. Public relations involves some writing and some speaking on your part. As a photographer, you are mainly visually oriented. If you are one of the lucky ones, you can express yourself almost as well on typing paper as well as you can with photographic paper. However, don't let this turn into an ego trip. Make absolutely sure that you can handle the words, whether you have to put them on paper, or make them up as you go along when you are talking to a few hundred people at a Rotary-sponsored meeting.

To help you make the decision, let me tell you a little of what you might expect when you deal with a public relations agency. First of all, they will probably charge you a monthly fee for their work. If you buy their services, be absolutely sure that the agency spells out in detail just what they will do each month for the fee. It is impossible for them to guarantee any specific results, such as a feature story in the local paper, or an interview on a TV show. But, if they put in writing their objectives on your behalf, you will have guidelines for a practical working relationship.

Now, here is a little trick that may work in favor of you and the agency: It's the old barter game. Suppose the PR counsel wants a couple of hundred dollars a month to do a job that you feel will be well worth it, but is simply beyond your budget? Why not offer to trade services? You know your rates, and you should know something of the clients in the PR shop. Why not offer to trade work for work? More than good PR will probably accrue from this arrangement. The chances are very good that if the PR people like your work they will use you for assignments beyond the amount specified in the barter agreement. Think about using an agency on such a basis before you undertake all the work that is necessary to put together and run a good PR campaign yourself.

If you are thinking about going this route, talk with several PR agencies before you decide on one. Usually, these agencies specialize in certain types of business. Make sure that the clients handled by the agency mesh with, but do not conflict with, you and your business.

What can you expect to pay an agency? There is no pat answer to this question. Away from major cities the rates are generally lower, but this doesn't necessarily mean that the quality of the work will be lower. The services may be as good, better, or worse. Only you can judge the quality of talking to other clients who use the shop, and by evaluating the successes they have had. Most agencies work on a monthly fee for a specified amount of work. Any work outside the specified effort will be billed extra. Make sure you know exactly what the extras are and what you will be billed, if the need arises.

Creating the Theme

Unless you plan to photograph everything, and very few professionals do, you should develop your PR program around the type of business you want to emphasize. I'm sure that you understand that the nature of business is to make money. You may like the idea of photographing machinery, but if you live in an area of few factories and no industrial advertising agencies, you should rethink your specialty.

Let's say that your specialty is portraiture. How might you develop a theme that would tie your PR program together? There is hardly a photographer that won't take a portrait assignment, so you will have competition. The idea is to make sure that you stand out as *the* portrait photographer everyone thinks of when a face is to be captured.

For the moment, let's refine portraiture, and say that because you live in an industrialized area, full of prosperous businesses, you are going to specialize in executive photographs. What would you do to set yourself apart from your competitors to make sure that you get the assignments?

Most people like to see themselves in a photograph, but are not especially enamored of what they have to do to get the picture. Most executives begrudge a photographer more than a few minutes, and then fidget all through the sitting. If you can come up with a way to make the whole thing a positive experience, you have a strong hook for your public relations campaign.

More often than not, you and your executive will meet once: when you take the picture. During those few nervous minutes, you want to know everything there is to know about this individual so that you can portray him not only as he sees himself, but as he should be seen by others. Even a first-rate psychologist would be at a loss to get that kind of understanding in the time allotted. But you are not only expected to get it, you are supposed to produce a print that meets with everyone's approval.

How would you solve this problem, and make strong public relations points? How about developing a printed questionnaire that you send to your subject a few weeks in advance of the sitting? Ask all sorts of questions that are designed to give you personal insights, and to provide a topic of conversation when you meet for the picture. Think about hobbies, sports, business, and anything that would make him relax and open up while you are shooting.

This is nothing new. But, the way you use it will be if you are public relations minded. Once you have used the questionnaire successfully, arrange with a local newspaper editor to do a story on your technique. Imagine what a headline like this in the business section would do for your practice: *Photographer Takes the Fuss Out of Executive Portraiture.* In addition to the story, there would be several of your best executive prints for all to see.

This is what I mean by an underlying theme. A hit-or-miss public relations effort that makes you look like a jack-of-all-trades and master of none will do very little for you. Unless, of course, being a jack-of-all-trades is your thing. If this is the case, play it up, but make sure that it is the theme of every PR effort, and that you don't come off as a master of none.

Keep Your Name in View

This is the old bromide of every public relations person who never got any further than writing stories about a local group that wants to diaper dogs. However, as trite as it is in the hands of a hack, it is a maxim that has meaning when properly used.

Memory is short, and because most people don't use a photographer often, you should think of some way to remind them you are in business. Even if you work with people who use your services often, such as advertising agencies or department stores, it still pays to remind them that you are there, working, and looking for more assignments.

How to keep your image alive depends mainly on your specialty. To give you an idea of how to think about this problem and some practical solutions in specific areas, let's look at some of the ways photographers make a living.

The wedding photographer. You only get one chance with each couple. If they think of your competitor, you'll never know that the decision was not made in your favor until the announcement picture appears in the paper.

Good public relations is more thinking ahead than applying a bunch of rules. Let's think about the wedding process and see just where and how you can mount an effective public relations campaign.

What does a bride buy besides wedding pictures? A wedding dress. She hires a hall and a caterer. A band. What about the stores that sell presents to those who will attend the wedding? The point is this: There are a number of other businesses the bride will use as she plans her wedding. Why not arrange with some of these suppliers to display samples of your pictures? Perhaps one of the best places to do this is with the store that creates wedding dresses. Every bride would like to see how others have looked in different styles of wedding dresses. Why not arrange to photograph a number of styles, without charge, if the dressmaker will display them and give you appropriate credit?

The industrial photographer. There are a number of opportunities in this field for business-building public relations. In heavily industrialized areas, for example, manufacturers often form organizations that meet regularly, usually for lunch. If you offered to shoot publicity pictures of *one* of these meetings, at no charge, you would be in a position to meet people who can influence the purchase of photography. You will have a chance to showcase your ability, and to make personal contacts. However, be careful not to let this activity get out of hand. Be sure to let them know that photography is your business, and that you do get paid for taking pictures of meetings as well as machinery.

If there is an industrial development commission in your area, you might consider offering your photographic services. These organizations are usually made up of volunteers from area industry as well as elected officials. Again, this is an excellent place to meet the people who should be your paying customers.

The general studio. The photographic generalist usually locates in an area that has heavy foot traffic. It's not exactly walk-in business looked for, but walk-by interest. Therefore, make the most of your window to display your work. It is very important that you change prints frequently. When people realize that there will be new pictures every few weeks, they will be more attracted to your exhibit. This will also show that you are busy and popular.

The exhibit doesn't have to be limited to your window. You might arrange exhibits in other places that could benefit from the traffic such an exhibit would bring. Be sure to get appropriate credit.

If you plan to exhibit portraits and baby and wedding pictures, select the prints very carefully. Not everyone is beautiful or handsome. Only you know what they really look like. If you select prints that reflect your technique and artistry only, and are not of particularly good-looking people, you can be judged a poor photographer. Stout people expect to be seen thin, and others imagine themselves in ways not reflected by reality. In plain English, show the prettiest and most handsome people you photograph.

I used these three examples to give you an idea of how to think about making the most of public relations. Rather than go on describing what each photographic specialist could do, I think that I can be most helpful by detailing techniques that can be used by most photographers.

Some Successful Public Relations Techniques

Here are some public relations ideas all photographers can use.

1. Where do your potential customers congregate? Perhaps most of the industrialists in your area eat lunch in a local restaurant. Why not arrange with the restauranteur for a free exhibit—with appropriate credits, of course. You might also try to exhibit at a golf or country club, at a church, a social club, and even at a school where PTA meetings are held. The possibilities are limited only by your own imagination.

2. Just because pictures must been seen to be appreciated doesn't mean that you can't do a good PR job during a radio interview. As I mentioned, however, you will need some facility with words, and this situation is probably the most demanding of that skill.

   Don't just call the program director and say that you would like to appear on so-and-so's show. Have an idea that will appeal to the listeners of the show. You could become the local photographic guru by doing regular spots on the state-of-the-art for the snapshot taker—who, incidentally, can become your biggest customer for general photography. You might plan seasonal appearances, during which you tell the listeners how to make the best holiday photographs. You might even try to get some regular exposure by moderating panel discussions with other professionals, or by running an amateur camera club of the air. Non-network stations are usually more receptive to these suggestions, but the major networks are always looking for good local programming, so don't rule them out.

3. Television is an obvious choice because you can show your work. But, getting on TV will be more difficult than getting on radio. For one thing, there are more radio stations than TV stations, and most of the TV stations take their programming from the networks. But don't stop because it sounds tough. Give it a try. If you hit with TV, it can be one of the best ways to get your story across.

4. Local newspapers provide an excellent outlet for your public relations efforts. Apart from simply sending them releases on your activities (discussed later in this chapter), you might offer to write a regular column—for no charge. Oddly enough, there is not too much syndicated material available on photography, and most papers that carry photographic stories usually generate them themselves.

Newspapers have lost the immediacy they had before the full impact of television was felt. Because of this, newspapers are publishing more and more service material, and providing news interpretations rather than trying to scoop TV. This situation is ideal for you, if you feel that you could crank out 800 to 1,000 words a week. It shouldn't be too difficult, and the effect can be good for business.

5. Don't miss an opportunity to address a group on the subject of photography. It sure beats talking to one person at a time.

   What kinds of groups? That question must be answered with another question: What is the market for your specialty? You can waste a lot of time talking to people who will never buy your services. When you have decided on your specialty, the next step is to identify the people in your community who would be prospects, and to find out if they belong to any organizations that might like to hear a lecture on photography.

   Remember that these people will be snap-shooters who would like to get better candids and vacation pictures. This isn't a competitive situation, and a little favor can often result in a big portrait or wedding job when the time is right.

   Local groups are usually looking for interesting speakers and anyone who promises to tell them how to make better pictures should be welcomed. Again, remember that you are the pro; you will be respected for your skills and your willingness to share enough information to help people make better snapshots.

Your Public Image

The techniques I have described so far will work for just about anybody, but before you run off to try them, you must decide who you are. This is not a rhetorical question, or an introduction to Philosophy I; it's a serious question that can contribute to success or failure of not only your public relations effort, but your entire business.

There are photographers who feel that they prefer to shoot a lot of pictures, and charge less than the next person. Others prefer to make one or two exposures a week and collect fewer, but larger fees. It all boils down to what you feel most comfortable with. This is really a business decision, but its impact on public relations is very important.

If you are a gutsy type of person and feel that you can afford to turn down the less profitable jobs, you had better be prepared to have the image and the courage to make sure the big assignments end up in your studio. And, if you prefer the security of a high-volume business, you must be prepared to handle the jobs in such a way that you are not worn out at the end of the day.

Whatever image you decide is you, stick to it. Build it every step of the way. And never vary from your intentions. It is this consistency that makes the difference. You know photographers, I'm sure, who are self-declared experts in one area, and never let you forget it. The chances are that they deliver the goods, but for every individual with this high self-esteem, there are many others with equal skill and talent, but without the stamina to pull it off.

Bear in mind that I'm not talking about being a phony; I'm talking about taking yourself very seriously when you have the appropriate skills. And when you do start to build these expert credentials, it will be very difficult for anyone to take any business away from you. It's a strong position to be in, and one that requires considerable attention to the public relations effort.

Just as important as your personal image is the image of your premises. If you are doing executive portraits, you will want a studio that will be in keeping with the surroundings familiar to your subjects. A pot of coffee and a box of doughnuts might not be enough; how about a mini-kitchen in which your assistant can whip up a quick lunch for your executive portrait clients? From a public relations point of view, be sure to consider the needs, interests, and backgrounds of the people who will be your customers as well as your own photographic convenience.

How to Use Publicity Techniques

This time, I will begin with a definition: Publicity is a message about your activities prepared as editorial, rather than advertising, material, and published or broadcast without charge.

Apart from the public relations techniques I have described, you can get a lot of mileage by keeping the newspapers, radio, and TV stations in your area informed of your activities. However, before we get into the details, remember that these activities must have some interest to the people who will see or hear them, or the editors will throw away your material.

In all publicity work, keep this in mind: What's in it for the reader or listener? It may be exciting for you to announce that you have just added a wing to your studio, but this means nothing to potential customers unless you translate this information into something that will benefit them. In this example, you might have built the new wing as a bridal studio. If this is what you have done, say so, and tell in detail just how this will benefit the bride who comes to you for pictures. Tell of the dressing rooms, the make-up center, the accessories, and the lighting that will make them look perfectly natural.

Later in this chapter, I will show you how to write a publicity release, but first let's look at the organizations to which you can send such a release.

The main use of publicity is for communicating with publication editors and radio and TV programming people. Often, these releases will lead to other things. The publication may run your story, but see in it material that could turn into something else. For example, a release on your new wedding wing might lead an enterprising editor to call and ask for an interview on the subject of how a bride should prepare herself to be photographed. The spring editions of most papers usually abound with such material. It helps the advertisers as well as the readers.

You can also use your publicity releases as a form of direct mail. Although direct mail is covered thoroughly in the chapter on advertising, you should consider this as an inexpensive way to reach the special groups you would like to impress. If, for example, you just added new processing facilities that would be of interest to local businesses who buy considerable product photography, a release on the subject can do a lot of good. See chapter 9 for details on direct mail.

How to Write a News Release

Before you write a word, make sure that you have something that will qualify as news for the editor to whom you are sending the story and for the readers of the publication. One of the most common editorial complaints is that of the newsless news release.

It may be important to you, but is it news and important to the reader? If you can answer "yes" to this, you can start on the release.

When people were writing longer sentences, and there was little reader resistance to their length, editors would insist on the Five W's being in the first sentence. Who, What, When, Where, and Why are still the main building blocks of every news story, but don't try to cram every thought into one unmanageable sentence. Writing today is characterized by brevity and simple clarity. If it takes two or three short sentences, forget the old city-room folklore and give the editor a break.

Every major detail should be in the first paragraph and the rest should be a mini-story that could stand by itself if all the rest of the copy were eliminated.

Let's see how a lead might look for Lynn Parker, who just announced the addition of a photo restoration service to her custom lab:

"Lynn Parker, president of Apex Photographers (WHO), has added an antique photo restoration service (WHAT) to her Middletown facility

(WHERE). Apex Photographers now (WHEN) offers this service because of the rising interest in old photographs (WHY)."

In two short, uncluttered sentences, the entire message has been told, but readers are seldom satisfied with such meager detail. For this reason, the story will follow in what journalists call the inverted pyramid format. That is, details are presented in a descending order of importance. This is done for the convenience of the newspaper make-up person. A paper has just so much space for advertising and editorial material. If a story runs too long, the make-up person can cut from the bottom without damaging it.

When you write a news release, try to avoid using adjectives or adverbs that are not absolutely necessary. The rule is prune, prune, prune. When you have trimmed away the modifiers, you will have a story that should be acceptable to the editors for whom you write. Even if they do some editing themselves, when they see that you have spared them the misery of too many modifiers, they will be more likely to give your story serious consideration.

News release format. Don't be tempted to design an ornate form; this often turns off an editor. If your story has news value, your regular letterhead with a rubber-stamped legend, "NEWS RELEASE," will be quite effective.

There is no concensus on the headline. Some editors prefer to get the release without a head, and then write their own after reading the material. Others prefer to have the headline because it gives them an idea of what they will be reading in the release. They can then rewrite the heading if it doesn't conform with the style of the paper. I have always preferred to include the headline, and leave it to the editors to either use it or change it.

In addition to the name and address of your company, you should always include a phone number where an editor can reach you for more or confirming information.

The date of the release mailing should be included as well as any specific time the release should be used. When a release is to be timed with a special event, the date should be specified, but if timing is not especially important, the release will usually carry the line, "FOR IMMEDIATE RELEASE."

Try to keep your release to one side of a piece of paper. If you must go beyond this, don't type on the back of the sheet. On the bottom of the first sheet, centered, write the word "more" and enclose it in parentheses.

At the end of the release, whether it is a single or multiple sheet piece, write the word "end" and enclose it in parentheses.

It's general editorial practice to use words for the numbers one to nine, but to use figures for 10 and beyond.

Because abbreviations vary so much, it's usually best to avoid all but those most commonly used.

Here's what a one-page news release might look like:

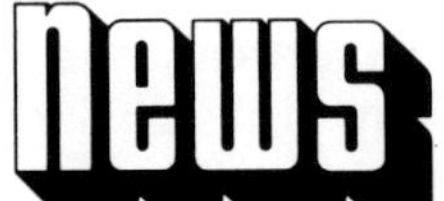

APEX PHOTOGRAPHERS - 123 River Road, Middletown, NJ

DATE February 24, 1980

RELEASE DATE March 1, 1980

CONTACT Tom Parker (201) 568-0760

ANTIQUE PHOTOGRAPH RESTORATION SERVICE NOW BEING OFFERED BY APEX PHOTOGRAPHERS

Middletown, NJ.- Tom Parker, president of Apex Photographers has added an antique photo restoration service to his Middletown studio. Apex now offers this service because of the rising interest in preserving old family photographs.

According to Parker, "Many people have have old photographs of friends and family that they would like to keep. Unfortunately, the paper on which many of these pictures were printed years ago deteriorates, as does the photographic image. However, we can recapture the sharpness of the image and print the pictures on a new plastic based photographic paper that will ensure endurance."

Parker recently completed a course in antique photo restoration and has expanded his laboratory facilities to handle the work. He will be happy to quote restoration prices before any work is undertaken, and he will also help people evaluate any old photos brought to his studio.

Apex Photographers is located at 123 River Road, Middletown, New Jersey. The studio is open from 9 to 5, Monday through Saturday.

(end)

There it is, the short course in public relations. It won't make you a pro, but it will make you look like one. See you in the papers.

10 | Legal Aspects of Photography

Steve Delloff

You, the professional photographer, are a business person. If you're just preparing to set up your own business, getting organized is probably one of your primary considerations. Will you operate in your own name or use a trade name? Will you organize as a partnership or a corporation? Do you have to fulfill any state or local requirements to open up a business? What are your legal responsibilities as an employer? How do you negotiate a business lease? These are some of the questions common to almost every person starting a business, regardless of the type of business. The photographer has other questions to consider as well: copyright requirements, model releases, invasion of privacy, and photographic libel, for instance.

It is difficult, if not impossible, to give blanket answers to legal questions. Laws not only differ from state to state, but are constantly changing through actions of legislatures (amending, passing, and repealing laws) and courts (interpreting laws as cases come before them). The best advice to follow is: Don't be your own lawyer *unless* you have the necessary training and experience. Don't sign legal documents or enter into agreements without having a lawyer review the materials and advise you of your rights and obligations under them. Many times the wording of a lease, contract, mortgage agreement, or loan note will seem simple enough, but contain legal terminology whose legal meaning may be quite different from its apparent meaning. When you deal with governmental agencies, you may get correct information from agency personnel, but then again, you may not. It is best to consult a lawyer before problems arise.

You should discuss with your lawyer the types of business entities open to you: sole proprietorship, partnership, and corporation. Based on your particular needs and goals, the lawyer will be able to suggest the appropriate form of organization and explain what you have to do to comply with applicable laws and regulations. Having a lawyer review business documents before you obligate yourself is really a matter of common sense. If you are aware of the possible consequences before you take an action, you may want to reconsider, renegotiate, or forego an action entirely. Prevention of problems in the beginning is far less costly than trying to remedy them later on.

How do you choose a lawyer? Recommendation by a person in a business similar to yours is the best way. Then see if you can develop a working relationship with the lawyer you have chosen. Unless you have confidence in your lawyer and are willing to listen to his or her advice, you cannot have an effective lawyer-client relationship. Your lawyer, too, must be willing to listen to suggestions.

Finally, it is helpful if your lawyer is acquainted with photography as a business. It's rather difficult for a lawyer to advise you properly on the contract for the purchase of an expensive package printing set up if all the lawyer knows about film processing is that he takes the film to the local camera store to be developed. You should remember that some legal areas of photography, notably those dealing with libel and copyright law, are highly specialized. Just as your family doctor would probably refer you to a specialist for a condition that he did not feel qualified to treat, the general practice lawyer would refer you to a specialist in those areas in which he did not feel specially qualified.

Accidents

In chapter 7 is a detailed account of some of the state and federal requirements for business people. That chapter also explains the various types of insurance that you should be aware of. Two types of insurance that deserve special emphasis are liability insurance and worker's compensation insurance. Liability insurance protects you from financial damage in the event you do something which results in injury to a person or damage to property. The name describes it well: It insures you against occurrences for which you may be liable.

Having liability insurance does not make you immune from lawsuits. Any accident you are involved in brings with it the potential of a lawsuit. It is important to remember that all the circumstances of every accident, no matter how trivial, that involve injury to a person or damage to property should be reported to both your insurance company and lawyer as soon as possible. Don't rely on your memory; take notes of what happened, when and where the accident took place, who was present, and why and how it happened. Remember to take pictures if you possibly can. They are not a substitute for a written report, but a valuable adjunct to it. Remember that insurance company adjusters normally don't come to the scene until sometime after an accident has taken place. In large measure, they begin their investigation based on the information they have received from their insured: YOU. Since you were there, you have the events fresh in your memory. Write them down immediately; your memory can play tricks on you later on. Why notify your lawyer in addition to the insurance company? Insurance companies are usually only obligated to defend you to the limits of your policy coverage. It is possible that a lawsuit against you will be for a higher sum of money than your policy covers. If this occurs, the insurance company will suggest that you have your own lawyer defend you in addition to the defense they provide. It is also possible for an insurance company to argue that the occurrence is outside the provisions of the policy. There, too, you will have to have your own lawyer represent you. The more a lawyer knows about a case and the earlier this information comes into his possession, the easier it is to plan a successful defense. In the case of an accident, you should not make statements to anyone without your lawyer's approval. A hasty statement of "I'm sorry, it was my fault" made at the time of an accident can be very costly in a subsequent lawsuit.

Allied to liability insurance is worker's compensation insurance. This type of insurance is designed to compensate a worker injured on the job. The definition of who is a "worker" and what constitutes "being on the job" is constantly changing as cases come before the courts. As with all other legal matters, don't assume you know about this type of coverage because it looks self-evident; consult a lawyer. Each state has requirements for which employers have to be covered by worker's compensation insurance, how much coverage is required, and so on. Your lawyer will be able to advise you of the requirements for your state. As with accidents covered by liability insurance, make careful notes of all occurrences for which you may be liable under worker's compensation insurance. While worker's compensation insurance is designed to prevent lawsuits between an employee and an employer for on-the-job injuries, it is possible, in certain instances, for an employer to be sued.

Put It in Writing

One way to help in maintaining good relations with your customers is to make sure that the *customer understands* what you are going to do and that *you understand* what the customer wants. Terms of delivery, payment, adjustments, and other details should all be spelled out in advance. The best way to do this is with a written contract, signed by both you and the customer with a copy given to the customer. There are many contract forms used by photographers. Let your lawyer look them over and then tailor one to your particular needs. However, don't rely on a preprinted contract or legal form to solve your problems. These stock forms may or may not have the legal language appropriate to your situation. Since each business is different, a legal form has to be modified to do what it is intended to do. Don't try to save money by using a legal form and by-passing the lawyer; you may have an expensive and time-consuming lesson in the interpretation of legal language if you do.

A contract need not be lengthy, but it must clearly specify the rights and obligations of both parties: you (the photographer) and your customer. Before your customer signs the contract, you should make sure that he or she understands what is being signed. A good contract can be made into a valuable sales tool by showing the customer the benefits that will accrue by coming to you for photographic work where everything is spelled out in advance, in writing.

No matter how well written your contract is, there will be times when something happens that leads to a dissatisfied customer. Regardless of your legal rights under the contract, make every attempt to satisfy the customer since it's good business practice to do so. Keep records (such as copies of letters and notes of telephone calls) of things done in an attempt to satisfy the customer. Should things progress to the point where your customer wants to sue you or vice versa, your written record of steps taken to resolve the matter amicably will be quite helpful to a lawyer in the conduct of a lawsuit. Remember that the contract is always subject to interpretation if there is a lawsuit. Both *your* prior practice in dealing with a similar problem as well as the general trade practice of photographers is usually important in interpreting contract terms.

Your relations with others in the conduct of your business, such as suppliers, your landlord, and repair people, are made easier if each side knows, in writing, what it is to do and what it is to receive. Usually, large businesses with whom you deal will have contracts prepared in advance by their legal departments for you to sign. It's a good idea to have your lawyer review such a contact *before* you sign it. The contract may be fair to both parties, or it may be weighted in favor of one side. If you learn that the contract is weighted against you, you may still want to sign it, but at least you will know what the possible consequences are. Remember that your signature on a contract means you have agreed to the terms and will be bound by them. A business person has a very hard time defending a lawsuit by saying he or she really didn't understand a document. While this is sometimes a valid defense in the case of a consumer contract, persons in business are presumed to have "business sense" and presumed to have inquired about the possible consequences *before* signing.

As was the case in your relations with your customers, keep records of telephone calls and letters which relate to a contractual relationship with a supplier or anyone else with whom you do business. These notes are very valuable to show what you have done in an attempt to rectify a situation in the event of a lawsuit.

Lawyer vs. Accountant

The chapter on accounting contained a discussion of the various taxes and the need for professional help when you prepare them or have dealings with the state or federal tax authorities. You will find that the division of knowledge between lawyers and accountants falls somewhere in the area of taxes. The accountant's specialty is numbers and the lawyer's is words. Don't rely on only an accountant or only a lawyer for advice; make use of the specialty of each. Let the accountant set up the numbers and let the lawyer advise you on the law. It may be that the lawyer you use is well versed in tax accounting and is well qualified to prepare tax returns. Unless you are positive that the work the lawyer or accountant is doing is within the scope of their individual experience, use each profession according to its specialty.

How do you know if a professional is experienced in an area? Ask questions. The professional who has the requisite experience will be able to answer your questions in a clear, logical manner. There is no subject too complicated to be explained to a client by either a lawyer or accountant in language the client can understand.

Photo Releases

Each of your customers usually orders work for a particular purpose: the bride wants pictures of her wedding; the executive may want a portrait for publicity purposes; the factory wants pictures of its products for advertising purposes, and so forth. Normally, the prints are delivered to the customer and the negatives are retained by the photographer; the photographer owns the rights to the pictures. However, this is not always the case. A written agreement between you and your customer may specify that the prints and negatives will be the property of the customer and that you, the photographer, or anyone else may use copies of the pictures only with the permission of the customer. That's why it is important to put the exact understanding between you and your customer in writing so that there is no misunderstanding at a later date. Later on in this book, you will see that the protection of the copyright law may be bargained away by a signed agreement.

Suppose you do a portrait job and the prints turn out so well that you want to use one of them for a sample. Can you do it? Yes, if your customer agrees. Of course, it's best to get this agreement in writing, signed by the customer. Such an agreement is very much like a model release, which is a contract between you and your subject by which the subject gives you permission to use the photograph in which the subject appears for specified uses. A typical model release would read something like this:

In consideration of the value received, I hereby grant to (photographer's name), his legal representatives and assigns, permission to copyright, sell, publish, and/or use photographic portraits or pictures of me or in which I am included, in whole or part, for advertising, trade, or any other lawful purpose whatsoever.

I hereby waive any right that I may have to inspect or approve the finished product or products or advertising or printed matter that may be used in connection with this picture or the use to which it may be applied.

I hereby release, discharge, and agree to save harmless (photographer's name) from any liability by virtue of any blurring, distortion, alteration, optical illusion, or use in composite form as well as any publication. I hereby warrant that I have every right to contract in my own name in the above regard.

DATE:

____
SUBJECT'S NAME

____
SUBJECT'S ADDRESS

____
WITNESS

If your subject is a minor, the release must be signed by a parent or guardian. If you are not sure of your model's age, insist on a birth certificate or similar proof of age. The model release, signed by a minor will *not* protect you, even if the model lied about age.

This sample release is as broad as possible to cover the uses for which the photograph may be used as well as what may be done with it technically. Remember, that as airtight as this release may seem, under certain conditions, it may have loopholes.

Usually, a model release will be required if you have a recognizable person in a photograph that is to be used for a commercial purpose. The definition of "commercial purpose" when used in this sense is quite broad, so if you have any doubts as to what you might want to do with the picture, get a model release. Much the same holds true with any picture you take in the course of your business that you may want to use for some purpose other than the one for which it was originally taken. Get written permission from the person or firm commissioning the picture to use it and make sure the written permission clearly indicates what it is going to be used for.

Property, as well as people, may need a release. If you intend to make commercial use of a photograph that pictures someone's personal or real property, e.g., a dog, machine, or house, get written permission of the owner to do so, spelling out what the picture will be used for. A trademarked item or a well-known setting (a famous hotel or restaurant, for example) may be considered property. You should get written permission before making commercial use of any photograph that contains a recognizable person or piece of property in it.

Privacy

The photographer who wanders around taking pictures is constantly involved with questions of invasion of privacy, although it may not appear that way. The nature of privacy is such that it is impossible to give precise answers to what is or what is not an invasion of it. A convenient rule of thumb is that a person in a public place or attending a public event can expect to be photographed as part of the general scene, but not singled out and featured without express permission. A public personage or an actual participant in a public event or some newsworthy incident affecting that person has only a limited right of privacy. Thus, persons who are either public figures or who are involved in newsworthy events are usually photographed without permission or model releases. However, definitions of public figures, public places, and newsworthy event are constantly subject to interpretation. There is at least one photographer who was sued by a public figure who got very tired of constantly being followed and photographed in public places. Remember that news is not a continuing thing; yesterday's news story is tomorrow's memory. A repeated use of a photograph after the time the incident has ceased to be news may be an invasion of privacy if the photographer has not gotten permission to use the picture. A commercial use, of course, always requires written permission.

Restaurants, stores, movie theaters, and the like are *not* public places in the sense that they are privately owned and operated. The owners and operators of these establishments "invite" the public to enter for specific purposes: eating, shopping, watching a movie, and so on. There is not an implied invitation to come on to the premises for the purpose of taking pictures. If you do come to the premises for the purpose of taking pictures, you may be considered a trespasser if you have not gotten permission to do so. Signs stating "keep out," "no trespassing," and "private property" are specific warnings to you not to enter for the purpose of taking pictures without permission. The safest rule to follow is to ask permission to enter onto private property to take pictures, get the written consent of those persons you are photographing (or whose property you are photographing), and clearly indicate to your subject and/or property owner what you are going to do with the photograph. If you can't get permission, don't use the picture.

Libel

Even if you have gotten permission and a model release, it is still possible to get into trouble. If the usage of your picture affects the reputation of your subject by holding the person up to ridicule, contempt, shame, disgrace, or scorn, or tends to induce an evil opinion of the subject in the mind of the general public or causes injury in a trade, profession, or occupation, you may be sued for libel. Remember our example of the model release; no matter how airtight it seems, if the usage is harmful enough, a suit for libel may be successful. You need not have had malicious intent (usually necessary for libel) to be successfully sued for libel. For example, suppose that your model was female, modeling a bathing suit in an advertisement for a sun-tan preparation. She signed the sample model release and thereby "waived any right to inspect or approve the finished product or products . . . or the use to which it may be applied." Suppose you were contacted by a magazine that needed a picture of a young woman in a bathing suit; since this particular picture seemed to fit the editor's requirements, you sent the picture and the model release. However, the editor wanted to use the picture as an attention getter for an article on prostitution.

There is no question that the magazine is a legitimate one and that the photograph is being used for a lawful purpose. However, your model's reputation may be badly damaged by having a picture of herself in conjunction with an article on prostitution, particularly if there is no explanatory text to indicate that she is a model, not a prostitute. Your intent wasn't harmful, but the net result to the model might be. Despite the release, if the model can show damage to her reputation or loss of earnings as a result, you may be the loser in a libel action.

Regardless of the wording of the release, common sense dictates that you ask about the use to which your pictures are going to be put and get it in writing. If you think that the use might cause trouble, even though you have a release, contact your lawyer. Naturally, if your model consented in writing to this use of her picture, there would be no problem.

Obscenity

No legal discussion on photography would be complete without a word about obscene pictures. "Dirty photographs" have probably been around for as long as there have been cameras to take them. Unfortunately, there is no one definition of what is or is not an obscene picture. Court decisions dealing with obscenity have been rather vague and usually relate back to notions of "community standards." This simply means what the average citizen in a given area would consider obscene. If this is not too helpful, one judge once gave this explanation of how he determined whether something was obscene: "I know it when I see it."

Under the First Amendment you have a right to express yourself. How far you can go before your right of expression turns obscene is a subject of continuing interpretation by the courts. If you contemplate doing work that could conceivably run afoul of the obscenity laws, probably the best way of keeping out of trouble is to consult your lawyer. You should be aware that most of the interpretations of obscenity laws that have liberalized what adults can see or read have come about because someone arrested for violation of obscenity laws fought and won. Even if you win in the end, being arrested for violation of obscenity laws probably won't be too good for your reputation if you're a small-town photographer. Tasteful nudity, of course, (your definition of "tasteful") will not present any problems with obscenity laws. Remember, however, to obtain a model release from every nude you photograph, even if you never intend to make use of the picture other than the one for which it was ordered.

Copyright

In January 1978 the copyright law was changed to provide added protection for copyright holders. This extensive law covers more than photographs. The Register of Copyrights (Library of Congress, Washington, D.C. 20559) has a pamphlet entitled "Highlights of the New Copyright Law." However, if you have a problem involving copyrights, or need specific information, it is best to consult a lawyer who specializes in copyright law.

In general, copyright protects your pictures, not the idea behind your pictures. If someone improves on your idea with their pictures, they have not infringed on your rights. You own your picture for your lifetime plus fifty years. If you are employed by someone to do "work for hire," your employer may have you sign an agreement stating that you temporarily relinquish your copyright to the photograph. A photograph that is specifically commissioned or ordered by a company is work for hire if you sign an agreement to that effect. Your rights on work-for-hire photographs revert back to you after 35 years. The same holds true if you give someone, in writing, exclusive rights to your photograph.

To obtain this protection, it is necessary that you register your picture with the Register of Copyrights. You may register either published or unpublished pictures. Write to the Register of Copyrights to obtain the necessary forms and registration materials. While the old law required you to send two copies of the entire publication in which your picture appeared, the new copyright law allows you to group register your pictures by supplying one tear sheet and one masthead for each photograph you've published in any twelve-month period after January 1, 1978. These pictures, under current copyright rulings, must have a bona fide copyright notice adjacent to your published picture to be group registered. Since this area of law is subject to change, make sure you have current information before you attempt to register anything.

Under the new copyright law, you may use the copyright symbol © without registering your photograph with the copyright office. However, your rights in the event of infringement are greatly reduced if the photograph is not registered. Until there are enough actual cases to establish a definite precedent, it is difficult to determine what remedies are available to the owners of unregistered photographs that are infringed upon. It is possible that a photograph's copyright could be invalidated if you were to publish your photograph without a copyright notice or with some error in the copyright notice (such as the misspelling of your name or an incorrect date of copyright) and you did not register a claim to correct the error with the Copyright Office within five years after the photograph was published without the copyright notice or with the wrong information. This would mean that the photograph would not be protected by the copyright law and would be in the public domain. A photograph in the public domain can be reproduced without payment to anyone.

In the event of infringement of a registered photograph, the owner of the copyright has the burden of discovering the infringement and bringing suit within the statutory period (three years). To be successful in an infringement suit (recovering a substantial sum from the infringer), the injured party must prove damages, specifically the profits received by the infringer and corresponding loss to the copyright owner from unauthorized use of the picture. It is possible to have "innocent infringement" with little or no award to the copyright holder. An innocent infringer is one who acts in reliance upon an authorized copy from which the copyright notice has been omitted. If you as the owner of a copyrighted photograph that is registered in accordance with the law discover that your copyright has been infringed upon, consult a lawyer who specializes in copyright law. It may be possible to work out a settlement with the infringer, or a lawsuit may be necessary.

Some Final Advice

The old adage about an ounce of prevention being worth a pound of cure applies to all your legal problems. Just as you would take your car, photographic equipment, or yourself for periodic checkups to prevent problems or discover them quickly, discuss potential legal questions with your lawyer before they become problems. You're in the photography business and should concentrate your time and talent on taking pictures, not dealing with legal troubles.

11 | Associations and Continuing Education

William J. Anton

Associations, including technical societies, can, if used properly, be one of the most important resources available to the professional photographer. The cost of participation in proportion to potential benefits makes membership one of the best expenditures a photographer can make.

The success of associations depends primarily upon the exercise of power from collective and cooperative action. This leverage is directed toward achieving goals and objectives that are focused on the problems and needs of the industry and of its members. There are many forces at work in business today that increase the importance and value of associations. These forces include consumerism, government regulation, intensified competition, technological change, and economic and social instability. In addition to these forces, there are unique characteristics of photographers that make membership in an association important.

The Professional Photographer

A better understanding of the personality and characteristics of a professional photographer is helpful in evaluating entry into photography as a business career. With this understanding, it will also be easier to accept the value of association programs and association membership.

Photographers are, as a general group, creative individuals seeking expression as artists. They are more introvertive than is generally imagined. In seeking material rewards for the practice of their skill at the request of clients and customers, the professional is faced with a number of conflicting choices. On the one hand he or she seeks rewards and recognition from peers and from the public. On the other hand, the professional has elected photography as a means of earning a livelihood. A photographer often fails to realize that his technique is less crucial to success in business than skill as a manager and salesperson.

All three of these desires can be satisfied through association participation, but the photographer all too often chooses an interest in developing his technique at the expense of the other requirements.

A true professional is equipped with basic talents and skills required to meet all obligations to a buyer. In order to do this, the professional has acquired an acceptable body of knowledge that can be brought to bear on the problems of various clients. The professional is reliable, demonstrating consistent, competent performance, and takes pride in the result of his or her work. Finally, the professional has a high level of integrity and helps to maintain professional standards and defend the profession against detractors.

To grow and demonstrate these qualities, the practicing professional needs assistance. A large measure of this assistance is available through membership in professional associations.

The Role of Associations

There is only one reason associations exist: to satisfy individual interests and common problems facing members of an industry or a profession. Why else would natural competitors join together, pool their resources and their efforts, and work toward important goals?

A point is reached when unsatisfied needs become overwhelming and competitive organizations form associations while individual specialists form professional societies. People have learned over the years that their individual interests can best be advanced by collective action. In some cases this is the only way in which worthy objectives can be achieved.

Two primary needs motivate individuals and organizations into forming associations. One need is generated by the forces of business competition and the instinct for survival. Competition from other photographers is often perceived as a major threat. A more sizable threat to a growing photographic industry and to an individual photographic studio is the consumer's pursuit of products and services outside of photography. The second need is for psychic reward—not only personal recognition, but a catalyst to release an artist's creative impulse. Associations have developed programs to satisfy this latter need very successfully. These two needs have created immense demands for various types of services and programs from associations and professional societies.

In addition to the direct benefits to an individual that are available through membership, associations contribute to the overall welfare of an industry. Competitive pressures generated by new technology, restrictive legislation, a bad public image or a lack of any image at all, and the pressures for new standards and protection resulting from consumerism create problems too large for any one individual, company, or studio to face. As a result, associations have devoted great efforts to improving standards, developing educational programs for its members, creating consumer and member awareness, enhancing the public image of the industry, and perfecting the skills of its individual members. They have also very successfully provided forums for the exchange of ideas.

Representing professional photographers in general, there is the Professional Photographers of America, Inc. This international organization is headquartered at 1090 Executive Way, Des Plaines, Illinois 60018. There are also 180 regional, state, and local affiliates of the PP of A throughout the U.S. and the rest of the world. A complete listing can be obtained by contacting this organization.

Many associations of other photographic specialists exist also. These include the American Association of School Photographers, Society of Cinema Photographers, Association of Architectural Photographers, Evidence Photographers International Council, and many others. A more complete listing, with the addresses where these organizations may be contacted, can be found in *Photography Market Place,* edited by Fred W. McDarrah and published by R.R. Bowker Company, 1180 Avenue of the Americas, New York, New York 10036. This guidebook also contains the names and addresses of allied associations in the photographic industry including associations that represent color labs, picture framers, studio suppliers, and photographic dealers.

Purpose of Professional Standards

The professional's success is dependent upon a satisfied clientele. In this age of consumerism, the public demands the best product at the best price. Buyers are no longer willing to accept work that is low in quality, not delivered on time, or overpriced. Government agencies and courts are taking every step to protect the rights of consumers. It is a matter of principle, therefore, that professional photographers' best interests will be served from careful attention to the welfare and interest of the buying public. The confidence of the buying public can be earned if the profession establishes standards of competence and presents a positive image to the general public.

The purpose of standards is, therefore, not only to satisfy the needs of clients, but to also protect them from shoddy photography and unethical business practices. This protection can be provided through the establishment of standards of performance, codes of conduct that insure good work and services, and industry peer-recognition programs.

Standards may be established by various controlling or influencing organizations. These may be organizations representing the public such as government agencies or by organizations representing the suppliers, such as industry associations.

From a business person's standpoint, self-regulation has many advantages over regulation by those outside the profession and unfamiliar with the profession's technology or interests. It provides customers with information about the competence of the seller without creating a barrier to entry.

Standards are no more than bench marks against which performance is measured and evaluated. Unfortunately, photography is an art form and as such can be described in qualitative terms according to general criteria, but cannot be evaluated in specific measurable terms. This is true for all art forms where the evaluation is much a matter of subjective opinion. This is not an insurmountable obstacle, but a different method of evaluating the quality of professional photography is necessary.

Although the typical customer may be unable to judge good technique, he and the targeted consumer will soon sense any perceptible differences among the work of competing photographers. On what basis other than the fact that the photography meets the needs of the client and is acceptable to his values should professional photography be evaluated?

It would be ineffective to depend upon the public to serve as judge for acceptable photography. This judgment certainly could not come before the fact and afterward it would be too late for corrective action. [There is a way in which subjective art can be evaluated, and we can draw on a source for opinion and judgment.]

Good evaluation of professional photography has to come from the people successful and experienced in producing photography for others (or those buying photography for the commercial use of others).

An elaborate scheme for judging professional photography through exhibitions and competitions has evolved within the profession. This scheme, along with the establishment of codes of ethics by associations of professional photographers, is the most appropriate vehicle for judging, maintaining, and upgrading the quality of work offered customers by photographers in business.

This method of evaluating professional photography and thereby setting standards for comparison, while imperfect, has been validated by wide application and acceptance.

Professional Photographers of America, Inc.

The Professional Photographers of America is an association of individual photographers numbering about 15,000. These members are mostly in the United States, but there is a sizable representation in Canada, Japan, Mexico, and other countries around the world. The traditional mission of the PP of A since its founding in 1880 has been to advance photography as a profession, exchange information, provide training and education, protect photographers' rights, and cooperate with and inform other interested groups.

These are broad objectives pursued vigorously and well by the PP of A and its more than 180 local, state, regional, national, and international affiliated organizations.

In the beginning, the thrust of the association's program was directed toward technological development and the enhancement of photography as a craft. Little effort was spent on reaching the general public. The initiative, resources, and competition of equipment suppliers has long since negated the necessity for the association's effort in technological development. Occasionally, however, photographers provide useful feedback for changing equipment specifications and application needs to the manufacturers for the industry's benefit.

Photographers are by nature equipment-oriented and generally have kept pace with technological advancement. New technology in the last few years, however, may make additional training necessary for photographers, particularly in the film processing side of the business, and association programs may be developed to cover this need. A more important influence on the association's programs, however, has been the effect of consumerism and the need for photographers to upgrade their image through the development of standards of performance and attitudes of professionalism and to project that image to the public. The programs of the Professional Photographers of America have focused on these goals. During the past 50 years heavy emphasis has been placed on these areas: exhibitions and the development of a merit and degree program; education and continuing development of the practicing professional; marketing, including such specialized programs as a qualification program and a certification program; a high-quality magazine and a convention and trade show for the sharing of new ideas, techniques, and application information, as well as exposure to new equipment and supplies.

Photographic Exhibitions

Although exhibitions of photography go back to the origins of the craft, a giant step forward was taken in 1937 when the Professional Photographers of America tied demonstration of skill to a degree program honoring individual competence and technique. With this development, the recognition motive has been utilized to upgrade skill and improve standards of work. Consistency of performance is another underlying principle of the Merit and Degree Program. The Master of Photography (M. Photog.) is awarded to those photographers whose superior competence and technique have been repeatedly recognized in exhibition competition. To gain the degree, photographers must earn 13 exhibition merits and 12 more exhibition or achievement merits. Exhibition merits are earned when a photograph receives a score of 80 or better in the General Exhibit at the Exposition of Professional Photography held at the association's annual convention.

Categories included in the PP of A's annual photographic work competition are: general works (photographs and transparencies); works by masters (for persons already holding the degree of Master of Photography); displays by photographic specialists (for retouchers and color artists); and industrial and technical photography. The best of the general exhibit is selected for a traveling loan collection that can be reserved for display in photo and slide form by members and affiliates.

Each year the association develops a new list of approved judges. Inclusion is based upon experience as a photographer and as a judge at affiliated competitions. Reference testifying to the photographer's ability, integrity, and skill as a judge are required to be included on the PP of A's Affiliated Jurors List. A seminar for judges is conducted by the association each year and judges on the list must attend once every three years in order to maintain their status.

In the evaluation of photographs in the annual PP of A works competition, all photography is judged under controlled lighting conditions by panels of five jurors. A provision is also made for other opinions if there is a question about the panel's evaluation. The execution of each photograph must, in the judges' opinion, meet professional levels of technique including the use of lighting, proper exposure, print quality, the handling of subject matter, the selection of background and setting, the application of color harmony, and composition. In addition, heavy weight is given to the entry's ability to make a visual statement and its impact upon the viewer. The judges also give consideration to the creativity and imagination shown and whether or not the photograph is interesting and has a compelling portrayal of concept in finished form.

Detailed rules have been prepared for the PP of A's annual works competition. Any photographer can enter by completing the application, paying the fee, and following the rules. Figure 1 is a reprint of the rules for the national competition.

Photographers may also enter exhibition competitions held in connection with annual meetings of affiliated associations and groups of associations. These exhibitions are authorized by the PP of A and have special rules similar to the PP of A rules. Information on participation in these exhibitions may be obtained from the Chairman of the Jury of the PP of A Affiliates. In entering print competitions, it is vital that the photographer read carefully all the instructions concerning the exhibition and follow them to the letter.

Continuing Development of the Practicing Professional

One of the major activities of the Professional Photographers of America is the Winona School of Professional Photography. This nonprofit educational institution is designed to meet the educational needs of the working professional photographer. It is also open to individuals serious in photography or who are contemplating entering the profession. The school offers a series of week-long courses covering a wide spectrum of specific fields in photography.

The faculty is selected from the finest and most experienced working professionals, each teaching the subject he or she deals with daily. Students learn through lectures, demonstrations, informal discussions, and hands-on sessions where students carry out assignments under the direct supervision of the instructors.

Small classes and an informal approach mean individual instruction is available for each student.

The school's four-building complex is located 45 miles west of Fort Wayne, Indiana. Class size is limited and registration is on a first come, first served basis. The courses occur primarily during the summer months and include students from all states, most Canadian provinces, and several overseas locations. Twenty percent of the more than 1,200 students entering each year are women.

Membership in the PP of A is not a requirement for acceptance. A few scholarships are available from the school and from affiliated organizations of the PP of A. A free catalog describing the program is available on request by writing to the Winona School of Professional Photography, 1201 College Avenue, Winona Lake, Indiana 46590.

The association also sells inexpensive slide cassette programs of various topics of interest to the professional. This series of "Learn from the Professionals" tapes is presented by outstanding practicing photographers. The following is a typical list of available programs:

Architectural Approach to Commercial Photography

Public Relations Photography

Small Product Photography

Basic Commercial Photography

Basic Portrait Lighting

Laboratory Special Effects

A Photography Bag of Tricks

Commercial Lighting on Location

Information on the cassette tapes may be obtained by writing to the Professional Photographers of America, Inc.

The PP of A also conducts a cosponsored seminar program with its affiliated organizations. The purpose of the program is to bring instructors of nationally recognized caliber to the many members who cannot attend the association's convention. This makes it possible for photographers to attend sessions at a time that does not interfere with their working hours and at a cost well within their reach. The program is also designed to acquaint nonmembers with the benefits of belonging to the PP of A.

The programs are developed and administered by affiliated organizations with promotional assistance from the national organization.

Instructors participating in the approved cosponsored seminars earn achievement merits toward the association's photography degrees.

The Professional Photographer's Image

During recent times, the association has attempted to develop programs to upgrade the image and promote the services of professional photography. The division representing commercial photographers in the PP of A was the first to develop a program of this type called the Qualification Program. This highly successful program maintains high standards of commercial photography to assure clients' satisfaction. Since 1957, the Commercial Division has maintained rigid control of member studios' procedures. Since that time about 500 studios have met the rigid standards of photographic proficiency. To earn and maintain the Qualified Studio status, a studio must continually demonstrate its ability to produce top quality photography by regularly submitting samples to selected bodies of review. A responsible individual of that studio must certify that he or she operates an established place of business equipped to perform assignments in its photographic specialties. The person must also provide references from clients. A studio may apply for Qualified Studio status in only two portrait categories: business portraits and executive portraiture. Most of the "Qualified Studio" listings are for studios in the commercial field, many of whom represent business and industrial clients. Qualified Studios are listed in a special directory that is distributed to almost 100,000 advertising agencies and commercial, business, and industrial organizations. A modest advertising program is also maintained with ads appearing in a number of important business publications.

In the last five years, the thrust of PP of A's programs have evolved more and more toward enhancing the professional image of the photographer and informing the buying public. In 1978 the Professional Photographers of America launched a program to certify individual professional photographers. The program evaluates participants on the basis of business success and ethics as well as technical skill and competence. The essence of the concept of the Certification Program is that the confidence of the buying public can better be earned if the profession establishes standards of competence and requires photographers to demonstrate abilities to meet these standards.

The Certified Professional Photographer Program was developed jointly by the Professional Photographers of America and its state affiliated associations. It is designed for administration by the state associations. The basic steps of certification are: 1) application to the state organization, 2) written examination, 3) evaluation of photographic submissions, and 4) renewal of certification between the third and fourth year. To apply, a photographer must belong to the national or state organization for at least two consecutive years immediately preceeding application. The applicant must have been employed in photography full-time a minimum of 35 hours a week for three consecutive years immediately preceeding application. The three-year requirement can be lessened by applying formal education credit, but a minimum of two full years' employment is required. The application form requires the applicant to indicate the percentage of his work by photographic specialty, employment history for the preceeding three years, and to provide four personal references and three trade references. Each applicant must also agree to abide by and sign the Certified Professional Photographers Standards of Professional and Personal Conduct.

After the application is approved, the applicant will be eligible for the written examination and to submit samples of his work for review by the

Certification Review Panel. The confidentiality of the applicant's identity is maintained throughout the examination and review process.

The purpose of the exam is to test the applicant's knowledge of the techniques of photography and his understanding of professional ethics.

After passing the exam, the applicant is asked to submit 15 samples of actual job assignments completed within the last 24 months. Photographic submissions must be accompanied by the client's specifications and the purpose of the photography along with a description of how the photo was handled. This evaluation of actual work is the key feature of the certification program.

If the submissions are accepted, the designation of Certified Professional Photographer will be earned and the photographer can make appropriate use of the logo and other materials available for advancing his professional career and practice.

Periodic renewal of certification is an important part of the program. Recertification between the third and fourth year requires proof of continuing education and five submissions of current work.

Additional details on the Certification Program may be obtained from the Professional Photographers of America, Inc.

In those rare situations where direct satisfaction with the photographer has not been obtained, a consumer redress program is available. This program was instituted by the PP of A in mid 1976. In the program the association acts as a catalyst and mediator obtaining all facts and fosters communication between individuals in an attempt to obtain a mutually agreeable solution. This program has been an aggressive, positive one directed toward increasing the credibility of the professional photographer and helping to make him aware and more responsive to consumer attitudes, thus enhancing his professional image.

Keeping Abreast of Current Developments

The association's annual convention and exposition is a major educational service for photographers. The convention provides a platform for exchanging work information, new ideas, and the latest techniques among photography practitioners.

A major trade show of the latest in photographic equipment, services, and supplies is held in conjunction with the convention. An exhibit of the best in professional photography also accompanies the convention.

Normally, five to six thousand photographers, photo suppliers, and business people attend the five-day convention, usually held during the summer in locations around the country. Most of the affiliated organizations also conduct annual conventions and trade shows at various times of the year in their locales.

Every member of the association receives a copy of *The Professional Photographer.* This monthly photographic magazine is the official journal of the association. The magazine offers technical and business features, industry news, advertising and promotion ideas, general interest features, and articles written by leading photographers in the United States and abroad. Special sections are included for new products, technical questions, legal affairs, and educational news.

A nonmember edition of the magazine is available to subscribers, but emphasizes educational development rather than business acumen.

There are many ingredients for success in business. In photography these include technique, marketing, and financial management skills as well as adequate resources. Over the long term, perhaps the most essential factor is the attitude the photographer brings to bear on his business objective. For the professional this includes not only a positive approach to life's challenges, but an awareness that he is serving a client and therefore the needs of the client must be paramount. Active association membership and participation can be of great assistance in helping the photograher achieve the essential degree of professionalism and success in his business. Photography today is one of the greatest communications media. It needs people whose skills and intellect are well developed and whose understanding of life is broad, varied, and in perspective.

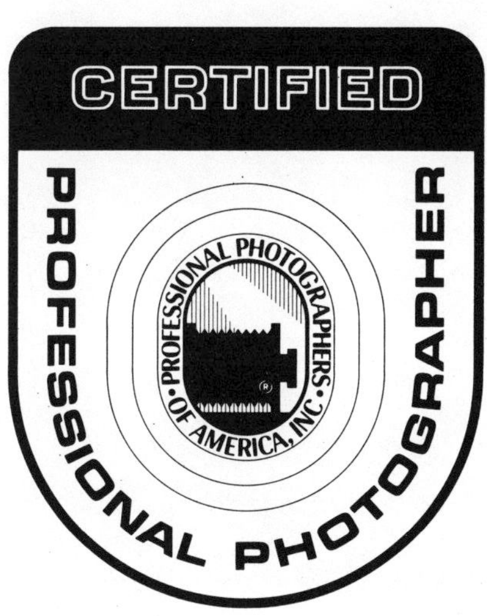

12 | Freelance Photography

Art Shay

I am a freelance photographer. I've been one since 1951 when I left *Life* as a reporter to explore the possibilities of spending my life behind the camera. Adding up the years, I've been at it for over 25 years, and at this precise moment I am absolutely thrilled to be driving to Elkhart, Indiana, to take pictures of some female weight lifters for a magazine.

I am especially delighted because my career as a freelance photographer began on a day in 1951 with precisely this kind of assignment. I had done perhaps 140 stories for *Life* in three years as a reporter. In those days, a reporter was merely an assistant—somebody who got an idea for a story, helped make the phone calls, took care of the film, wrote the captions, and in many cases had to pamper such great *Life* photographers as Francis Miller, W. Eugene Smith, Alfred Eisenstadt, Leonard McCombe, and many others.

I learned my trade from these *Life* photographers, these people with extraordinary ability of capturing whatever was happening in the world and putting it on film. Of course, these people got a kind of fame and status that only now is beginning to re-emerge for the photographer. I envied them and I knew that I wanted to be like them.

I felt that the camera was a sacred instrument. My introduction to photography had come with my father's old Kodak when I was 14 or 15. I had taken it on Boy Scout trips and learned in a converted coal bin in the basement of my Bronx apartment building how to develop and make contact prints. It was at that time that I first began to see the possibilities of photography as a way of making a living. Later, I became a flyer in the war and something of a writer, and traveled across the world taking snapshots. I differentiate between snapshots and pictures. A snapshot is a mere record, something that passes before you as a photographer and that you've managed to put on film. A picture is a statement and contains a point of view.

How did I get to Elkhart, to do a female weight lifting story? To test a new lens I did what photographers often do: shoot a picture of some newspaper to see how sharp the lens is from corner to corner. I looked at the negative under a magnifying glass and saw a clipping that said, "Weight Lifting—2 p.m. Sunday," that very day just a few miles away. One line that followed interested me: an "Event for the Ladies." It was then about an hour before the event.

I had shot pictures of female weight lifters before, but there was always something missing, something I had come to understand from *Life* that was essential to a story: the opening picture. That one big picture tells the story.

In this assignment, I had a 110-pound woman weight lifter appear to be picking up a 230-pound male weight lifter. The way I arrange this was to have her stand behind him, hold on to his elbows, and have him jump. At the highest point in his jump, I clicked my shutter, and had a picture with an *idea*.

Freelance Photography as a Career

Each week I get several calls from people who have seen my by-line and they usually ask me to take on a son or daughter as an assistant. Not long ago a banker for whom I had done several annual reports asked me this question: "Would you let my daughter work free for you for a while?"

I said I would under one circumstance: "My 21-year-old son wants to be a banker. Could he stay in your office every day and work free with you and learn banking?" To this day he thinks I was kidding because it is not possible to learn banking just by hanging around a bank. Photography as a career is a serious undertaking and a highly competitive one, much more so now than it was when I was starting out.

The best training a potential photojournalist could have would be to work as a reporter on a small-town newspaper, or if possible, a large newspaper. You should learn all the "W's"; the Who, What, When, Where, and, of course, the "Why?" and "How?". Most journalistic events that become picture stories, or partly picture stories, can be broken down into one of those categories: a Who, a What, a When, a Where, a Why, and a How. Your captions should contain all of this information. At some point the working newspaper photographer must understand that it's a relatively low-paying profession. I don't know anybody on a small-town newspaper who is earning as much as $15,000 a year. However, I do know six freelancers who do annual reports at $750 a day and up, and who are earning more than $60,000 a year.

The photojournalist who starts out to be a pure freelance photographer very soon ends up taking commercial pictures. For five or six years after I became a freelance, I was thrilled to get all these by-lines: *Life, Saturday Evening Post, Fortune, Time, Sports Illustrated, Forbes,* and *Business Week.* I was turning down such commercial accounts as Standard Oil of Indiana, drug companies in Chicago, and food processing companies. After five or six years I began looking at my bills and my income. I had gotten my income up to some $30,000 a year, working at $100 and less a day for magazine rates. Looking at the calendar and looking at my income tax statements, I realized that it wasn't possible, even with space rates getting better and better, ever to earn more than $40 to $45,000 a year as a "pure" magazine photographer, or a photojournalist. I suddenly made myself available to such companies as the ones I had photographed for *Fortune* magazine, and within two years I had just about doubled my income.

How to Start

Photography is a business. If you have a job as a photographer, your assignments are given to you. However, if you are planning to become a freelancer you must start building up contacts with the people who buy pictures: public relations people, secretaries, assistants, or presidents of various organizations. It is a good idea for freelancers to be on good terms with the local newspaper columnists. They run into good stories and you, as a photographer, will often run into items that columnists will be glad to have.

If you are serious about photojournalism, cultivate civic officials and your local police and fire department. Police and fire departments are most receptive to photographers who follow through and send in prints of pictures they may have taken of policemen and firemen on duty. Two or three prints like this will go a long way toward having somebody call you in the middle of the night with a news tip.

The serious freelance photographer should not leave his place of business for less than $200 a day. Magazines such as *Time, Life, Fortune, Sports Illustrated, Forbes, Us,* and *People,* now pay $250 a day plus expenses. Space rates are also paid; that is, approximately $500 a page against space rates. If you shoot for one day and come up with two pages, you've earned $1,000. If the magazine doesn't use any pictures, you will get $250 plus your expenses.

Commercial rates are generally much higher. A major company expects to pay between $400 and $1,200 a day for the services of a top ranked photographer. When starting out you might have to charge $250 or even $150 a day to get your foot in various doors. To generate business it might even be wise to build up your portfolio by asking your local industrial plant if you might come in and do a few pictures without charge. As a beginner, you shouldn't let your prints go for less than $35 a shot. If you don't respect your own value, your potential clients won't either.

Your Portfolio and Your Ideas

A portfolio shouldn't contain more than thirty pictures. The prime fault made by many young people is that they cannot decide between picture A or picture B of the same subject, and so put them both in. Force yourself to choose. Show your ability to handle diversity. A woman I know asked me to look at her son's portfolio. I looked at the portfolio and told him the truth. He had perhaps three or four situations covered in forty pictures. The rest were repetitious; the pictures were what I call "thereness" pictures. The idea was absent.

For more than 25 years as a freelancer, I have always felt that the idea is central to an effective picture. Magazines need ideas, publishers need ideas, advertising agencies need ideas, and Sunday Supplements need ideas. I persist in telling younger photographers to get ideas, write them down, and take them to editors. When I started I shot many stories on speculation. You have to know *what makes news.* When you make a suggestion, the average editor will say, "So what." If you can answer that "so what," then you have the germ of a story going. I could name a dozen stories that resulted from column items, clippings, and from preposterous overheard conversations.

I once did a picture for a story that I had suggested on an animal trainer whose specialty was dogs. I shot pictures of his well-trained dogs diving through the air, landing in the water, and retrieving a tame, but very cocky wild duck that was wearing a khaki protective sweater. Afterwards, driving through traffic, it occurred to me that I had done the wrong story. I turned around and reshot the story from the point of view of the duck. The duck's name was Melvin and the story turned out to be the story of Melvin, the Dog-Training Duck.

I was so taken with the way the duck quacked at these dogs and brought them around when he wasn't being retrieved that I later visited the trainer at his quarters, taking the sleeve of a red sweater long discarded by one of my daughters to replace the dull khaki sleeve Melvin wore. I showed Melvin sitting on the back of a station wagon quacking orders at dogs. I showed him in the water; I showed dogs shying away from Melvin; and I showed Melvin sitting on his trainer's head quacking away at the blue Wisconsin sky. The picture ran as a cover on a Sunday supplement and also ran as an inside spread. I wrote the story for it and earned approximately $2,000 for two or three days work. Ultimately, the story ended up in fifty newspapers and magazines around the world and made something like $15,000. This is the power of *The Idea*.

How to Avoid Clichés

The best way to avoid clichés is to always try and see the familiar from an unusual angle. Some time ago I was in my dentist's chair looking at a set of large training teeth. It occurred to me that I might use them for a funny picture in a children's book on dentistry I was doing. I wanted a picture of the dentist working on teeth as seen from inside the throat, looking out over the tongue. I made a tongue out of Spam, covered the upper and lower plate with black cloth and got the dentist to drill one of the front teeth. Using a wide angle lens just behind the piece of fake tongue, I was able to photograph the dentist through the teeth. To my pleasant surprise, I got many letters from readers who had seen the picture in their books and wondered how I had done it. When the gas shortage hit, I did the same picture from inside, presumably, of a gas tank looking up the gas nozzle, past the rushing stream of gas.

The Equipment You Need

A freelancer can start a photo business with one 35mm camera and a 35mm medium wide-angle lens. Later, a normal 50mm lens might be added. Then add a 24mm lens, another camera body, a small electronic flash, a light tripod, and two reflectors able to take number two photofloods. That's really all the basic equipment a photographer needs, whether he or she is starting to take pictures of babies or of factories. For color you should have a CC 30 Magenta filter for most fluorescent light situations.

For black and white assignments, which are 80 percent of my assignments, a 35mm camera is just fine, and half your picture could be done with the 35mm or 28mm lens. The addition of a 2¼-inch square format camera is useful because some clients want larger color images from which to reproduce. Contact prints made in this size are easier to look at than 35mm.

You should retain a contact sheet of every roll of black and white you shoot. If you are naturally neat and orderly, your equipment will be spotless and you will be able to retrieve pictures taken years ago as easily as you'd locate pictures taken last week. Look at them and keep trying to improve, trying to change for the better, and above all, try not to keep your talents a secret. I will repeat: *The idea* is basic to your success as a freelancer.

13 | General Commercial Photography

Ted Schwarz

The typical commercial studio is likely to handle the widest variety of photography imaginable. The day might start with the photography of a new line of fashions to be featured in a department store advertising brochure. Then one or more members of the staff will photograph a steel mill for an annual report. A new office building is next, the photographs being taken for the architect who designed the structure. Then there is a series of portrait photos for an insurance company honoring its million-dollar salespeople. Finally, a kitchen area of the studio is utilized to whip up a soufflé as part of a publicity photograph to be taken to promote a new cookbook.

The commercial studio is obviously a "jack-of-all-trades." Depending upon the size and location of the community in which it exists, the studio may handle a broad variety of subjects or limit itself to one or two specialties. In the Detroit-Cleveland-Pittsburgh megalopolis, a studio can specialize in industrial advertising and public relations photography. Such a studio will be involved with steel mills and major manufacturers of cars, earth-moving equipment, and numerous other products. In a more rural location, the commercial studio must seek all types of business, from pictures of a slaughter house to photographs of the high school prom queen.

In general, commercial work falls into a number of specific headings. Portraits and weddings are the mainstays of numerous commercial studios and are covered in depth in other chapters. Such jobs are available anywhere you might live and are the easiest types of work to obtain. Depending upon your location, you might even get walk-in clients for such work.

Advertising, Public Relations, and Illustration Photography

Advertising photography is another area of commercial photography. The idea behind advertising is to sell. It may be a specific product, such as a line of clothing. It may be a business such as a new restaurant. It may even be a less tangible concept such as a new rate schedule for an airline company.

Public relations photography is somewhat akin to advertising but is usually done on location. Instead of the hard sell that is found with advertising, public relations photographs often tell a story.

To better understand the difference between advertising and public relations, suppose a department store wants to put money into an intense promotion designed to improve its image and sell its products. The advertising manager will call a commercial studio and arrange for the photography of products from one or more departments. These photos will be placed in a mailer that will be sent to credit card holders. The mailer will offer special buys in the various department lines and each picture must sell the item involved.

The public relations department of that same department store may contact the same commercial photographer, but this time the request will be different. The photographer will be requested to photograph a "day in the life of a great department store" or something similar. The photographer will record people shopping, sales clerks waiting on customers, home sewers in the sewing class sponsored by the store, children watching a puppet show, civic leaders meeting for lunch in the store's coffee shop, and maybe kindly old Mr. Peabody, buyer for the shoe department, who volunteers his free time helping at a home for the handicapped. The pictures are assembled into a booklet that will go to schools, the news media, and others. The pictures are meant to tell a story that, indirectly, will bring new business. There is no hard sell and the store's products are shown incidentally, if at all.

Annual reports frequently fall into the public relations category. So do pictures taken to illustrate magazine articles the client is having placed in various publications. Another area, debatable as to whether it is public relations or advertising, would be photographs of a work in progress, such as a construction project. Thus a public relations photographer might take a daily record of a new hotel under construction and an advertising specialist will be called in to record the finished hotel in a way that will insure that people will want to stay there.

The similarity of advertising and public relations work results in most commercial photography studios handling both fields, at least to some degree. Advertising pictures can require extensive studio floor space and elaborate set-ups beyond the capacity of many photographers who prefer to shoot as much as possible on location. Such photographers are going to take all the public relations work they can get but will limit the types of advertising projects they agree to photograph.

Illustration work is a third major area of commercial photography, but one that is usually limited to cities with a heavy concentration of magazine and book publishers. The commercial studio is asked to take a story, book, or even a concept and create a photograph that captures its essence in a single visual image. This could range from a damsel-in-distress photograph for the cover of a crime magazine to something more abstract, like illustrative photographer Robin Perry's much reproduced photograph for an article on a terrorist who was killed while in her early twenties. He superimposed her image on a cracked eggshell in a manner that is eye catching, dramatic, and vividly speaks of a shattered life. Sometimes the illustrative photographer will have to develop the entire picture concept based on the material provided. Other times the photograph must duplicate the concept an artist has developed. It is probably the most creatively demanding type of work you can handle and thus one of the most rewarding for those who can equal its demands.

Legal and Insurance Photography

In many communities the commercial studio is asked to handle legal and insurance photography. This is done in a variety of ways. For example, suppose there is an automobile accident at an intersection. One driver claims that improperly placed signs and dense foliage blocked the view and caused the accident. With this type of case, a photographer may be called in to help settle the case.

The photographer will be asked to photograph one or more aspects of the accident. Sometimes photographs will be taken of the damage to the cars. There may even be a request to photograph the tire skid marks, if any, though this may also have been done by the police. Then there will be photographs taken of the scene of the accident. Pictures of the intersection will be needed, as well as of the offending sign and shrubbery. The photographer may even be asked to take pictures of the intersection from the viewpoints of each of the drivers just before the crash. This may be done from another car or on foot.

The photographs will be used during negotiations and trials to help determine who will be paying for damages resulting from the accident. The judgment may be made against the offending driver or perhaps the owner of the land where the shrubbery was allowed to become a traffic hazard. The pictures will make the situation clearer for the judge, jury, and opposing attorneys.

Insurance and legal photographs require great accuracy and detail. They comand high fees when done well because they can win large sums of money or prevent a company from having to pay huge settlements.

The first step toward entering this field is to contact area lawyers and insurance companies to see what interest they may have. Sometimes police and newspaper photographs are relied upon. Other times the agents are equipped with either Polaroid or 35mm cameras and take their own pictures, crude as this approach is likely to be. Still other firms will be interested in you and will discuss their needs in depth.

Generally it is hard to put together a portfolio of related prints since this specialty is so far afield from normal commercial accounts. Detailed product photographs probably come the closest, but even these do not relate all that much. Fortunately, the potential clients recognize this and are more willing to give you a trial than clients for advertising and other fields of commercial photography. Once you have worked on one or two cases, you will be accepted regularly.

Theater Photography

Depending upon your location, theater photography can be another specialty. In communities with extensive professional theater, such as New York, Cleveland, Chicago, San Francisco, and similar areas, theater photography can be a part-time studio specialty. This is handled either by recording a dress rehearsal or by carefully creating a scene on stage to represent the meaning of the play. This created scene may be quite different from the blocking of the director and the image may not relate to anything the audience will see. Instead it is an illustration meant to capture the essence of the story rather than an image taken during the performance. At times such illustrations may be handled in the studio where there is more lighting and background control.

To obtain theater photography assignments you will need to talk with the theater manager, director, and theatrical booking agents. All of these are likely to hire your services and each will want a slightly different type of photograph. The director is concerned with the play, for example, while the booking agent may be concerned only with a performer.

Theater photography has several different branches as well. Your studio can handle night club photography of singers, musicians, and comedians. These prints will serve as club publicity, personal publicity for the entertainers, and may even have subsidiary sales potential to various magazines connected with the performing arts.

Many contacts can be made through the various unions related to the field. You should see if there are area branches of the Musicians' Union, the Screen Actors' Guild, and the American Federation of Television and Radio Artists, among others. If there are, the officers will be good sources of information concerning the photographic needs of the members and how to contact them.

Your studio should try for a long-term arrangement with each club, theater, or other entertainment center. Try to line up the job of photographing each new performer, show, and group of musicians. Some of the coverage will be for displays and posters. Other prints will be used for newspaper and magazine promotion. Still others may be purchased by the entertainers. The more effort you put toward selling your work for every possible use you can imagine, the greater your gross profit from a minimum amount of effort.

Analyzing Your Market

The first step toward establishing a commercial studio is to analyze your potential market. Are you an urban or rural dweller? Are you in an area with heavy manufacturing and/or several corporate headquarters? Are you in a publishing center? What types of businesses are the major employers? Do area businesses spend money on advertising or just hope they get by on word of mouth? Do department stores and specialty shops use photographs in their advertisements or just line drawings? Are area businesses likely to be repeat customers or are they the type that will hire you to photograph the exterior and interior, then display those same prints for the next ten years?

If you don't know where else to start, go to the yellow pages. Look at page after page and think about the businesses that can genuinely use a photography studio's services. Analyze what types of photographs they might need and whether or not their requirements can be met in a small studio, on location, or in a large, controlled studio that might need several thousand square feet of space.

Once you determine the potential work, think about what you can realistically handle. For example, department stores in some larger cities regularly use color advertising supplements in the daily newspapers. These supplements appear once a week and the time between when the pictures must be taken and the transparencies delivered to the art director handling the advertising can be as short as 24 hours. If you go after this work, you must either have a color darkroom where you can process your film or access to a custom lab that can give you immediate service. If you have neither, you cannot handle this type of work.

The Pros and Cons of Having a Darkroom

At this point in the discussion of the commercial studio it is important to digress for a moment and mention the darkroom. The importance of a darkroom to a commercial photographer is an often debated topic among professionals. Although the "right" answer is totally an individual matter, a few observations may help you decide what is best for you.

A darkroom is a major financial undertaking for a commercial studio. Even the smallest darkroom takes up space that could otherwise be used for photography or office work. This means a greater square footage and higher rent.

Next is the matter of equipment. If you already own a certain amount of quality darkroom equipment, you can probably get away with spending around $1,000. If you own nothing, your bill can rise dramatically.

Finally there is the matter of who will run the darkroom. A skilled technician is expensive. His or her salary might be greater than your own income the first year or two of operation. An unskilled technician is even more expensive because the saving in salary is offset by waste and redoing poor quality work. If you handle the work yourself, you cannot charge what you would earn behind the camera and you are also losing time that could better be used soliciting new business.

The end result is that a darkroom should not be an automatic aspect of your studio. If you have the volume of work to justify such an expense, then by all means have one. You might also want to have some basic equipment you can call upon in a rush when even a custom lab cannot give you the speedy service you need. But so long as you have access to a custom lab, the darkroom can be a serious drain on your profits when you are first starting out in business.

The rural photographer may not live in or near a community where there is a custom lab available. This means working through the mail, a minor problem except for time. However, this does not mean that a rural studio should have a darkroom. Analyze your assignments and, if time is not a critical factor, you will probably find that working through the mail presents no difficulties whatever. Just be certain you understand the *maximum* in-lab times for the type of work you regularly order and advise customers accordingly. Also, be certain you increase your charge to cover mailing and packaging costs.

Assembling Your Portfolios

Returning to types of assignments, once you know the kind of market your studio will be handling, the next step is to obtain the jobs. To do this you are going to have to become a salesperson, no matter how hard such a role may be for you. Many photographers are rather introverted, as the nature of the profession allows a person to stand back from an event and simply act as recording observer. However, you will have to be aggressive, if only by adopting such an attitude as a "front," in order to compete.

The first step is to put together one or more portfolios of your work as it relates to the jobs you will be seeking. This can be a tremendous problem, especially if you have nothing in your files. For example, suppose you want to go after industrial photography accounts, a subject with which you are familiar because, before going on your own, you worked in the photography department of a manufacturing plant. You are experienced and know how to handle a camera for this specialty but all your previous work belongs to your former employer. You were not permitted to make extra prints at your own expense to use as a personal portfolio. Thus you are highly skilled yet have no way to prove it.

What is the answer? You have got to arrange to photograph a business or industry of the type you want to handle as a studio specialty.

Contact the office of the director of one of the industrial plants in your area. Explain that you are a photographer with extensive experience in industrial work, but as an employee, not as an independent studio owner. Say that you are going into business for yourself and need examples of your work in order to obtain assignments. Then relate the fact that, due to the nature of your previous employment, you have no samples.

Once the director, or the person to whom you've been referred, understands the nature of your plight, ask permission to photograph the plant at your own expense, specifically to prepare a portfolio. If the business wants prints, you will provide them at your normal rates. The only break you will give the company is to not charge for your time since they are doing you a favor in helping you get samples.

The same situation is true for any other type of photography for which you lack samples. You will find that in the vast majority of cases you will receive cooperation. If one turns you down, an unlikely event, the next place you call will undoubtedly agree.

The reason for charging full price for any prints purchased is to be fair to competing professionals. You cannot really charge a day rate "after the fact," especially since you initiated the request to photograph, but you can earn the full measure of your worth for any prints you sell.

Once you have your pictures, you should make as many different protfolios as possible with 15 to 20 prints each. The reason for this is that each time you return to the same potential client to discuss your work, it looks impressive if you can show the person a new set of quality photographs. It is also a good idea to separate black and white from color work as the color often is so dramatic that it detracts from the black and white.

Each portfolio should relate to the work you are trying to sell. An advertising portfolio might contain product work, fashion modeling, some architecture, and similar pictures. A general commercial portfolio designed to get many types of jobs might contain advertising pictures as well as food, illustrative, and industrial photographs, and/or anything else that might apply to your community. Naturally, wedding photography samples, if handled by your studio, will be limited to specialized albums for brides. It will not be a part of a portfolio shown to business people, though one or two executive portraits will help.

Selling Yourself

The first step toward getting assignments is to make the rounds of potential clients. This means having a portfolio, business cards, and letterhead paper for writing follow-up letters. The latter must be typed and, if this is not one of your skills, it will pay you to hire a part-time typist.

Contact potential photography buyers by telephone and arrange for an appointment to show your work. With advertising agencies, this will mean account executives and, occasionally, the art director as well. Siince each account executive usually operates independently of the others, you should obtain appointments with everyone within an agency. You may find that while one person rejects your work, someone else thinks you are a genius.

If you are uncertain whom to contact, go to the head of the organization. Sometimes that is the right person. If it isn't, you at least will be referred properly.

When you get into areas such as fashion work, you will find that you have numerous potential clients within the same organization. For example, the advertising personnel of a department store will want fashion photographs for newspaper advertising. The fashion department of the store will want pictures of a fashion show, staged in the store's coffee shop, in which the same clothing was worn. The manager of the coffee shop will want pictures of that fashion show for promoting the varied entertainment offered people while eating there. And the manufacturer of the clothing may want pictures to show how the fashion line is being promoted. If the store is part of a chain, additional pictures may be purchased by public relations people for use in the home office, perhaps as part of an annual report. Each section has a budget and needs that are independent of the other departments. In addition, the models may want to buy prints for their own portfolios. Obviously, the more contacts you make within a store, the more business you generate.

The portfolio you present should be filled with pictures no smaller than 8 x 10 and no larger than 11 x 14. Some photographers like the idea of 16 x 20 prints because of the dramatic impact of the enlargement. However, the larger the print, the greater the distance someone must maintain to view it effectively. Many account executives, even with large agencies, have far smaller offices than you would anticipate. They may not have the room to properly view a portfolio of 16 x 20 prints, though the 11 x 14 prints will be no problem.

Never use slides for presenting your portfolio. If you bring just a slide tray, it may not be compatible with the projector the client uses. Even worse, the client may not have access to a projector or light box. If you bring your own projector, there may not be enough space to properly project the work. Color prints are the only practical approach to color work.

If you have tear sheets of published work, these should be placed at the end of the portfolio. Each print and each tear sheet should be inserted in a plastic page protector and mounted in an album. Portfolios with zippered sides and a collapsible carrying handle can be found in most art supply stores.

Once you have an appointment, dress fairly conservatively and arrive early. It is a good idea to have the receptionist be able to announce your presence at least ten minutes ahead of time. You should explain that you are early when you arrive and say you will be happy to wait. Often the client's schedule is tight enough that someone else will be in the office when you get there and you will have to sit around until the appointed moment. So why arrive early?

The answer is strictly psychological. Most people feel guilty when they have to keep someone waiting to see them. They forget that the person arrived ahead of schedule. All they notice is the fact that someone is there to see them and they are too busy to get to them for five or ten minutes. The end result is that the client is likely to feel guilty and will grant you more time to present both your photographs and your sales pitch than might be possible otherwise. Instead of giving you fifteen minutes of attention as planned, for example, the person may give you 30 minutes or longer. If by chance the client doesn't give you extra time, you have not lost so many minutes as to have made the maneuver a bad gamble.

When you get into the office, explain that you are starting a new studio and are interested in showing the person what you can do. Give the account executive, art director, or whomever you are seeing your portfolio and discuss a little about your background. Explain that since you are new, you do not expect a major assignment the first time out. Say that you are willing to tackle any job he or she might have, no matter how small, to show what you can do. Sometimes this will result in an immediate assignment. More likely nothing will come of it except a promise to call you when something comes up. You leave your business card and are probably forgotten ten minutes later. If you are not forgotten, the card may get lost or thrown out with no one knowing how to find you again.

The sales pitch will be repeated over and over again in the course of each day you spend seeking business and the end result will usually be the same. Do not be discouraged, though. This is the nature of this business. Most people tend to continue working with reliable, familiar names. You are an unknown entity. However, once you get someone to try you and the person is pleased with your work, you suddenly become the familiar face who gets first call for an assignment.

Upon returning home, make a list of the names and addresses of every person you have seen. Then write each person a letter. You can use a form approach but type and sign the letters individually. Do not have a form letter printed. The note should read something like the following:

> Dear ________________________________:
>
> It was a pleasure meeting with you and having the opportunity to show you my portfolio today. As I mentioned, I run a new studio in town but have a strong background in (name of specialty) photography and know I can effectively handle your special needs. I will be happy to handle any photography work you might need done, no matter how minimal, in order to show you more of what I can do specifically for you. I am confident the results will please you.
>
> Thank you again for your time today. I look forward to hearing from you concerning possible photographic work I can handle for you.

Sign your name, address, and telephone number. You might also include a business card.

Wait two weeks and, if you haven't heard from the potential client, follow up by making a second appointment. Bring the second of your portfolios, assuming you have one (portfolios generally run from 15 to 20 prints so you will need a minimum of at least 30 exceptional photos), to show during this session. Everything else will go as before.

This third contact (the letter was the second) is often the time you get an assignment. If not, keep trying. It is very difficult for a business person to break old habits and call you instead of someone used in the past. Thus it is up to you to keep trying, bringing your studio to the client's attention over and over again until you are either convinced you will never be called or an assignment is obtained. Never show your annoyance or sound like you are pleading for work. The impression you want to give is one of a competent, self-assured professional who recognizes that he or she is capable of handling the jobs the client may have. In effect you are saying that you have so much to offer, you do not mind the understandable delays in obtaining that first assignment.

Building a business is a long, slow process, which is why undercapitalization can be so serious. You are going to spend much of your time on the streets seeking that first assignment and almost as much time going after that second or third chance. You must never take clients for granted, no matter how long you have had them, because there will always be new photographers coming along who will also be aggressively seeking their business. For this reason, some established photographers have their receptionists telephone their regular business clients at least once every 2 weeks if no assignments have come in, and ask about any services they might provide. By showing you want the client's business and will go out of your way to keep it, you will stand the greatest chance for long-term success.

Figuring Prices

When you finally get your first break, the client is likely to ask you what your rate will be. Do not be pressured into quoting a set figure. You will lack the experience to name a fee off the top of your head and be certain that price will result in a profit.

Instead of quoting a price, talk with the client about his or her needs. Be wary of the client's casually using such technical terms as "available light" and "candid" pictures because the person may not be so familiar with those terms as you think. Clients have been known to speak of "available light" when, in reality, they wanted carefully illuminated images that could only be taken with flash or floods. When a photographer delivers "candid" industrial photos, the client might complain because certain machinery wasn't cleaned and then highlighted or certain operations weren't dramatically illuminated. Only when you are positive you understand the client's needs can you begin to consider a price.

Next return to your home or studio to figure the charge, promising to call the client with a price quotation later in the day. If the client is in a hurry, retire to a neaby coffee shop to think. Whatever you do, don't make a snap judgment.

Start by figuring your expenses. What equipment will be needed for the job? Do you own everything or will you need to borrow, rent, and/or make some items? How much film will you need? Remember, you should plan on taking several more rolls of each type of film than you expect to use. It is better to have too much film for a job than to carry too little and run short. However, you will only be able to bill the client for what you use unless the job requires a special purchase, such as Infra-Red Film, which you are unlikely to ever need again. Only with such a special purchase should you charge the client for all film purchased, not just the film used.

What will your processing and printing costs be? If you use a custom lab, you will have to pay for packaging material and postage in both directions. If you do the work yourself, how much waste can you expect?

Will you have to hire models? Rent props? Use tungsten or quartz bulbs with a known life? (If a six-hour bulb is burned one hour to handle a client's work, the client is charged one-sixth of the cost of the bulb as part of the bill.) Will you have to travel a long distance? Buy special props?

Next figure your time for the job. Many photographers feel that there is one hour of preparation for each hour worked. Depending upon the assignment, such lengthy preparation may be unrealistic. However, there is also the chance that preparation will be far longer than the actual work. In either case, it must be included in your time. Darkroom work should also be considered.

Finally, when you have all your expenses, add these to your hourly rate, including a percentage for overhead. Overhead means camera wear and tear, studio rent, utilities, and similar items. Even if you are working from home or a small office area, less space than the studio you hope to open shortly, charge as if you were renting full studio space. Not only does this make you a fair competitor, it also prevents you from having to raise your rates when you do open a studio. Just be certain you check with business property realtors to be certain you know expected rents for the size studio you will rent or buy in the area you feel should be the location of your business.

There are any number of ways to figure the final charge. One rule used by most portrait studios is to charge a set multiple of expenses. Thus from three and one-half to five times all costs is considered a fair charge for the work.

Others carefully determine the hourly rate they want and add all expenses including a fraction of the overhead. This latter is determined by figuring the costs for a given year, then dividing them by the number of assignments you will be handling each day. For example, suppose you know that your equipment will have to be replaced every five years and that you have $10,000 invested in it. To find that portion of your overhead, divide the 10,000 dollars by the five years. This leaves you with $2,000 to be covered in the course of 12 months.

Next decide how long your working year will be. It is not 52 weeks because you will lose some time for days off, illness, vacations, and holidays. It is not even an eight-hour day because many studios are involved with work-related matters only seven hours a day with the remaining time spent taking breaks for one reason or another. Naturally, as a new professional, you may put in many more hours than just seven a day, but the basis for this example will be seven. You can then adjust it to your personal situation.

In the course of the seven hours, approximately an hour and a half will be spent on nonproductive tasks that can't be charged to the client. You will be ordering supplies, checking mail, maintaining record books, telephoning potential clients, and handling similar chores. This leaves five and a half hours per day that can be charged to clients. Assuming a five-day work week and a 48-week working year (four weeks off for vacation, illness, holidays, etc.) you are left with 1,320 productive hours. This means that every hour, approximately $1.50 must be charged to a client just to cover the cost of your equipment depreciation. The rent, utilities, and other overhead must be similarly determined and charged to a client. And this is all in addition to the specific costs per job.

Now add to all this the salary you will pay yourself plus that which you must pay any employee. If you want to earn $15,000 that first year, you have to spread that figure over the productive hours, which means an additional charge of almost $11.40 an hour just to cover your income. Suddenly you are charging $13 an hour just for salary and depreciation. You must also figure your hourly need for the rent and utilities. Then you add all your other expenses and you find the minimum you have to charge to stay in business.

To make matters worse at first, you will not have so many productive hours the first year or two as you will experience later on. However, there is a limit to what you can charge if you want to avoid greatly exceeding the rates of the competition.

There are some sources for information concerning pricing your work that can be of great help to you. One is the *Blue Book of Photography Prices* published by the Photography Research Institute Carson Endowment, 21237 South Moneta Avenue, Carson, California 90745. This is a regularly updated, loose-leaf publication that gives theoretical assignments that are typical of the kind experienced by most commercial photography studio owners. Professionals are contacted and asked to explain how they would plan the assignment, figure costs, and set their prices. A broad range of professionals participate around the country and the material provides their comments as well as the range of prices from low to high. It is a way of learning how to think your way through assignments and to see how the competition is cutting costs or handling unusual financial problems.

Another periodically updated publication of help to you is the *Estimating Manual for Professional Photography.* It is published by Professional Photographers West, Inc., 1665½ Veteran Avenue, Los Angeles, California 90024. This gives information on pricing your work and shows what others are charging.

Two organizations can also help you. One is The Society of Photographers in Communications, 60 East 42nd Street, New York, New York 10017. The other is Professional Photographers of America, 1090 Executive Way, Des Plaines, Illinois 60018.

Certain types of specialties will take careful planning. For example, catalog photographers will have a period of days or weeks in which to prepare product photographs for catalogs ranging in size from the telephone-book type offered by Sears, Penney's and other major chains to small pamphlets for local department stores. You will be told how many items there will be and the deadline. Then you will be asked to estimate the charge, the time to set-up and take down the objects and props, the time needed to obtain models for the clothing and similar matters. So long as you have the items in your studio, you can work on the project continuously, stopping only when you are tired. Such catalogs allow an extremely efficient use of time and can be quite profitable, even when you charge slightly less than normal due to the volume.

One cost factor will be the use of models. Professional models are available for fees ranging from little more than minimum wage to well in excess of $100 an hour. The difference is determined by the model's training, fame, and location. A top model in rural Dead-At-Night might get $5 to $10 an hour while the same model, handling herself the same way, could be earning $75 an hour or more in New York.

Using Models

Models are an essential part of an advertising business. They will wear the clothing being shown in the photograph or add background for a picture of a restaurant. You are going to have to know what agencies serve your area, their cost, the quality of their models, and the alternatives available to you.

Not all modeling agencies are the same. A large number of them are connected with schools and it is the school that gets the owner's attention. The agency is an afterthought, meant to give a professional gloss to the operation. The charge for attending the school is high, but the models who make it through are assured of being listed with the agency. Unfortunately, in a number of cases, little concern is given to the skill level of the models who graduate from the school. Sometimes they can take three or four poses, then don't know what else to do with themselves.

Before working with an agency, talk with the director. Find out what type of training the models receive. Ask about the instructors. Have they ever modeled? If they have, where did they do it and what types of assignments did they have? Ask about clients as well, taking names of people you can ask to determine whether or not agency models have performed satisfactorily during assignments similar to the ones you will have.

The model agency should have composite photos of the models showing them in a number of different poses. Is there a sameness to the images or are there different facial expressions, body movements, and hand positions? Were the pictures taken by more than one photographer? Sometimes a model seems to come alive with one photographer and looks deadpan with anyone else. One clue to this fact is found when the model has only worked with one photographer. Admittedly this may have been to save money or because the community was too small to have more than one photographer taking such portfolio pictures. However, it may also be a warning sign.

Finally, ask to interview in your studio the models with whom you might work. Set specific appointments and see if they are prompt, decently dressed, and professional in manner. They should be able to sell themselves to you. You might even put them in front of some seamless background paper and take a half dozen test shots to see how you react with each other.

Once you are satisifed that the models available to you can handle the expected work, find out what the price will be under all possible conditions. There may be a fee charged for travel time. You may be expected to supply the models with clothing or the models may be expected to have a reasonably versatile wardrobe for use when posing for photographs other than fashion pictures. You cannot estimate the costs for an assignment unless you know all the expenses you might encounter.

There are some alternatives to working with professional models that you should consider. In some communities the quality of the models is very poor. They are trained by people with no practical experience and the models who complete the courses could never compete in larger communities. Since a poor model wastes your time and costs you money in the long run, you should consider using students and teachers from area dancing schools that teach ballet. Ballet utilizes every position the human body can take while still remaining graceful. A ballet dancer can easily show off clothing to best advantage just by taking basic positions. A dancer is also likely to have a good figure and appear attractive in the photographs.

If you use a dancer, you can pay slightly more or less than the going rate for models, depending upon the area, your budget, and what the dancer will accept. An added business advantage is that you may also find yourself getting paid to photograph the dance studio and the students.

Studio Space

The space you will need when you specialize in a particular type of photography can vary greatly. Much product work does not require large space if you stay with the items normally sold in department stores. Photographers working in an area such as Detroit may need facilities to handle the photography of new cars and similar large items but this is a problem common to a very limited section of the country.

How much space do you need? The larger your studio, the more you can do. If you are going to photograph a single person full figure, a minimum of 18 feet should be available to you. This will enable you to set up the paper, lights, and model, then step back far enough to get the full figure visible in your camera with a normal lens. The width of the room can be limited to the width of the seamless paper.

Catalog work can require a fairly wide studio since you will be periodically working with several models at the same time. You may also have to build fairly large light tents for individual items.

One studio design concept that can save you money while providing you with great flexibility is to have an expanded design. Sliding panels or accordian doors can separate the studio from the office area and the office area from the reception room. When more shooting area is required than you normally use, the doors can be folded back and the furniture in the previously partitioned room moved aside.

The accordian-door studio design is most practical for the larger advertising studio located in an older building with extensive square footage. Often this is part of an older warehouse or similar structure. It may also be a loft such as can be found in cities like New York. Since clients will not be coming to the advertising photography studio, as they would with a portrait photograph studio, the physical appearance is not important. What you want is large open space divided to suit your special needs.

Scheduling

As your commercial studio begins to have several fairly regular accounts, you should try to schedule personnel time so that you make the most efficient use of your day. If you will be handling location assignments, try to schedule several for the same day, in the same part of the community. As your staff increases, train each member to handle multiple duties so that those with the greatest skills and highest pay are working only on assignments that bring top dollars. Your finest portrait photographer, for example, should be handling your larger budget clients while the receptionist does double-duty handling passport photos. If your best photographer handles passport photos when he or she could be doing something more productive, chances are the salary will be enough greater than the hourly income that you will take a net loss for the hour. With your receptionist doing this relatively simple task, the person is learning something about photography, gaining a new skill, and bringing income to the studio that will be in excess of his or her salary.

How you run your commercial studio and the particular specialties that you go after will vary with the area in which you are located, your interests, and your skills. By exploring all the possibilities and aggressively seeking clients, your studio can be profitable almost from the start.

14 | Wedding Photography

Rocky Gunn

Professional photographers today use many styles and approaches in photographing weddings. Some professionals rely on a photojournalistic approach and offer lots of candid pictures to capture the feeling and emotion of the event. Others favor a portrait concept and produce photographs of impeccable quality that reflect the dignity of the ceremony. Lastly are the photographers who emphasize the illustrative approach and inject a number of multiple exposure and special effects into their wedding pictures. Many younger photographers offer a combination of all three styles, but the most successful professionals have usually developed one definite "look" or identifiable style.

For any photographer, artistic success can be defined as being able to produce photographs that are acclaimed by both clients and fellow professionals. Financial success can be defined as the ability to generate enough income to become financially independent. Overall, then, there are four "keys" to success: product, marketing, sales, and management.

Since this book is about business, the only point I'll make about product is that the pictures must have a market value. The strength of your artistic skills will dictate how much emphasis will be needed in marketing and sales in order to stay in business. In other words, if you have a great product you need less skill in marketing; if you have only an average product, you're going to really have to sell your work.

Marketing

Let's start with marketing. People have to know what you have to offer them, and you have to know both your clientele and your product. What are you placing emphasis on? Candids? Action photos? Portraits? Groups? Double exposures? You must know what aspect of your photography is attracting your business. Are you emphasizing service or quality? Are you after high volume of average prices or low volume at high prices? Do you have a truly distinct product? Do you offer something that cannot possibly be copied by anyone else? You must analyze your product with an unbiased and critical outlook. Should you determine that your photography does not offer a distinctive style, that does not mean you cannot succeed. It means you need to emphasize another area, such as service.

After knowing your product, you must know your clientele. Do you know the economic and educational background of your prospects? You have to know this to determine how to present your product in the most effective way. People's tastes vary with their cultural background, and you've got to find what appeals to them and then build interest. This leads us to the golden key of wedding marketing: literature, or a brochure. A photographer should produce a piece of literature that completely represents the product being sold. The brochure must be clear and to the point, and avoid complex pricing schemes. Above all it should include pictures. The pictures should be striking and reflect the style the photographer is offering. The copy should be written in language that relates directly to the young adult because this is the age group that produces wedding business. Be brief and be informative. In wedding advertising, price is usually an important consideration, so an easily read price list should be included in any literature. Black-and-white brochures are fine, but many sales promotion companies specialize in producing color brochures at reasonable costs. Imprinting them with your name is relatively inexpensive.

Direct mail is one of the best methods of getting your message across. A very attractive brochure and a well-written letter can bring a great deal of success, especially if followed up by a phone call. You can also arrange to have your brochures distributed by local bridal shops and wedding caterers.

Firms in some cities specialize in gathering names of brides and selling the list to subscribers. A more direct way of building your own list is associating yourself with certain stores and businesses that could supply a list of prospective brides: caterers, bridal gown shops, churches, florists, and bakeries, for example. Special shows like bridal, home, and garden shows can also be of some help in securing names.

Referrals are an excellent way to build a business. The good will of your past customers can be the most valuable producer of leads, but it takes years to build a business from referrals alone.

One of the most effective ways to get your work in front of brides is by imaginative display. There are many places to show your work: theater lobbies, restaurants, and display windows and showcases in stores or shopping malls can all be good places to display your photographs. However, display of your work alone will not usually produce direct results unless accompanied by some of the other methods of marketing such as direct mail and phone calls.

The yellow pages, circulars, and magazines are excellent places to advertise most businesses. However, because wedding photography is a little different from most other businesses since it demands an artistic and personal relationship, referrals and personal interviews are more often an effective means of contact.

The telephone is such an important selling tool that it overshadows many other forms of marketing. Many studios would not be in existence without their phones. I have compiled a book of scripts for answering phone queries. By having a script to guide you, it is much easier to answer your clients and potential customers in an orderly and efficient fashion. This does not mean you can or should memorize a script, but only have a general idea of how to approach the different types of questions.

Even though many weddings are taken on location, there can be good reasons for establishing a studio. Your studio can permit space for several presentation areas for the purpose of looking and selling. A good display or presentation can make an ordinary selection of photographs seem outstanding. A studio designed to aid the marketing and sales program must be attractive, appealing and be able to pull business in on its own merit.

Once you meet your prospective customers for a presentation, there can be no stronger method to close a sale than a good audio-visual show. Many photographers are not aware of the advantages of this approach and are missing a great deal of business. A show with slides and music can do wonders.

Sales

There are three basic concepts in wedding sales. The first is the finished print presentation. In this situation, a photographer prepares all the photographs taken at the wedding that he wishes the customers to view and presents them in the final form that he wishes to sell. This method usually consists of presenting fifty to eighty 8 x 10s finished and ready for sale. This system is unquestionably one of the most powerful. Aside from visual impact, there is no better method to first impress your customers with their wedding pictures. The disadvantage is that you must invest a great deal of money and effort that you may not recover.

The second method is the package system. In this method the bride chooses a number of pictures and albums for a given price. For example; $445 might include twenty-four 8 x 10 prints in a bridal album, two parents' albums of twelve 5 x 5 prints each, and one 11 x 14 portrait. The strength of this system is its ease of presentation and approach. Anyone can sell with this system. A business specializing in wedding photography can project sales and estimate profits because wedding buying behavior is so predictable. The weakness of this system is the difficulty in increasing the order substantially if you want to.

The preview system is the third. This system uses the 5 x 5 or 4 x 5 proofs that the lab first runs. You base your sale upon the entire set or part of it. In any case the previews become an integral part of the wedding sale. Many photographers use the proofs as an incentive to sell more prints and/or use them later to get new business.

Most wedding sales packages come under one of these three basic systems, or combine the methods into an integrated system that is designed to produce the net income desired. The average wedding picture package currently runs about $485 and includes twenty-four 8 x 10s in a bridal album; 24 proofs, and an 11 x 14. However, there are great differences in price depending upon quality, the photographer, the clientele, and the area. These prices can run as little as $39.50 to $1,400 as an "average" for a set of wedding pictures.

The business side of wedding photography is very complicated because wedding photography is usually bought by a client only once in a lifetime. There are many people who pick up a camera and trot right out the door and begin to take weddings. And usually these people turn out work that is extremely below par. On the other hand, there are people who have studied very hard and have devoted a lifetime to the practice of wedding photography; they deliver excellent, creative work. Most brides have no idea who is good and who is not nor what is a fair price. A wise bride would seek a photographer whom she has met or whose work she has seen. There is no better way to find out about a photographer than to see at least three of his other customers' albums.

Management

Most of the people who just pick up a camera fail in business not only because their work is poor but because they don't know about business. Unless a person is extremely organized there is almost no chance of making a living from the wedding photography business. Every successful business evolves around organization. My business functions fall into different parts, and I place certain responsibilities in each department.

The receptionist's main duties include answering the phone, which demands a certain amount of proper training, keeping a schedule of all appointments, and making certain that the requirements of each assignment are posted and placed on a calendar. The mail is another of the receptionist's duties, as is following up inquiries.

The main responsibility of any salesperson is to generate dollars and keep the flow of dollars coming into the business. I think it is a good idea to determine an average that you want to attain from each wedding. To meet these financial requirements my sales staff is responsible for making sales presentations and billing. The sales department in my studio is also responsible for customer relations and keeping records of the proofs.

Making certain all the film goes in and gets back from your laboratory is a job in itself. Marking, storing, and classifying the negatives, cutting and preparing the order, checking the quality of the prints, and spotting and retouching must all be taken care of in a responsible manner. Sorting out, packing, and packaging the prints into frames, folders, and albums, recording the rejected prints, wrapping and packaging, and mailing and storage can take much time if you are not organized. You may be dealing with some 300 different prints and over a hundred negatives.

Without proper management you are usually lost before you start. The very first thing a photographer should do is set goals and objectives. You must determine before you start what you want to accomplish in photography. A lot of photographers don't do that and end up running around in circles.

In order to accomplish your goals you need to keep records. The dread of many photographers is their inability to keep adequate records. A good bookkeeper is the best way to insure a working knowledge of where your business is headed financially. See chapters 6 and 7.

A good rule of thumb is to multiply your costs by three and use the total as your sales price.

The business side of wedding photography is complicated by many variables. However, there are a good many full-time photographers earning excellent livings from wedding photography. For those who study hard and are willing to work, wedding photography can be artistically and financially rewarding on a part-time or full-time basis.

15 | Advertising and Fashion Photography

Ed Nano

Quite often a client or a friend will ask what I mean when I refer to a photographic illustrator. My answer is that a photographic illustrator is one who photographs an idea to create a photograph for a client that persuades the viewer of the ad, brochure, catalog, package, or billboard that he or she should have the product being sold. This can be anything: a new car, the latest fashion, a razor, beer or food, or any other commodity or service. Furthermore, the illustration may have to engender in the viewer an emotion of tenderness, love, hope, hunger, or fear, even if the product is not in the main illustration or is an abstract subject such as insurance or banking.

Markets for Photographic Illustration

What are the markets for these photographic illustrations? All one needs to do is to go to the local public library and thumb through the hundreds of books and magazines displayed there to get an idea of the markets. Look through the women's or fashion magazines—*Ladies' Home Journal, McCall's Family Circle, Woman's Day, Vogue, Seventeen,* or *Glamour*—to see the large number of food illustrations, cosmetic ads, and fashion and accessories ads and you will start to realize how many photographic illustrations are being made to supply these markets. Glance through *Time, Newsweek, Forbes,* or

Fortune and observe the corporate and consumer ads these magazines contain. Limited interest magazines such as *Golf Digest, Tennis World, Sailing,* and *Scuba Diving* are but a few among a rapidly growing number of magazines that cater to recreation and craft interests. While still in the library, look through some of the cookbooks and the many how-to books, another growing market for photographic illustration.

There are many more markets to explore. All the major corporations produce annual reports each year, most of them profusely illustrated with photographs. They are trying to impress their stockholders and potential customers by showing new products, new uses for established products, or new production facilities. These same corporations produce brochures showing their facilities and catalogs to sell their products.

Perhaps the largest growth area in photographic illustration is in retail catalogs. As the printing industry has improved the speed and quality of their printing with such advances as high-speed web presses and laser-beam color separators, the market for photographs has increased. Other factors in the growth of this market are the increasing costs for the retailer of selling merchandise in the traditional retail store due in part to staffing many clerks and more willingness on the part of the buyer to buy from sales catalogs, partly due to the improved quality of their illustrations.

Many of the catalogs are sent out by conventional department stores, but many others are produced by retailers who sell only through mail order. Yet other companies might have a few stores and sell nationally via their catalogs.

Another use of photographs is in envelope stuffers that retailers, oil companies, and credit card companies use to mail with their monthly statements, adding no cost to their statement mailing, at the same time exploiting more potential sales.

The airline takes advantage of their captive audience and include in their seat pockets a catalog of usually expensive and exotic items that can be purchased by mail or phone.

Many food processors expand their markets by mailing catalogs with well illustrated photographs of food and other gift items for individual or corporate gift-giving.

As in magazines, there are narrow-interest catalogs devoted to sailing, hunting, camping, woodcarving, lingerie, or about any subject you could imagine—and the market is still growing! Just observe the increasing number of catalogs and stuffers you receive at your home each month and you'll have some indication of the growth of this market.

Photographic illustrations are all around you each time you go shopping. The market for photographic illustration in packaging is endless.

Walk though a supermarket and you will notice that almost all the packaged products are illustrated with photographs, whether the containers hold ice cream, cereal, cake mixes, canned goods, or frozen foods. A visit to a drugstore will show how cosmetics and personal care items are illustrated with photographs. Taking a trip through a department store will reveal the use of photographs to illustrate underwear, small electric appliances, houseware items, and many other commodities. You will even notice full-color illustrations being printed on clear film, which is a recent perfection of an old printing process.

Where to Set Up Business

Where are the photographic studios making all these photographs? I think you can find capable and successful illustration studios located throughout the United States. It is obvious that a large number of these studios would be found in New York, Chicago, and Los Angeles because of the size of these cities and the presence of a large number of leading advertising agencies and their clients. Several large studios located in North Carolina produce many furniture and home furnishing photographs because of the heavy concentration of furniture factories and fabric mills in the general area. Because the home offices of the automobile manufacturers are located in Detroit, most of the photographs for the ads and brochures used by that industry are produced there. Most major cities usually have several photographers that do illustration, and there are photographers in smaller towns servicing local industries with high quality illustrations.

Fashion illustration is generally done in New York or Los Angeles, largely due to the concentration of manufacturers and fashion models. Dallas is emerging as a major photographic illustration center because of the increasing number of catalogs being produced there and its growth as a fashion center.

Do you need a studio to be involved with photographic illustration or can the world be your studio? As you look at all the photographs in the ads and on the packages, you will note that there is a mixture, some made in the studio in sets or on simple backgrounds, while others were made on location. The location photographs may have been made in local areas, close to the studio, or they could have been made anywhere in the world, depending on the budgets available and the sites called for in the layouts you are working on. A studio certainly makes photography a lot easier, but a lot of work can be done without one.

How large does an illustration studio need to be? Some of the larger studios may be 25,000 to 100,000 square feet and employ 25 to 100 people, with as many as 10 to 20 photographers on staff, while small studios may only be 1500 to 6,000 square feet and only have one photographer, one or two assistants, and possibly a salesperson.

Some of the larger studios employ set designers, stylists, carpenters, painters, home economists, and many others, beside maintaining complete lab facilities for film processing, printing, quantity prints, and other capabilities. The smaller studio may buy all darkroom and printing services from custom labs. Some very successful photographers work almost exclusively on location, only renting studio space on the rare occasion that they need a studio.

Even in this age of specialization some illustrators work in broad areas of photography. But many others work in very narrow areas of illustration. These people develop and perfect their lighting and other techniques and tend to specialize in food, fashion, still life, or people. The location specialist has to literally know the world for he or she is often called on not only to make the photographs but to locate the shooting site. The photographer must also handle the logistics of models, props and products, and select the right photographic equipment that will accomplish the job without having the full resources of the studio.

Related Skills

Whether the photographer works in the studio or on location there are many skills other than making the photographs that are important. One of these skills is the ability to work with models. He or she must be able to help the art director or client in the selection of the models, often based on experience gained in working with them, and how they respond to direction and work with other models. Helping in selection of proper clothing or costumes might be required along with efficient scheduling. Of course, in the larger studios the stylist or studio manager might help with these details. Depending on the size of the shooting budget, he or she may be called on to secure models for jobs in remote areas away from large cities, in which case it may be necessary to scout the area for usable local people.

In fashion illustration the photographer has to know how to work with the stylist and make-up person, dressing and accessorizing the models. He or she should be aware of fashion trends, hair styles, make-up, and whatever else would help produce contemporary fashion photographs.

In addition to the usual model agency sources, many photographers use their neighbors or other people that he or she feels can follow directions and will fit the "character" that is being portrayed. Some photographers keep files of these people to show clients or they may resort to "instant photographs" to see how they photograph. Quite often photographers will also "test" shoot models who are just starting to see how they photograph and follow directions.

On major jobs it is not unusual to interview several models in the studio with the art director and client, at which time a selection is made.

Another area in which a photographic illustrator must exhibit his nonphotographic skills is the selection of props. The selecting of props usually follows a meeting between the art director and the photographer (or his rep), at which time the layouts are reviewed and the general direction of the assignment is determined. If models are involved, clothing is discussed. If the assignment calls for still life photographs, the kinds of props are determined. Details are settled, such as whether props are from a modern or earlier period. Wallpapers, carpeting, wall colors, and other decorating details may be determined at this time. In many of the larger studios the prop stylist, the set designer, and the other craft people may sit in on these meetings without the photographer being present. The studio might even prepare working sketches based on the client's original ideas and have them approved before set construction begins. In smaller studios, free-lance stylists may be used and outside people may be employed to construct the sets. It is not unusual for the photographer who does much illustration to have a good selection of props in the studio. These props are usually collected over a period of time from jobs that have been done in the studio. Often the photographer may select props for a job himself, knowing specifically what he or she is trying to accomplish in the illustration.

Many photographic illustrators have a much closer working relationship with their clients, the art directors, and advertising managers than most photographers. These clients tend to depend on the illustrators' ideas on photographic design, lighting, photographic technique, and prop selection. It is not uncommon for the involved people to sit around a drawing board, layout pad and felt-tip pen in hand, and arrive at a solution to a concept. It is interesting to note that many of the contemporary photographic illustrators either have some art background or are former art directors.

This should suggest that a person trying to improve his photographic skills to do photographic illustration should try to learn as much as he can about layout, design, and printing capabilities and limitations, thereby being able to better understand the problems involved in these areas and be able to help solve them. Our opening suggestion about the use of the library to study the use of photography can be expanded to suggest that these same magazines would be a good source of information and inspiration in studying good photographic illustration. Much can be learned by looking at the ads and trying to duplicate them.

Acquiring Clients

How do you sell to the photographic illustration market? You could run ads in art director and advertising trade magazines and in the yellow pages, but most likely no one would call you for most of the selling is of a more direct nature. If you are now a commercial or a free-lance photographer, your selling problems will not be too much different. You will need a portfolio of examples of your work, in the form of transparencies, prints, or tear sheets of published photographs. The portfolio must be well-disciplined, showing only your very best work in limited quantities, not more than 20 to 30 examples, preferably the fewest examples that will show the range of your work. It is best to try to direct some of the samples toward the kinds of accounts the art director or the advertising manager is involved in. If it is a food account, try to show some examples of your work with food, not just cars on location or machinery or people.

If you have a large studio, you probably will have salespeople making calls. If you work alone, you will have to make the calls yourself or have a rep out making calls. You may care to reproduce some of your examples and do a direct mailing to art directors and advertising managers, then make personal follow-up calls on the people on your list.

Equipment

What equipment do you need to do photographic illustration? Many camera formats, from 35mm to 8 x 10 view cameras, are used; lighting can be electronic or tungsten light. Generally you will find a wide variety of photo equipment in studios that do general illustration. The more specialized studios will concentrate on the kind of equipment needed for the type of illustration they do. Food and still life studios would most likely have 8 x 10 view cameras and location photographers will work with more portable 2¼ x 2¼ or 35mm equipment. Most likely each would rent equipment for any jobs for which he did not have the proper equipment.

I think a broad characterization of advertising or fashion illustrators is that they are people who understand advertising and fashion. They must be able to interpret the client's ideas and contribute to them. They must observe things around them and have good taste in all the things they do. They must be able to design photographs in the camera. And they must have a good range of equipment and facilities and be able to use these tools to make photographs that accomplish what is wanted.

16 | Handling Customer Complaints

Kermit L. Buntrock

When the telephone rang and I sensed that I had an incensed female customer with a full head of steam at the other end of the line, I said, "You talk and I'll just listen while you nail my hide to the wall."

"That's exactly what I intend to do," she replied; and that she did—in precise language that left little room for misinterpretation.

When her anger had run its course I asked what she felt was needed for us to live up to her expectations of us. She proposed a solution that was reasonable and the conversation ended on a pleasant note, with her telling me about a grandchild.

A Sane Method

Customer complaints should be grasped as opportunities—not shied away from as ulcer-causing irritants. When they are handled in the proper manner, a stronger business—client bond can be forged than existed before the incident.

Outlined here is a method for handling complaints that should prove a goodwill builder for you.

1. *Listen politely and attentively.* Hear the customer out without interruption. Keep calm. Reflect concern. Be sympathetic. While you listen, don't let your expressions or actions show that you doubt the story or

consider it unimportant. Customers become justifiably furious when they feel they are being ignored. Above all else, don't take an adversary position.

2. *Repeat your understanding of the complaint.* This shows the customer that you were listening and understand what he or she has been saying. This makes sure that you both agree on the substance of the complaint. Also, when you get everything out on top of the table, the complaint will often seem less important to the customer.

3. *Ask the customer for an opinion on a fair settlement.* When the customer is given such an opportunity, he or she will often propose less than you would have been willing to offer. At this point, if you can, give a little more than the customer asks. This small investment in goodwill often pays dividends for many years.

4. *Follow up with a letter.* Explain that customer satisfaction is basic to your business—that the only way you can live and grow in the tough competition existing today is by pleasing those who come to you. Emphasize that feedback from those on the firing line is important to you; and thank the customer for having the courage to speak out. Handling the complaint satisfactorily offers opportunity for the future. You have established your integrity—and nothing works for you over the long haul more effectively than that important asset.

Be Sensitive to Needs

As you become more and more successful and thus busier, you will run the danger of becoming less sensitive to the needs and feelings of your customers. Avoid this trap.

When you convey by thought, word, or deed that your customer is no longer of prime importance to you, the downhill slide has started and it will be only a matter of time before you become a business casualty.

Here is some oft-quoted advice given by an unknown author:

> *What is a customer?* The customer is the most important person in our business. He is not dependent upon us—we depend on him. He is not an interruption in our work. He is the very purpose for it. He is not a cold statistic, but a real flesh and blood human being, just as you and I. He is a vital part of our business, not an outsider. He is not a person to argue with or match wits with. He is a person who brings to us his needs and wants. Our job is to fullfill them. He is the very lifeblood of our community. He is the one who buys our services, pays our salaries. He deserves the most courteous and attentive treatment we can give him.

Copies of this should be over every work counter in your studio and its message indelibly ingrained in your philosophy of doing business.

Become a "Go Giver"

Being a "go getter" is commendable. Becoming a "go giver" is better. Both routes lead to success. The latter makes it a more pleasant journey.

When you change from a hard-driving philosophy of seeing how much you can get out of people to one of seeing how much you can give them in kindness, thoughtful service and more value for their dollars, a wonderful thing happens in your life. You leave a trail of smiles and happy hearts behind you and business will often flow to you from unexpected sources.

17 | Industrial Photography

Ross Sanddal

An in-plant industrial photographic department is generally defined as any photographic group established within a company whose end product is photography to produce images for that company. This definition covers photography in a wide variety of fields, many of them quite specialized, such as medicine, governmental agencies, and research facilities, along with more conventional manufacturing.

We are primarily concerned with the organization and functions of the most common industrial photographic department, a general, all-purpose facility that is very similar to a general commercial studio. The main difference from a general studio is that the industrial photographic department is usually a captive group; its customers are obtained from within its own company and it usually does not draw customers from the open market. A small number of industrial photographic departments do compete for accounts outside of their own company, but this is not a common practice.

Although most in-plant industrial photographic departments are relatively small (one to five employees), there is a significant number of large departments with thirty or more employees. At first glance, it frequently appears that the in-plant department is a luxury item for a company. When such things as wages, fringe benefits, inventory, capital investment, and space are taken into consideration, the in-plant department is not inexpensive. Adding up these costs, it would appear that purchasing photography from an outside source might be less expensive than maintaining a captive photographic group.

This brings us to a major question: "How does management justify the existence of an in-plant photographic department?" Maybe a better question is, "How does the in-plant department justify its existence to the company?" It is doubtful that the existence can be justified by comparing the true cost of photography with the cost of purchasing it outside. Probably the in-plant department is best justified by offering services that the commercial studio cannot offer, such as immediate availability of photographic personnel, ability to deliver rush jobs when necessary, knowledge of the company's photographic needs, and familiarity with company policies, facilities, and personnel. It has often been said that one of the main purposes of an in-plant photographic department is putting out photographic brush fires.

How does an in-plant photographic department get its start? Although some departments are planned from their very beginning, the majority of in-plant photographic departments evolve. An employee whose hobby was photography might have begun doing a few pictures for the company utilizing his or her own equipment and time. The next step was to assign the person part-time duties as a photographer and finally it was discovered that he or she was of more value to the company as a photographer than in the former position. Or the general photographic work may have evolved as additional duties for a group already doing specialized photography part-time, such as photomicrography for a research laboratory or even photographic reproduction for an engineering department.

No matter how the in-plant photographic department originates, its success within the company and even its continued existence is usually directly related to the photographers themselves. Industrial photography requires a constant sales effort on the part of the photographic personnel. Accurate records must be kept concerning the work being performed showing the volume of work, costs of operation, and any other pertinent information. The photographic department must at all times be able to justify its existence in a way that management understands: a complete set of records with a favorable bottom line. The in-plant photographer needs to be alert to potential new uses of photography within his company. He or she also should be aware of when it is best to do a job in-plant and of when it is best to go to an outside source for photographic requirements, and he or she should not hesitate to make these recommendations to his company.

If the photographer has no experience in setting up labs, it is desirable when setting up a new in-plant facility to visit other industrial photographers and to call upon various manufacturers' technical representatives to obtain all available guidance and advice before making the initial request for capital expenditures from management. Care must be taken to insure that not only is the equipment adequate to do the anticipated volume of work, but that provision has been made to handle the increased volume that is sure to follow. Remember that once the photo lab has been established, it must then justify new capital expenditures and compete with other departments for the available funds. It is much easier to secure adequate funds in the beginning than to try to correct a difficult situation at a later date. Before the photographer makes the requests, he or she should make sure that the planned facility can turn out quality work at prices competitive with commercial labs. Proper planning of facilities will pay dividends for many years in the future.

Many photographers feel that the industrial photographer has an easy time because he works his eight hours and can then forget his work; he has none of the pressures of selling or running a business that confront the freelancer or the small studio owner. While this may be true in some cases, in general, the industrial photographer faces the same or greater problems than the freelancer. In-plant photographers are usually subject to call at any time; they must constantly be selling the need for photography but they must do this to a limited market. They must also keep accurate and detailed records on a day-to-day basis. And above all else, they must carry on a program of continuing education in order to keep up with the fast-changing field of photography. The in-plant industrial photographer quickly learns that if it is photographic, he or she is supposed to be familiar with it.

What kind of assignments or what kind of photography can be expected of the in-plant photographer? To some extent, this depends upon the type of photo facility since some photo labs may be set up for a single purpose, such as processing and printing photomicrographs, or photographic reproduction (photostats or blueprints), or report and progress photographs of a specific project. These are special situations and we will leave them and limit our discussion to what can be expected by the general purpose industrial photographic department.

The assignments usually handled by the general purpose in-plant photographer are similar to those handled by the small commercial studio. The assignments will range from service-pin presentations and retirements to engineering report photographs; from passport and ID photos to portraits; from simple color slides to multimedia productions; from simple motion picture footage to finished sound film productions.

If the photo lab is a part of a research facility, the photographer may also be required to be familiar with such techniques as high-speed motion pictures, schliern photography, and exploded views.

As in a small commercial studio, in-plant photographers must also be accomplished darkroom technicians. They must be well-versed in various processing and printing techniques.

As the in-plant photographer's reputation gains stature within his company, he or she will begin to receive assignments that are a little more glamorous. Assignments such as catalog and brochure illustrations, public relations photography, and advertising illustrations are all available to photographers who sell themselves to their companies. It is usually the advertising assignment that gains recognition for the photographer within the company since it is this work that is seen by upper management.

Probably the prize assignment within any company, and the assignment that is most difficult for the in-plant photographer to obtain, is that of the photography for the annual report. Since the annual report is the showcase for the company, this assignment is usually reserved for an outside photographer who specializes in annual reports. Before the in-plant photographer can expect to do his company's annual report photography, he or she will have to demonstrate an ability to turn the routine assignment into a photographic stopper; to demonstrate creativity and individuality with a camera; as well as ability to handle and pose subjects, and a thorough knowledge of the company and its products. Once the assignments are begun he or she must consistently produce work of a quality that is acceptable to the advertising department. The photographer is only as good as the last assignment, which is a polite way of saying that the photographer must produce the desired results every time.

Advertising assignments will also test the photographer's skills as a darkroom technician because there will be calls for color printing, posterization, solarization, and other specialized darkroom techniques in order to complete these advertising illustrations.

The industrial photographer, whether working in-plant or freelance, faces the problem of being competent in all phases of photography. He or she cannot usually afford the luxury of being a specialist in any one field. Because of this, photographic education is becoming increasingly important to the industrial photographer. Photographic technology is advancing at such a rapid rate that it is difficult for a photographer to keep abreast of the field without a basic technical education and then maintaining proficiency through a program of continuing education. Attendance at conventions, seminars, workshops, and trade shows is a must. Time must be set aside for a planned program of selected reading and studying.

To give an idea of how our technology is expanding, a few years ago a book was published concerning photomacrography and photomicrography. Today this same subject is covered by seven separate books. New products and new techniques are being introduced at a rapid pace. In order to keep pace, the industrial photographer must schedule time each week for experimenting with these new products and techniques. Assignments that used to be difficult, such as existing light photographs of plant interiors, have become much easier because of the new high speed color emulsions. In almost every type of photography, there has been vast improvements over the last few years. Lasers have come into common usage; for many photographic applications, new and improved optics have opened new fields that were unobtainable only a few years ago.

The question often posed: which is better, to be an in-plant industrial photographer, or to be a freelance industrial photographer? There are advantages and disadvantages to each situation and it is up to the individual to make the decision. While the freelance has the freedom of working the hours of personal choice, within certain limits, the in-plant photographer has the security of steady employment and regular working hours. While the freelance has the right to accept or reject assignments, the in-plant photographer must accept all assignments. While the freelance demands a rate of payment commensurate with his ability and reputation, the in-plant photographer has the security of a steady and predictable income including fringe benefits such as retirement, insurance, savings plans, sick leave, vacation, and others. While the freelance photographer has the freedom of being his or her own boss, he or she also has the responsibility of overhead, depreciation, sales, production, and collection of accounts. On the other hand, the in-plant photographer is furnished a work area and equipment; there are no collection problems but there are sales and production obligations similar to those of the freelance. The freelance industrial photographer has the opportunity to build business to whatever level is desired; in most instances, the in-plant industrial photographer has the same opportunity to build a department to the level desired. In each case it is a matter of personal sales ability coupled with the capability to produce the required product.

18 | Other Areas of Specialization

Fred Schmidt

As far as the public is concerned, you are in a glamorous business. It is glamorous in a way: You get paid for taking pictures. Even though most people believe that anybody can take pictures, there is a mystique in being able to produce a photograph with that special quality that makes it professional, that sets it apart from the rest. What the general public doesn't realize is that very few photographers get to go to exotic places and photograph the beautiful people, or photograph history-making events. As we who are involved in photography know, most of the day-to-day work in the life of a professional photographer is rather routine. But photographs cannot be bought off the shelf, like groceries or hardware. Photographs are created and the photographer has a responsibility, not only to the client, but to himself or herself. It's a responsibility to produce the very best photographs possible.

Twenty years ago all one needed to go into business as a photographer was a 4 x 5 Speed Graphic camera, flash bulbs, a supply of film, a bathtub for processing, and a business card with the all-inclusive list of services.

Today you can get into the photography business with a camera, an electronic flash, a supply of film, a telephone, and the services of a processing lab. But the chances of survival are mighty slim. Getting into business is one thing. *Staying* in business is quite another matter. Each year, hundreds of qualified photographers are launched into the marketplace; the competition is extremely keen, and one must have a good head for business in order to survive as an entrepreneur.

Today, when there are more students in photography than ever before, we are seeing the photographers' traditional markets being eroded away by new talent. Each year, additional hundreds of graduates from photography courses are eager to begin working as photographers, and there are more job seekers than can possibly be absorbed by the business community. The most talented and best qualified persons—and the most aggressive—will fill the vacant positions and will get many of the choice assignments.

With all of this activity, the total effect should be positive. Those who don't make it as full-time photographers will always have an appreciation for things visual. These people will become the buyers of photography—in companies, in agencies, in institutions, in government, and in families. And they will demand top-quality photography. They will have a greater appreciation for images (and sound) that communicate, that deliver a message, and that help solve problems.

Opportunities for business in the traditional photography-related fields are covered elsewhere in this handbook. The purpose of this chapter is to review other areas of imaging not included. Most of the specialties that follow have been part of photography for many years. Some are recent developments. A few are beginning to be recognized as entities.

The specialties discussed here, with few exceptions, have three common denominators: 1) Travel is usually necessary to carry out the performance of most jobs; 2) the specialist can be based at a home laboratory-workshop; 3) staff positions for these categories are part of many photography studios and industrial photography departments. Also, again with few exceptions, each specialty could be combined with one or two others as a business. Most could be offered as a strong complement to an existing commercial photography business.

Photography is a service business and a specialist in imaging must realize that service to clients is of paramount importance. Through practice and continuing education this person becomes known as an expert in a specialty. Consultant status generally comes with achieving a reputation as an expert in a particular field.

In most cases a specialist can operate from a home-based office and laboratory or workshop. Since travel is essential to the success of most specialties, you can live in nearly any part of the United States or Canada where you have relative ease of communication and transportation. You can utilize the conveniences of a telephone answering device or service, and possibly the services of one person to keep records, answer correspondence, and handle the details of running a business office. Many times the specialist's spouse or partner will serve as the business and office manager.

How does one start specializing? Usually as a part-time effort. Sometimes a person will have a staff position either with an established studio or with an industrial photographic department. As the photographer's reputation grows, opportunities for "outside" work will arise. One who is exceptionally talented will soon find that there is a strong desire for independence. Sometimes an understanding management will help you launch a new career.

Another avenue to specializing lies in pursuing a specialty while performing other types of photography for support. At one point, the specialty will overtake the other work and it will become obvious that the specialty must be developed fully.

Anyone in the image-making business should be aware of the developments and changes in audio-visual communications, if you expect to be of real service to your clients. It will pay you to keep up to date by reading journals and attending seminars, conferences, and trade shows. There is a wide choice of media among still photography, cine, video, and slides. Learn to select those that will do the best job for your client.

Our society is increasingly visually aware. Sophisticated users and buyers know of the visual literacy awareness among a growing segment of the public. Users and buyers in business, industry, government, and even families, have a greater appreciation for good photography. And the specialist would be well advised to make every effort to produce only the best results.

Aerial Photography

The space program has made the public aware of the importance of aerial views of Earth. We have grown accustomed to seeing satellite photographs on television newscasts. Distant aerial views of geography are quite common in newspapers and magazines. We know that, in addition to aesthetic value, each photograph offers valuable information.

Although aerial photography has been practiced since World War I, it matured as an outgrowth of space photography. Aerial photographs are used in city planning and real estate development; for locating sites for factories, airports, marinas, and railroad and highway systems; and as aids in maintaining power lines and fuel transmission lines. Other uses of aerial photography include surveying farm crop conditions and timber production, recording the changes in rivers and shorelines, and showing building progress.

Markets for aerial photographs are found among owners and developers of property and real estate agents; municipal, county, state and federal governments; educational institutions; air terminals; and newspapers, magazines, and public relations firms. Aerial photography can be used as evidence in product liability court cases and for crop damage determination. Aerial views can be sold for displays at airports; for business, office, and home decor; and for post cards. Air-to-air photography is a specialty itself, and with the current growth in private aircraft ownership will come a demand for photographs of these craft while airborne.

There are a few companies specializing in the science of photogrammetry, a field that has grown out of aerial photography. Today, photogrammetry has a much broader meaning than before. Aerial surveying and topographic mapping are only two items in a long list of uses for photogrammetry.

Although it takes time to build a file of stock aerial photographs of a particular community, it is possible to develop a profitable business. Aerial photography can be offered by a commercial photography studio, but few businesses can make it on aerial photography alone.

A variety of equipment and film is available for aerial photography. In addition to access to small aircraft and a knowledge of where one is allowed to fly, it is extremely important to have the services of a pilot who understands and appreciates the aims and problems of aerial photography and the special problems of making commercial aerial photographs. It is essential to know the best time of year and the best time of day for successful aerial views.

Architectural Photography

North America is on a building and remodeling spree. In spite of occasional dips and temporary lulls in the economy, the construction industry continues to grow. And where there is construction and remodeling, there is a need for photographs.

One of the oldest specialties in photography is recording pictures of buildings, inside and out. Of the specialties covered in this chapter, architectural photography requires more effort and concentration than most to develop a particular style. Traditional clients for architectural photography are architects, manufacturers of building materials and furnishings, and publications. Many home owners and building owners also like to have photographs of their property.

While most real estate sales firms use straight photographic records (barely more than snapshots) of property to aid them in their sales efforts, there are a few that handle high-priced real estate, and the principal selling tool is a distinctive brochure of photographs. Whether black and white or color, the photography is of top quality, and always produced by a professional architectural photographer. The photographer usually photographs the exterior of the house from various angles to find the most advantageous views. He or she photographs interior views that will emphasize the most attractive features of the property.

Some architectural photographers only photograph exteriors and general interior views. Distinctions begin to blur, however, where the photography of interiors is involved. Here, the photographer can either be a photographer of interiors or an illustrator of furniture and furnishings in room settings for manufacturers or for editorial purposes.

The historic preservation movement across the United States and Canada opens another market for photographs. Restoration of residences and business properties ("gaslight square" restorations) in nearly every major city and many smaller communities is part of this movement.

Some architectural photographers are developing a market in photographs for decor in business buildings, industrial plants, offices, and homes, by working with designers and decorators. The subjects of their photographs are buildings and interiors and settings of the areas.

The architectural photographer should develop an understanding of design, and continually strive to broaden his visual awareness in order to build an image of quality. Architectural photography can be a major service of a commercial photography business.

Art Service

Traditionally, a photographic artist is a person who paints portraits in oils, usually painting over a photograph printed especially for this purpose. "Oil coloring" is still recognized as a craft of skill by the photographic profession. However, many photographic artists today use other media, including airbrush, not only on black-and-white photographs, but to enhance or retouch color photographs as well.

Airbrush art is used on portraits, in copy and restoration work, and in the finishing of photographs for commercial and advertising purposes.

Usually, the photographic artist works in a studio at home, dealing with several photography studios as a subcontractor. Most are self-employed. Some are on the staff, employed by photography studios and other art services.

Some photographic artists are negative retouchers for portrait photographers. While the retouching of black-and-white negatives for portraiture is dying out, there is a need for those who are skilled at retouching for copy and restoration work.

Color negative retouching requires a knowledge of dyes, separation filters, and color-compensating filters, as well as experience in portrait negative retouching. Primary use of color negative material is for portraiture, although an increasing number of industrial and commercial photographers produce color prints and transparencies from negatives for publication, display, and for salespeople's portfolios. Color internegatives are retouched as a corrective measure.

A few businesses in metropolitan areas offer a service of retouching color transparencies for commercial, industrial, and illustration photographers. These transparencies are used primarily in advertisements.

An art service can be operated from a home base, and pick-up and delivery made by local messenger services or by mail. Services include negative and print retouching, color correction, and restoration work.

Audio-Visual

Nearly every business and industrial firm has at least one slide projector; many firms have projection facilities of some sort; most high schools and colleges have a learning resource center, with a variety of AV equipment. The tools are there. Consider how you can put them to work.

Meetings and conventions are big business, and there is a growing need for audio-visual (more properly, aural-visual) presentations, from the simplest slide show to a full multimedia production with all the dazzle of a show business production. Most hotels and motels can accommodate meetings of organizations and companies. Many of the newest motels and hotels are designed with built-in AV facilities, including provision for closed-circuit television. Some motels within certain chains are equipped for teleconferencing—the use of television and satellite transmission to hold concurrent meetings of people in scattered locations.

Producing AV programs for meetings and conventions can be a profitable venture. Equipment is available to help simplify production of slides and to aid in the production of AV presentations, from simple to complex programs. There is a developing body of talented producers, writers, programmers, and technicians capable of producing full programs or any part thereof, from filmstrips to motion pictures. Some independent producers offer full-service production; a client may choose any or all services.

This market should be investigated, either as an independent business or as an adjunct to an existing commercial photography business. In the latter case, the photography required would be furnished by the studio. Travel

Fred Schmidt, "The New Multimedia Environment," Public Relations Journal, September 1978.

would be necessary in order to present completed productions on a road show for a client. Trained personnel is usually required to stage multimedia productions.

Biomedical Photography

Biomedical photography provides an essential service for medical schools, hospitals, research institutions, and veterinary facilities. Scientists, physicians, and dentists require biomedical photography for much of their investigative and clinical routines.

The images produced by biomedical photographers are used in research, medical education, and mental health, to cite three prime examples. Still photographs are published in journals, brochures, and magazines and displayed at conferences and seminars. Other photographs, from photomicrographs to clinical studies, are produced by biomedical photographers. Motion picture films and television tapes are also among the media offered by medical AV departments.

With the increasing national interest in health care and in health care facilities, there are more opportunities to establish biomedical photography services. Equipment required for a biomedical photography facility can be rather expensive. There are instances where the hospital or other institution will equip such a facility and hire, through a contract, an outside service.

Biomedical photography offers the people involved an opportunity to contribute to the accumulated knowledge of photography as well as to advancements in medical and biological science. The biomedical photographer is usually required to produce public relations and copy photographs, in addition to photography of tissues, patients, and operating room procedures. The biomedical photographer must have a thorough knowledge of photography as well as a basic understanding of and interest in the medical and biological sciences.

Decor

Photographic collections are displayed in banks, public buildings, offices, industrial plants, homes, and of course, in museums. Certain photographs by certain photographers are now considered favorites among investors. Akin to collecting photographs is decorating with photographic art.

There is an opportunity for photographers to expand into the market for photographic art. Many architects, designers, and decorators are learning to appreciate the possibilities of utilizing photographs as decoration in public places. While it is rare to build a full-time business on making and selling photographs for decor such a service could be built into a sizable segment of a commercial or freelance photography business.

Contracts can be negotiated either through interior designers or directly with motel or hotel chains, fast-food restaurant franchises, department stores, and national and multinational corporations. Furnishings contractors and specialty shops are also promising outlets.

Galleries sell photographic art, and publish certain pieces in limited editions. Gallery commissions to the artist range from 40 percent to 60 percent, depending upon circumstances and arrangements agreed upon between the gallery and the photographer. Several photography studios are opening their own galleries of photographic art, dealing in work by their own photographers, as well as by others.

Evidence Photography

Expertise is required to perform legal photography assignments, and to use special photographic techniques as they apply to forensic photography.

An evidence photographer must be familiar with the procedure in offering photographic evidence in a court of law. An evidence photographer must:

1. Possess a reputation as a reliable and expert witness in court.
2. Be able to present photographic evidence for a client.
3. Be able to produce photographs that will stand up in a court of law.
4. Have the knowledge and ability to use photography to preserve evidence and as an aid to investigation.

Offering a service as evidence photography can be a successful balance to a commercial photography business. An evidence photographer can be of service to attorneys, insurance companies, and to law enforcement agencies and fire departments. (Staff positions are available with municipal, county, state, and federal agencies.) A specialty within this specialty is that of questioned documents examiner. This involves, primarily, examining documents in order to determine whether or not a forgery has been committed.

Specialties can be developed in any of the following categories of legal cases in which photographs are frequently used:

- Arson
- Burglary

- Construction
- Maritime
- Medical malpractice
- Motor vehicle accidents
- Personal injury
- Product liability
- Workmen's compensation
- Zoning and licensing

In recent years, special photographic techniques and procedures have been developed in most of these categories. Equipment has been designed to help the evidence photographer meet requirements for admissibility of photographic evidence in a court of law.

Filmmaking

A working knowledge in still photography could be an asset to anyone considering film as a specialty; but that is only the beginning. Filmmaking is a complex procedure. It is also the most expensive of the photographic arts. It takes a variety of skills to produce a film.

What is variously known as private or corporate or industrial film production accounts for over $1 billion in annual expenditures in the US, according to recent research. Some five thousand 16mm films are made annually for a variety of sponsors in business, industry, and government. Major topics include training, sales, health, medicine, safety, public information, and education.

Traditional outlets for sponsored films are theaters, schools, public showings, and television. Now that we are entering the era of the living room education/entertainment center, homes—and offices—will soon be considered as new outlets. The growth of the videodisc will require new and better "software" programming.

There is a trend away from large film production companies, in favor of independent producers who subcontract the talent and technical expertise needed to make a successful film. Much like the producer of audio-visual presentations, the sponsored motion picture film producer will hire creative talent and the technicians and be responsible for working with the processing laboratory, the postproduction team, and a distribution company.

It appears that there will be plenty of talent to call upon to fill vacancies that may occur in film production. The American Film Institute estimates that some 100,000 college and university students are taking film and television courses each semester. Approximately 30,000 students are pursuing degrees in film and television.

It is not unusual for a commercial photography business to offer filmmaking as a service. So-called quick-and-dirty industrial films that are made for one-time use can be produced with relatively little time, using a minimum of equipment. Filmmaking applied to science and engineering should be investigated as a service to offer, provided, of course, that you have a background in both film and science or engineering. Motion pictures are used extensively in training. Professional trainers design the programs and they usually call upon professional filmmakers to help them produce training aids.

Marine Photography

Public interest is rising rapidly in the sea and in marine science and the social implications thereof. People in industry, government, and education are interested in marine biology and in producing energy and food from the sea. Environmentalists are concerned with marine pollution and climate. Oceanographers' interests extend from ocean eddies to energy.

Those who are active in aquatic exploration and in marine science research depend upon photography to aid them in their work. Photography is essential to underwater research. Photogrammetry is used in coastal geography and underwater surveys. Deep-sea photogrammetry aids archaeological expeditions in search of shipwrecks.

Still photographs and films of life in the sea are used for research, for public information, and for entertainment. Television techniques are employed for remote sensing and recording. Special housings for photographic and lighting equipment have been developed. For many years, certain scientists have used special lighting techniques and procedures for underwater photography.

Obviously, an interest in the sea and whatever moves upon or within it will be beneficial to anyone who is considering photography as an interdisciplinary medium. There are a few photographers who specialize in still and motion picture marine photography; their products range from scientific photographs to "pretty pictures" for a variety of clients, including publication in books, magazines, and films. Travel is involved; one may work from a home base. Marine photography is considered as one of the most adventurous aspects of photography.

Photonics Instrumentation

William G. Hyzer, authority on scientific instrumentation, says "Photography today has completely overrrun its natural boundaries as a photochemical recording process and is penetrating deeply into the adjoining photo-electronic and photophysical disciplines." Mr. Hyzer has defined *photonics* as "that branch of science which treats of the emission, behavior and effects of photons, especially as it applies to detection, recording and/or near measuring systems in which photons act as principal communication carriers." He defines *photonic instrumentation* as "that branch of photonics concerned with the development, construction and application of photonic instruments."[2]

An independent photonics instrumention laboratory is usually headed by a person who also serves as a consultant. Such a laboratory can offer the application of photography in some form to the needs of industry, medicine, and government. A sizable investment is required to set up a photonics instrumentation laboratory. It is possible to rent some of the equipment as the need arises, or to rent time on a specific instrument or system. Clients may have the instrumentation needed for a certain project. Photoinstrumentation technicians are being trained in a few technical institutes and colleges.

Photonics is involved in many facets of research and development, production, and quality control in manufacturing processes. Photonics and scientific and engineering recording measurement are used in such diverse fields as biomedical research, underwater research, aerospace technology, and urban planning.

Processing and Finishing

Professional photographic processing laboratories offer services of film processing and printing to professional photography studios and to corporate photographic departments. Typically, a professional lab is established by a photographer who does his or her own processing and branches out to serve other professional photographers.

In a closely allied field, the amateur photofinishing industry is expected to continue to expand as the public becomes more and more involved in taking pictures. The trend to franchised photo kiosks in parking lots is indicative of this expanding activity. Investors are establishing photo service centers in affluent and developing countries around the world. These centers are supported by centrally located processing laboratories.

[2]William G. Hyzer, "Scientific Instrumentation," Photomethods, May 1977.

Costs for equipment and installation and for personnel will depend upon the volume and quality of processing and finishing anticipated. Technical schools are training qualified personnel to fill the positions necessary in the operation of a processing laboratory.

If you are a good craftsman and enjoy the challenge of creating photographic prints, regardless of who photographed the original, there is an opportunity for you to establish a custom printing service. In order to provide such a service, you must understand tone control for black-and-white photographs that will reproduce satisfactorily. In the case of color photographs, you must be familiar with the graphic reproduction process. The proprieter of a custom lab must be willing to meet deadlines with quality results.

In these days of extensive travel by photographers, it is increasingly difficult to find dependable labs in various parts of the world. A professional craftsman catering to professionals should do quite well with a quality custom lab.

Some photography studios will pay as much for a qualified darkroom technician as for a cameraman, some will pay more. For those who are willing to spend their working hours completing, at times improving upon, someone else's photography, the rewards can be quite satisfying.

Repair and Maintenance

A business devoted to equipment repair and maintenance can fill a continuing need. As photographic and audio-visual equipment becomes more complex and sophisticated, the need for dependable technicians who can competently repair and maintain such hardware will increase. As we move into a visually oriented age, we will all become more dependent upon the repair industry.

Independent photographers, photography studios, and AV and photography departments need repair and maintenance services they can depend on. Most corporations and institutions own AV and photographic equipment. Nearly every community of any size supports a learning resource center in the local school or library system. That center has equipment that will need repair and maintenance. A repair firm could offer a service contract to those who will use their services. Such a service could be operated as an independent business or in conjunction with a retail operation. An AV equipment rental service would be a complementary business to a repair service, serving local meeting facilities located in hotels, motels, and restaurants, and church, civic, and fraternal organizations.

A repair and maintenance service would be expected to offer some or all of these services: general photographic equipment repair; professional studio equipment maintenance; identification systems maintenance; non-broadcast video equipment repair; and visual aids equipment maintenance and repair.

Establishing a maintenance and repair service would require an investment in test instruments and spare parts. Personnel could include photographic equipment technicians, modification technicians, installation technicians, field service representatives, and customer service representatives. Provisions must be made for the safe handling of equipment and for the capability of meeting promised delivery dates. As in all service businesses, customer satisfaction is of paramount importance.

Restoration and Copying

The sociological impact of people in search of their genealogy, interest in the preservation of family history, and the romance of yesterday and "nostalgia" involves photography to a great extent. People are uncovering old photographs, mementos, and newspaper clippings. Some of the photographs and documents are cracked and torn and people want to preserve the originals and have copies made for gifts, records, and display. Among such memorabilia are snapshots, studio portraits, school pictures, and military photographs—for which no negatives are available.

Special skill is required in the craft of copying originals and producing photographic prints that are similar to the originals. Being able to please a client is perhaps more important here than in any other endeavor in photography. Client satisfaction is sometimes almost impossible to achieve. Being able to match the client's mental picture of what the copy should look like with an actual photographic print remains one of the challenges in photography.

Making photographic copies of photographs is traditionally referred to as restoration work. Materials and techniques for copying photographs have been improved in recent years. With careful workmanship, satisfactory copies can be made. True restoration of photographs is quite another matter. This is especially true if the photographs are of photographic historical importance, such as calotypes, talbotypes, or daguerreotypes, or if they were made with one of the rare print processes, such as gum bichromate or platinum. Deterioration or damage to these materials is usually irreparable. In many cases, however, deterioration can be halted and the photograph can be saved. Thorough knowledge of restoration processes as well as proper care and handling, are required to restore the originals, and can be a valuable asset to any such service.

Restoration and copying can be offered in conjunction with an art service business. Potential clients include individuals, photography studios, camera stores, department stores, specialty shops, collectors, galleries, and museums.

Retailing

The photo retail industry has not, in the main, kept up with the knowledge and sophistication of consumers of photo products. Too few photo retail establishments cater to the customer's needs and desires. Providing a retail *service* that shows a genuine interest in customers by answering queries, giving advice, and solving problems will pay off for the concerned and dedicated entrepreneur. Unfortunately, the economics of retailing make such a service difficult to establish and administer. However, it is being done successfully in increasing numbers.

As more corporations and institutions get involved in audio-visual media (from slide shows to video programming), there will be room for professional dealers who will back up sales with service. The National Audio Visual Association has set guidelines and members follow aggressive programs of finding needs for AV equipment and fulfilling those needs.

The prediction of a $10 billion increase in sales in the photography industry for the next five years emphasizes the need for more and better sales establishments and qualified sales and management people.

Television

Variously known as corporate, private, or industrial television, this field covers a wide range of activity, from a one-camera, black-and-white program to a full-scale production. Although there is competition among independent industrial producers, television is still growing. Experienced corporate video producers are breaking away from staff positions to form their own production and consulting services. Filmmakers are also getting into this special kind of video production.

Video is used in business and industry for training, sales, public relations, education, and research and development. Video is gaining momentum in the health field; soon it will be in the courtroom. Independent businesses are being built upon a service of recording inventories of household goods for insurance and legal purposes.

The responsibility of the industrial video producer is to get the most effective use of the media for a client by interpreting user needs, analyzing the audience, determining objectives, and establishing budgets. Then he or she must secure the necessary talent and production people; complete the production on time, within the budget and to the client's satisfaction; and evaluate the results.

The field of nonbroadcast television is not closed to those in traditional still photography, although any photographer would be well advised to thoroughly investigate this burgeoning medium before attempting to enter it. In choosing any medium with which to work, one should have a knowledge and understanding of it. Ideally, the enterpreneur should be somewhat familiar with all media and know which one or what combination will do the best job for a client.

Theatrical Photography

All across the country can be felt a rising swell of theatrical productions: plays, opera, dance, orchestras. Known as regional theater, this activity is all around us. Many so-called community theaters have progressed beyond workshop status. Several are on a par with Broadway companies and have, in fact, produced shows that have gone on to Broadway and Hollywood.

There is a developing need for photographers to record and interpret the various theatrical and musical events for publicity, for editorial submission to special publications, for records of performances, for programs and books, and, of course, for the performers themselves.

Theatrical photography is one of the few specialties in this chapter that could easily be an adjunct to a portrait photography business. Theatrical photography could also be an offering of a commercial photography studio; it would tie in neatly with publicity and public relations photography. Unless you are a full-time theatrical photographer, travel would not be a major consideration. However, some theatrical photographers will sign on with a motion picture production as the films' still photographer.

Workshops

A phenomenon of today's photography is the emergence of workshops and refresher courses. Courses are offered in just about every phase of photography and may last from one day to several weeks.

Workshops are a modern version of the master-apprenticeship system of the early guilds. Changing fashions dictate trends in advertising; styles of advertising illustration influence styles of portraiture; and advances in technology bring about changes in the way industry uses photography as a tool. Workshops, refresher courses, and conventions are necessary events for the continuing education of those in photography.

Several photographers and technical specialists now teach their specialties to other photographers and technicians for several weeks a year. And they do this at a profit. The student benefits through intensive, concentrated sessions with the experts. The students then respond to their particular market; for example, a photographer may subsequently offer new styles of portraiture to his public.

Those who teach these courses also publish books and manuals, produce slide-tape presentations, write articles for professional journals, and some serve as advisers to manufacturers of products for professionals. These "teachers" are also practicing photographers.

Another side to the education phenomenon is the private photography school. These schools operate at a profit. They are usually approved by the Veterans' Administration and other government agencies; some offer state-approved technical training certificates to qualified graduates. Although these schools are organized to teach young people, they also offer courses for adults. One such school offers refresher night school semesters for professional photographers in the area.

The widespread interest in photography by the public has spawned the photo safari or photo tour. A photographer with an interest in, say, animal photography will conduct a tour to wildlife refuge. He or she makes arrangements with a travel agency or an airline, who in turn organizes and advertises the tour. The photographer acts as tour guide and technical adviser. The photographer benefits by sharing in the proceeds and getting an expense-paid trip to a favorite locale. He or she also has an opportunity to make photographs in particular area of interest.

Yet Other Areas of Specialization

In this chapter we have considered those areas of specialization that are the most popular and share common denominators listed at the beginning of the chapter. There are many specialties that offer unusual employment opportunities, not necessarily business opportunities, although each of these listed below can be and has been developed into a business or freelance career.

Through perseverance, applying a specialty in solving problems, continuous study, writing, speaking, teaching, and *doing*—getting results—it is possible to become a full-time specialist in your chosen field. Perhaps the list below will give you an idea or two to consider.

Archaeological photographer

Archivist

AV programmer

Dealer in photographs

Director (film, television)

Editor (film, television)

Food economist

Holographer

Lighting director

Make-up artist

Marketing specialist

Photographer's agent/business manager

Producer (film, television)

Publicist for photographic manufacturer

Script writer

Statistician for the photography industry

Stylist

Technical troubleshooter

Specialties in Imaging

Specialty	Travel Required	Home-Based	Staff Position
Aerial	X	X	X
Architectural	X	X	X
Art Service		X	X
Audio-Visual	X	X	X
Biomedical		R	X
Decor	X	X	R
Evidence	X	X	X
Filmmaking	X	X	X
Marine	X	X	R
Photonics Instrumentation	X	X	X
Processing & Finishing		R	X
Repair & Maintenance		X	X
Restoration & Copying		X	X
Retailing			X
Television	X	X	X
Theatrical	R	X	R
Workshops	X	X	R

R: Rare

Home-Based: Freelance, working out of your home, with an office and laboratory or workshop. Some businesses require industrial or retail sites (Processing & Finishing, Retailing).

19 | Selling Your Pictures

Ted Schwarz

A commercial photography studio owner who becomes satisfied with the income from day-to-day assignments is a photographer who is earning only a fraction of his or her profit potential. There is money to be made from your files if you learn how to spot salable images and merchandise them effectively. However, before exploring ways to put your files to work for you, it is important to consider just how long your images will be reproducible.

Negative and Transparency Preservation

Perhaps the most important aspect related to the subsidiary sales of a studio's file images is also the least often discussed. This is the area of negative and transparency preservation. After all, it does you no good to have a photograph in demand by thousands of people if, when you go to print it, the image has faded. Yet this is precisely the situation in which many photographers find themselves. In fact, one photographer who specializes in file sales had to take a trip around the world to replace several years' images that had deteriorated beyond use. The pictures were needed to illustrate a book on world travel and the photographer had to take a reduction in profit as a result of the necessary reshooting.

Black-and-white images are the longest lasting in photography. Most photographers are aware of the necessary fixing and washing processes that insure archival life times. Even negatives treated with little thought to the future are liable to remain printable long after your death. This is the reason we have such excellent images of the Civil War and turn-of-the-century America. The work of the early photographers was exclusively in black and white and remains easily printable.

Three types of positive color film are used by the majority of professional photographers today. Ektachrome is the primary film used because it is available in every size a professional might need to call upon.

Next in popularity is Kodachrome. Some photographers consider this the most perfect color film ever made in terms of saturation, enlarging capability, and overall quality. It is currently not available in sizes larger than 35mm at this writing and thus cannot be used for view cameras, medium-format equipment, and other tools so frequently found in the typical commercial studio.

Finally there is the imported Agfachrome. Only a fraction of the positive color work handled by professionals involves films other than the Kodak line. Agfa color film is the most popular of the non-Kodak brands. The film's colors are somewhat different from the Eastman Kodak products and there are many circumstances when some professionals feels this deviation is superior for the subject being handled.

Color film is a relatively new phenomenon and even the longest lived color films are still products of this century. Thus none of the films have undergone the aging process experienced by black and white. As a result, much of the information provided here is speculation based on accelerated emulsion deterioration testing handled in the lab. The manufacturers contacted for this information feel that the tests are valid and certain films, such as Kodachrome, have been in use long enough to seem to verify in practice what is currently known through laboratory testing conditions.

Kodachrome is considered the most stable positive film available from any manufacturer. Its minimum expected life without deterioration is 50 years, assuming the film is stored properly. If extreme methods for preservation are used, such as freezing the positive transparencies, the film theoretically will last a century or longer.

What is proper storage? According to Kodak, this means that the slides are kept in the dark at room temperature with a 40 percent relative humidity. The darkness need not come from carefully sealing the slides in light-tight boxes, however. Slides can even be placed in plastic page protectors, then mounted in notebooks with several pages pressed loosely together. This prevents sun and other harsh light from striking the emulsion, a necessity for proper storage.

Projection of slides causes deterioration because of the harsh light and heat from the projector bulbs. If your studio is setting up an audio-visual display or will be having a continuous projection system set up for a client or for personal advertising, you should use duplicate transparencies. When viewing the slides for sorting, it is best to use a light box or portable viewer relying upon a flashlight bulb.

Ektachrome, at this writing, has a minimum life of five years with proper storage. Most professionals will tell you that the reality is considerably longer but certainly nowhere near the life of Kodachrome. However, the one property Ektachrome does have is relative stability despite projection. A Kodachrome transparency has a far greater storage life than Ektachrome but the slide projector life of an Ektachrome transparency exceeds that of Kodachrome.

If you have Ektachrome transparencies that have long-term resale value, you should keep track of their dates and have duplicate transparencies made very four to five years. Eastman has been making excellent gains in improving the storage life of this film, but there is no sense in taking risks. It most likely will deteriorate to the point of being unusable during the course of your career and the use of duplicates and "duplicates of the duplicates" will be important. Internegatives provide a solution for some photographers who later discover that their "solution" becomes the problem. Color negative film, including that which is used for internegatives, has no better storage capacity than the Ektachrome original. It can not be counted upon for the long term.

Agfachrome film falls somewhere between Ektachrome and Kodachrome. Transparencies made 20 and 30 years ago remain in excellent condition today. Most are printable to the identical image possible when the film was first processed. Those which have deteriorated generally remain printable for professional purposes and the image can be saved from further destruction by duplication.

Filing systems

From the moment you start your studio, filing of negatives and transparencies must be carefully planned. You want a system that will enable you to find a particular image five years, ten years, or even longer after you originally took it. You will also want to be able to retain knowledge of clients' birthdays, wedding anniversaries, and similar important events.

There are numerous filing systems possible and the best one is the one that works for you. Many photographers use a notebook for black-and-white negative storage. They purchase plastic pages designed to hold one of the following: a roll of 36-exposure 35mm film, 12-exposure 120 roll film, two 4 x 5 negatives, one 5 x 7 negative, and/or one 8 x 10 negative. The design will vary with the manufactuurer and the size negative it is to hold, but all will be punched to fit into a three-ring notebook. These negatives are alternated with contact sheets also placed in plastic page protectors. Each set of negatives contains a code number and each matching contact sheet bears the identical designation.

Next a set of 3 x 5 cards is prepared for each set of images. These will be part of your photo retrieval system. Each card has a particular name or topic and the file number(s) of the corresponding negatives and contact sheets. Thus the Peter Philpott and Marybethjo Terhune wedding will have a card marked "Philpott, Peter—Wedding," a card marked "Terhune, Marybethjo—Wedding," and "Philpott, Marybethjo—Wedding" to cover all possibilities. It is a good idea to include additional information on a corner of the card, such as the date of the wedding and the location. This protects you if you have similarly named clients in the future.

Use as many different cards as you feel you need. It is better to have a card with every possible topic listed on it than to one day go to the files looking for something and not be able to find it because the one topic you can remember isn't one of your listings. This if the studio that handled the Philpott-Terhune nuptial photographs has weddings as a very small portion of its work, perhaps not more than two or three a year, there might even be a card with the specific topic "Weddings."

A second set of cards might be set into a "calendar" box. This is a box divided into twelve sections, one for each month. If the Philpott-Terhune wedding took place in July, a card noting the anniversary date will be filed in the May or June slot. This advanced filing of at least one month is to give you time to contact the couple for follow-up work, as will be discussed shortly.

Transparencies can be handled any number of ways. You might have notebooks marked with the topic and assign a code number to both the topic and the slides. Thus you would have one notebook marked "Construction," another marked "Fashion," and a third marked "Food," and so on, according to your assignments and how they logically fit into categories. A card file is then made to handle the detailed classification. Just be certain that the mount for each slide is numbered.

Profiting from Your Files

When a studio handles portraits and weddings exclusively, the best way to use files is to have them serve as both sources for income and tools for generating repeat business. For example, when a couple's first wedding anniversary is approaching, why not print the couple's wedding picture on post-card stock available from most camera stores? Then send the card, printed with a message suggesting that an anniversary photograph be taken. A follow-up telephone call might suggest that now would be the time to add additional photographs to the wedding album. Or if the couple bought all the wedding photographs taken the first time, you can sell framed enlargements. If you know the family's address, you can contact them with a post card, suggesting that they might want to surprise the couple with additional wedding prints as anniversary gifts. Just be certain you keep track of what everyone orders to avoid duplication.

Once a couple has a first anniversary photograph taken, the following year another card can suggest they continue the "tradition." If the couple is reluctant, a somewhat stronger push can be made every five years as these are anniversaries to which people put special significance.

A wise photographer keeps watch over the birth announcements in the local paper to see if clients have had their first child. Again a sales pitch is in order, this time for a new photograph with the baby. Family photographs are easier to sell than anniversary portraits of childless couples. Again, an annual card with the previous year's family picture is in order for selling a new picture at about the same time each year.

The longer you are in business, the greater the variety of pictures you can sell from your files. For example, why not sell a montage of images showing a couple being married, having children, growing older, then having their own children marry? The more your photography studio becomes a tradition with the family, the greater your chances of having long-term, repeat business. You are also constantly making money from negatives on file that only need to be retrieved to start generating income. You do not have to take the time for a new sitting or go to the expense of buying and processing film. It is conceivable that a $250 wedding can eventually generate thousands of dollars in repeat sales.

Portraits offer the same opportunities as weddings. However, a portrait promotion should be run every five years. People usually change enough during that period to want a new portrait.

Are you taking portraits of business or community leaders? The city council might be interested in buying a series of photos of your community's mayors over the past few years. Companies may want a photo record of past presidents. Hospitals will want prints of administrators.

Obviously, the important point to remember is that you should think creatively about your files when you have wedding and portrait photographs exclusively. These are not one-shot sittings with no future value. So long as you use your imagination, you can constantly generate income from these files.

Take advantage of special photographic printing papers such as the post-card papers. There are also calendar overlays available and both can be ordered by your lab at your request, assuming you are using a custom lab and not one that is exclusively machine printing. Your family portraits can be converted into Christmas cards and gift calendars. You can even photograph children in spooky costumes and sell their parents Halloween cards. In future years, enlargements of those special pictures of "dress up" will be cherished by the parents.

The Magazine Market

Few photographers limit themselves to just portrait and wedding work. Even if your studio deals exclusively in these fields, you probably use your cameras in an avocational way. Perhaps you just take them with you when you travel. Or you might have a hobby photographing insects, birds, boats, sporting events, or any number of activities. What you probably overlook is the fact that because you are a professional, even your "just for fun" pictures represent the images of a trained eye. They are going to be far superior to the average person's snapshots. Your vacation pictures will be perfectly composed records of scenery, monuments, cities, and other subjects.

In other cases, your studio is involved with a wide variety of assignments. These might include fashion, architecture, annual report photography, and the myriad images commercial photographers are called upon to record in a given year.

Whatever your situation, these photographs all have sales potential. Even the vacation pictures will sell because your work will always be handled in the dramatically attractive way you have trained yourself to see. The only question is where to sell them and that answer may surprise you. There are literally thousands of markets for your file photographs and they are located throughout the world.

The magazine publishing field is one of the greatest markets for the photographs you have on file. And while the publishing world has mourned the loss of such giants as *Look,* at least in the form it had, the fact is that thousands of specialized magazines have appeared in recent years. Every year there is a new release of the annual *Writer's Market,* and every year it lists more markets. Certainly some new magazines fold, but many more take their place.

There are three general categories of magazines. Trade journals are those publications meant for the members of a particular business or job skill. There are magazines for nurses, doctors, photographers, hospital maintenance employees, construction workers, teachers, and every other job imaginable. The magazines' titles include *Church Administration, Apparel Industry Magazine, Baking Industries Journal, Parking Magazine, Executive Housekeeper,* and, of course, such familiar titles as *The Range Finder, Studio Photography,* and *Industrial Photography.*

House organs, also known as company publications, are magazines put out by a particular business for either the employees or the customers of that business. These include *Marathon World,* published by Marathon Oil Company, *Think* published by IBM, and *The Beaver,* published by the Hudson's Bay Company in Canada where beaver skins were the company's first product.

Finally there are general interest magazines. These range from news publications such as *Time, Newsweek,* and *U.S. News & World Report* to women's magazines such as *McCall's* and *Cosmopolitan,* to *Playboy, Saturday Review, Science Digest,* and all the others. Each is involved with a specific topic, such as news, or a special interest of the reader. In your field, *Popular Photography, Modern Photography,* and related magazines handle the hobby side of photography. Obviously the difference between the general interest magazines and the trade journals is that the trade journals address the business aspects of a field. *Popular Photography* is never going to talk about photography studio pension plans, but such an article might be found in *Studio Photography.*

Your public library's reference division is likely to have several books that list house organs, trade journals, and general interest magazines. The most readily available are the annually updated *Writer's Market* and *Photographer's Market,* published by Writer's Digest Books, as well as the periodically updated Where & How to Sell Your Photographs, published by Amphoto. This last book is not an annual and thus becomes outdated in some of its listings between editions. However, it has an extensive series of articles covering all areas of freelancing, which makes it worth purchasing even after it has been out for a while.

Before you can begin selling your file photographs, you must analyze what types of pictures you have taken and who might be interested. Perhaps the easiest of all photographs to sell are scenics. These might have been taken on assignment or during a vacation. They might show the downtown areas of your city or beautiful Lake Mosquito located high in the snow capped Outabreath Mountains. It really doesn't matter.

Next take a look at Writer's Market or a similar publication to see which magazines use pictures on an individual basis. You will quickly discover that many religious magazines, publications for the elderly, and general interest periodicals like to have black-and-white and/or color scenic photographs breaking up normal text. Sometimes these are used on the cover. Other times they serve as a noncontroversial centerfold. The pay is frequently low—often under $100—but the magazines are willing to buy one-time use, reassign copyright, or take an exclusive only among competing magazines. In this latter situation, a picture sold to a magazine for retired individuals cannot be sold to any other magazine deliberately aimed at the same target audience.

However, that picture can be sold to a religious youth magazine or other noncompeting publication without conflict.

Many cities have their own magazines. Some are chamber of commerce publications. Others are independents for the wealthier people in the community. Both are markets for unusual city photographs including those which have become historical photos due to a change in the skyline from the destruction of some buildings and the construction of others. General street scenes, especially of unusual sections such as ethnic neighborhoods, will also be of interest here.

Finally there are the calendar and greeting card companies. These firms buy thousands of scenics every year for use on their products. A few offer posters and wall hangings as well. (See Photographer's Market as an excellent source for company names.)

The calendar and greeting card markets are not likely to be high paying; \$25 to \$200 is the normal for one-time use. However, they seldom buy complete rights and usually will allow you to sell the same images to magazines and other noncompeting markets.

Pinpointing Your Market

Each time you handle an assignment, carefully analyze the photographs you have taken to see what possible subsidiary sales you can make. For example, suppose you have been hired to photograph a hospital for its annual report. Perhaps it has a new wing or some special equipment the administration wants to emphasize. There may be a new paramedic arrangement with which they want the community to be familiar. Or the hospital may just heavily illustrate all its annual reports, regardless of whether or not there have been major changes in its service during the previous year.

The first subsidiary sale will come if there has been a new wing added or the remodeling of an older area. The architect, builder, and others involved with the construction or remodeling will be possible purchasers of the pictures for use in selling other hospitals on their services. If there was something special about the building technique, a magazine such as *Engineering News Record, Lighting Design & Application, Hospital Forum,* or other special interest trade journals may be interested.

Next comes the reason for the changes in the hospital. Did the nurses work together to plan a more efficient use of space and equipment? Consider *RN,* the *Journal of Practical Nursing,* or *Hospital Progress* magazines for such stories.

Communication is always an important aspect of hospital care. Doctors and nurses have to be reached quickly in order to handle emergency situations. If the paging and/or communication system is innovative, *Emergency Product News* or one of the electronics industry publications might be interested. When closed circuit television is used for teaching and education programs, a magazine such as *Videography* will be receptive to your work.

Some of your photographs will be of specialized equipment in use. For example, you may have photographs of technicians doing blood analysis or an inhalation therapist might be using a new machine to help a patient learn to breathe more easily. A letter to the manufacturer may result in additional picture sales for use in the company's advertising, sales' brochures, and even company publications, if any.

Do your photographs show individuals in unusual health careers such as paramedics? Teen magazines whose readers are thinking of future jobs might be interested in such images. These include *Seventeen, Teen,* and others.

At times, a publication will prefer that your photographs accompany an article on whatever subject you are illustrating. If you lack the writing skills needed to handle it, talk with the public relations person at the hospital. Usually someone there will have the skill, the interest, and the time to write the article since it relates to the hospital's daily activity. If you have a problem, writers for weekly newspapers and similar publications are often happy to freelance. The pay scale isn't so great as with a daily newspaper so the reporters and editors frequently like to hustle extra income when they can.

Submitting Work

Before sending any material, write a query letter to the editor of the periodical to which you wish to submit your photographs. Explain that you are a professional photographer who has just photographed whatever hospital, business, etc. is involved. Describe the particular angle you feel will be of interest to the publication's readers and ask if you can send photographs *on speculation.* It is important that you add the notation that the work will be on speculation because some photographers assume that a request to see anything is the same as a purchase. They will frequently send photographs that are totally inappropriate for the magazine, then submit a bill for the work. When the magazine rejects the prints, the bills keep coming and the editor has a problem. By explaining that the images will be sent on speculation, you are telling the editor that you recognize that a go-ahead to send the prints is not the same as a purchased order.

Always include a self-addressed, stamped envelope with your query letter and with your work. In the latter case, the envelope must be large enough to allow for the return of the photographs and sufficient postage must be applied to allow for return by whatever class you specify on the envelope. Note that the class of mail (first, third, or whatever) must be boldly printed *in red* on both sides of the envelope used to send your prints. Otherwise it may be placed in the wrong container by the post office workers and sent a slower class than you had in mind.

The best mailing envelopes for photographs are the ones with corrugated cardboard inserts. Many camera stores sell photo mailers; these are heavy-duty envelopes stuffed with corrugated cardboard in a size slightly larger than the size of the print they are meant to hold. You can place a photo mailer for 8 x 10 prints, the pictures, and a covering letter inside a 10 x 13 regular manila envelope for best protection. The photo mailer serves as the return envelope and the cardboard protection benefits the prints that are loose within the package. These mailers are expensive but they are cheaper than remaking the prints returned with edge damage or crease marks from being folded.

Psychologically, most editors respond best to photographs sent first class. The prevailing attitude seems to be that if the photographer isn't proud enough of his or her work to get it to the editor quickly, chances are it isn't very good. The assumption is often made that either the work is inappropriate for the magazine's readers or it has been rejected by other periodicals. Usually this attitude isn't valid, but more than one editor has admitted rejecting material sent via one of the slower classes just because he or she didn't want to accept something some other editor hadn't wanted. Even if the work had been rejected before, it may have been because it was sent to the wrong market, not that it was bad. However, you cannot win an argument with someone using faulty reasoning. When playing the freelance "game," it is best to send everything first class. A slower rate is fine for the return envelope, however.

It is a wise photographer who knows the market before submitting freelance material. You can have great success submitting ideas based on the descriptions of a publication's needs found in guides such as *Writer's Market.* However, since editorial policies change faster than market guides can be updated, it is best to try to obtain sample copies of the magazines involved.

Most businesses and organizations maintain subscriptions to trade journals appropriate to their fields. Within the hospital in our example, for instance, there are probably a dozen or more different magazines being taken by the various departments. Usually these find their way to a small library maintained by almost every hospital. When this is not the case, a talk with the person in charge of public relations or someone from the administrator's office will guide you to where they are kept. It is doubtful that anyone will mind your looking at them—on your own time—especially since the publicity generated by these additional picture sales will benefit the hospital.

If all else fails, send for a sample copy of the publications. Ask for the magazine and include an envelope for the editor to use to bill you. Always say you would like to *buy* the magazine, not that you would like to be given a sample. With budgets increasingly tight, magazines can no longer afford to give copies to potential contributors. However, when someone ask to *buy* a copy instead of requesting a free sample, the request is unusual enough that most editors just send the magazine without charge. This can save you a considerable investment if you freelance from file on a regular basis.

What Magazine Publication Involves

Whenever sending photographs to publications, keep in mind the limitations of reproduction. Normally a studio sells a photograph meant to stand alone, frequently carefully displayed. It will be printed as large as necessary to have the greatest dramatic effect.

When you sell your work to magazines, it no longer matters how brilliant your images might be. The reproduction will be based on the space limitations caused by advertising. Your work must fit into available "holes," regardless of what that may mean.

Advertising is the most important aspect of publishing. A publication's personnel will sell as much advertising as they can for each issue. This is carefully laid out throughout the magazine and the remaining space is given over to regular features, articles, and illustrations. *If* there is space and *if* the photograph is of great interest to the readers, a picture may be given a full-page display. More likely it will be reduced to whatever slot is available at the moment. If the photograph is a horizontal one and there is only a vertical opening (or vice versa), the picture will either be discarded entirely or drastically cropped. If you send a sweeping panoramic scene loaded with detail and there is a one-square-inch hole for your picture, that sweeping panorama will only be visible to the person willing to take the trouble to study it with a magnifying glass.

What does all this mean to you? Simply that when you send a picture to a magazine, you must stop thinking only of the quality of the photograph and start thinking about its eventual use. This is something studios specializing in illustration must do all the time, but most commercial photographers never consider this. After all, even when you do advertisements there is flexibility because the client can usually buy whatever space is necessary to show the ad photo to best advantage.

When you photograph for magazines you must think differently about your work. First, study the file pictures you will be sending to the publisher. Consider what the images are supposed to represent (a new hospital design, an unusual construction project, or whatever), and try to locate a photograph that tells this story in a single print. Suppose you photographed a hospital's annual report and decided to send a series of pictures of open heart surgery to the company publication of the manufacturer of the heart lung machine used during the surgery. You have close-ups of the nurses, the doctors, the anesthetist monitoring the patient's vital signs, and other dramatic images. You also have a picture of the operation taken from such an angle that the primary focus is on the technician working with the heart/lung machine. This photograph instantly tells everything the magazine reader needs to know about the article. It shows surgery, the people doing the operating and, most important, the machine manufactured by the company for which the magazine is being published.

Ideally your one story-telling photograph will be taken from both a vertical and horizontal viewpoint or, in the case of 2¼ x 2¼, so it can be cropped to both dimensions. This is not something you normally consider when handling a studio assignment but is worth thinking about once you start selling your work from the files. By having both a horizontal and vertical image that tells the reader what the picture story will be about, you are certain of selling the image. If you just have one or the other, the picture conceivably could be dropped for lack of space.

Other images should be both vertical and horizontal. A magazine photographer might deliberately take each different image in both styles, but that is not always realistic for a commercial studio owner. However, the more variety you provide your primary clients, the more it will benefit your freelance efforts for resale.

Color is another consideration and the only way to determine what is appropriate in this regard is to study the magazines to which you are submitting material. Most magazines use very little color. The cover is likely to be in color and there will usually be color on advertising pages that are not completely sold. However, black and white is the preferred medium because of cost. Dramatic impact is usually less with black and white and every editor wants to increase the number of color pages that can be run. But the economics of the business are such that if you are only able to work in one medium due to the client's request, it should be black and white to get the most resale benefit possible.

Transparencies are always preferred over color prints, a problem for many studios because color negatives are so much a part of the business. However, most magazines will accept *glossy* color prints if necessary and you can have a transparency made from the color negative. If you can use slides, though, Kodachrome is preferred for 35mm and finer grained Ektachrome is desired for larger sizes. Agfachrome and similar non-Kodak products are also acceptable.

If you are trying for a cover photograph, be certain your transparency fits the proper vertical format. Space must be left for the logo at the top and most publications like to have one side of the transparency planned so that the blurbs of information about what is inside can be printed.

The number of photographs you send at any one time should be both limited and carefully planned. It is better to send a dozen pictures directly relating to the editor's needs than it is to send fifty, only a handful of which relate to the publication's interest.

In the example of the hospital photographs, you should not send thirty views of the hospital with a letter saying that there were many innovations in the construction and the pictures show them all. It is too general and, no matter how excellent the photographs or interesting the subject matter, such an unstructured approach will probably result in a rejection.

A better method is to isolate one small aspect of the hospital, such as a new surgical wing design. The pictures you send will include one or two overviews of key locations, close-ups of the staff working, pictures of the support facilities such as a sterilization area, and similar images. The dozen or so pictures will all be closely related to one another and will be limited to a single aspect of the construction. Later submissions can concentrate on other key areas such as the intensive care facility or the burn unit. In this manner you might sell a half dozen different short picture series even though a submission of numerous prints touching on the same areas would be rejected if mailed all at once.

Another source for additional income from your pictures is one you probably have never considered. This is the professional photography magazine market, which is always looking for how-to-do-it articles for other professionals. Have you taken a series of photos that required unusual technique? Special equipment? Unusual location and/or client demands? If there is anything the slightest bit different about your work, the publications will be interested. It doesn't matter that there are hundreds of studios doing the same work or even that a number of those studios have photographers with greater skills. Few professionals ever think of this how-to-do-it market as an outlet for their pictures and the competition for space is very limited. If you can communicate effectively and your pictures are at least of competent professional quality, they will be interested and the pay can run from a few dollars to several hundred.

Legal Considerations

There is always a question about who owns your photographs. Photography is an unusual business. If you head the industrial photography department of a major manufacturing plant, all your work belongs to your boss. This means negatives, contact sheets, slides, and prints. You have no right to any of it and may even be prohibited from making samples on your own time and at your own expense to use in a portfolio when you go on your own. However, if your studio takes pictures for a company but is independent of the organization, that business owns the prints and/or slides you provide and nothing more. The unpurchased images and the negatives remain your property to be used again and again.

Because of this unusual business situation, a situation not found with other fields of endeavor, there is some question about what you can sell to markets other than the original client. The safest approach is to tell the client that you feel some of the images taken during the time you worked for the business are of interest to particular publications.

The majority of clients are delighted to know that the pictures you took will be appearing in various publications. The work will reach a larger audience at no additional cost.

Are there people in your photographs? A book of this nature is not the place to spell out all the laws related to publication. However, in general it is wise to have a model release from everyone you will be showing. Often this will be signed when the work is first handled. You might carry release forms or a public relations person or other company official may accompany you as you photograph, getting the releases signed. In a hospital this may mean both patients and staff. In a manufacturing plant it will usually mean employees only.

If you do not have a model release for each person shown, chances are the work can be reproduced regardless. The photographs are going to be used editorially to help tell a story. So long as the person shown is not ridiculed, embarrassed, or utilized for financial gain, the editorial use will not require a release. Thus a picture of an x-ray technician taken as part of a hospital public relations assignment can be sold to a magazine to illustrate an article on new types of x-ray equipment. So long as the technician is not shown to be endorsing the particular x-ray unit, a release is no problem. However, if the manufacturer of the equipment wanted to use the picture in an advertisement, the technician would have to sign a release.

Model releases may also have to be obtained for readily identifiable pets, houses, and other property. For example, suppose you have photographs of champion pedigreed dogs in your files. A dog-oriented magazine wants to use some of the pictures in a story. The prints can probably be sold for this editorial use with no problem, providing the animals and their owners are given credit. However, if a dog-food manufacturer wants to use those same pictures, a release is essential. An expert on dogs could easily state the names of the specific ones you used and you would have legal complications.

The same situation prevails with architecture. Perhaps you have pictures of a uniquely designed old home, which you want to sell. If that home is privately owned, you may need to have the owners' written permission to publish the print. Again there is a difference between editorial use and commercial use.

Stock Agencies

Another way to make money with your files is to sell the pictures to one or more stock agencies. Basically a stock agency is nothing more than a giant file photo operation. Thousands or millions of transparencies and prints are kept on file. Sometimes these relate to just one particular subject; other times a full range of subjects is available.

Most stock agencies are located in the major advertising and publishing centers such as New York and Chicago. However, they might be found almost anywhere in the country.

When you work with a stock agency, the staff does pretty much what is being described in this chapter. They contact potential markets ranging from greeting cards companies to book and magazine companies to advertising agencies to post-card companies. They learn the client's needs, then show a selection of images on the particular topic requested. Your work is not personally represented but will be a part of the package presented. Your pictures may be buried among fifty or one hundred images, all on the same subject matter.

How effective are stock agencies in terms of handling what you do? They can be very effective, though most require a tremendous output on your part and a willingness to go many months without income from them. It is realistic to expect to have to provide at least 1,000 salable pictures a year to the stock agency, then have to wait a year or more before anything is sold. You will usually not be able to ask for the return of any of your images unless you want to pay a fee for the trouble of finding them for you.

If you are going to use a stock agency to handle your file sales, you might want to send only those images that you can longer sell yourself. You and your staff should make every effort to sell your work to subsidiary markets as described in this chapter. Then, when you can think of no further sales to make, turn the images over to whatever stock agency seems to have clients who could make use of them. Most stock agencies have far broader contacts than you could possibly obtain, so even pictures you can no longer sell may find a home and continue to earn income for you.

Before committing your images to any stock agency, try to learn who their clients are and what type of images have the best chance for selling.

Large stock agencies accept everything of professional quality because they never know who is going to want a particular image at any given time. However, such agencies also have a list of material currently in great demand that they cannot supply, at least in the quantity they would like. By talking with the staff about these topics, you can better pinpoint the agency that is most likely to regularly sell the type of photographs you can provide.

Additional Markets

In addition to domestic markets, there are numerous overseas magazines and book publishers who may be interested in your images. Even a small-town photographer whose images are unwanted domestically may find great demand abroad because of the aspects of American life they reveal.

When sending your photographs overseas, the same techniques used for domestic mailing apply, with a couple of exceptions. Of primary importance is the fact that American postage is of no value to foreign editors returning your work. They must use the postage of their own country for returning your pictures or the package will not go through the mail. Thus, instead of stamping your return envelope, enclose an adequate number of international reply coupons, which are available from the post office. These coupons can be exchanged at post offices throughout the world for the postage of that particular country.

Packages sent overseas that do not contain letters can go at a far lower rate than those which do. You would be wise to query the editor and, when given a go-ahead, send a letter explaining that you are sending the pictures under separate cover without a covering letter. Whatever information you wish to relate, you can relate in this letter. Then wait twenty-four to forty-eight hours and send the package of photographs at the special air rate, which is far cheaper than normal for a letter. You will need to paste a customs declaration form (small blue piece of paper available at the post office) on the outside. Mark the value of the package: "Photographs of no commercial value." If you feel you must rate them at least for the value of replacing them, you may have to pay extra. It is better to put no value on them and take a chance than to go to the extra expense.

There are other markets for your work. Consider producing post cards for your clients. In addition to making them fit advertising themes for restaurants, hotels, and other establishments, you might turn area scenics into cards.

Make your own calendars. Every subject with universal appeal can become a calendar. You might suggest that area businesses buy them for resale or give-away as a promotion.

Is your area's chamber of commerce or convention and visitors' bureau actively seeking people from other areas? Your photographs might make an ideal brochure or booklet.

Local newspapers may buy your photographs. Each time you take a picture with either a news or human interest angle, contact the managing editor of the paper. For example, suppose the local drama society hires you to photograph a play involving a monster. Your series of photos of the actor being transformed by make-up from human to "creature" will make a strong feature. The pay is minimal but the exposure, complete with credit line, generates business.

Newspaper feature syndicates are also in the market for photographs with broad appeal. They need illustrations to go along with articles supplied by regular stringers, freelancers, and staff personnel. Listings of such syndicates appear as an annual supplement within the trade journal *Editor & Publisher.* Most libraries subscribe to this magazine and the syndicate supplement usually appears around July. In addition, the market guides already mentioned have syndicated listings.

Framed prints of area scenes can be sold to restaurants, hotels, and similar businesses. Talk with the owners, even if they are normally not customers of your studio.

Do you have scenics, "adorable" animal photos, and similar subjects with broad appeal in your files? Why not make a portion of your studio into a gallery where these can be framed and displayed? You can promote these just as you would portraits. Clients can buy them and they can be sold separately from your normal studio work. Such a gallery is a good way to build traffic as well.

As you can see, the sales potential of your work is limited only by your imagination. Everything from images taken at weddings long past to scenic pictures taken on vacation can be marketed again and again, milking your files for all they are worth. With a little thought and effort, the initial client sale can be the starting point for income that eventually exceeds the amount received when the images were first recorded.

Index